French Illusions

From Tours to Paris

Linda Kovic-Skow

Dreamland
Press

ISBN: 978-0-9884640-4-9

In memory of my beloved parents —
George and Jean Kovic

Acknowledgements and Notes

First and foremost, I want to thank my husband, Alan, for his never-ending patience, love and support throughout the book-writing process. Next, I want to thank my mentor and friend, Kaylan Doyle, for sharing her writing expertise. You are a brilliant, talented author and I wish you much success. Special thanks to my amazing editor, Lizzie Harwood. You made some great suggestions and your help with France and the language was invaluable. I'd also like to thank Cheryl Malandrinos for her editing expertise. Finally, I want to thank my daughters Kelly and Jamie, and my beta readers: Judy Hollenbeck, Kimberly Yantis, Kathleen Martin, Karen Knight, Susan Jackson, Amanda Read, Judith Benson, Nancy Lynch and Patty Pacelli. This book is better because of all of you.

Out of respect, I've changed the names of everyone I met in France. My diary was my guide, but occasionally I filled in information from memory. Tours is a city in the Loire Valley, and along with Paris, I've tried to keep the descriptions of public landmarks and sights in these cities as accurate as possible. All of the diary entries, letters and notes throughout the book are real.

PART ONE

Unsettled in Tours

1

---◆✕◆---

A chilly gust of December wind blew hair into my face as I leaned through the car window to swap cheek kisses with Évelyne. "Thanks for the ride," I said, pulling my blue wool coat tighter.

She smiled, and her toffee-brown eyes sparkled as she steered her Citroën down the cobbled street.

Évelyne is so sweet. I still couldn't believe how lucky I was she asked me to stay with her. The entire staff at the Songais *Collège* had been wonderful, especially Director Moreau and Madame Bernard.

My guts twisted as unpleasant memories from recent events washed over me. The extreme reaction of my employer at the *Château de Montclair* shocked all of them. Huddled together, they pffted and shook their heads as they discussed solutions to my dreadful dilemma.

How could Madame Dubois be so heartless? Did she regret her actions? I doubted it.

A cheerful voice brought me out of my reverie. "*Excusez-moi, s'il vous plaît?* Do you know when the next train departs for Tours?"

I glanced at the young woman beside me and blinked. "Ten o'clock, I believe." *This girl can't be French—they're normally more reserved. Maybe she's American?*

"*Très bien.*" Grinning, she opened the door to the Songais station and waved me forward. I edged past her with my suitcase, mumbling a quick "*merci*" as we proceeded to the ticket counter.

Until today, I used a train pass supplied by the Dubois family for my excursions to and from Tours. Purchasing a ticket was a new experience, and I needed clarification on prices for one-way versus roundtrip tickets. Even though my French improved daily, I still struggled when conversations turned technical.

"Do you speak English?" I asked the man behind the ticket counter. He scowled and shook his head.

The friendly girl behind me stepped forward. "I speak fairly good English. May I assist you?"

Aha, definitely not American. "Yes, please."

She asked about ticket prices, translated his response and secured a round-trip ticket for me before purchasing her own fare. As we walked outside to the train platform, I thanked her and introduced myself.

"Nice to meet you, Linda. My name is Mireille." She extended her arm, and I lowered my heavy suitcase so we could shake hands. She seemed nice. I wondered if she was local.

Three other people joined us on the platform and, moments later, we all boarded the train, Mireille choosing a window seat directly across from me.

Pushing her copper bangs out of her eyes, she said, "Tell me, do you live in Songais or are you visiting?"

I massaged a knot in my neck. "Neither. It's a bit complicated." This should have been an easy question. Until two days ago, it would have been.

"Oooh, I love intrigue. Please tell me," she said, leaning forward.

I pondered the situation. Mireille seemed genuinely interested, but I didn't know how much I wanted to divulge. "For the past three months, I've been an *au pair* for a family here in Songais. I'd rather not mention the name . . ." I paused for her nod before continuing. "It didn't work out, so I'm moving in with a friend while I decide what I want to do."

"Are you American or Canadian?"

"American."

Mireille frowned. "I hope your employer didn't mistreat you."

"Some people might think I got what I deserved." My words came out raspy, so I cleared my throat, twice. "I pretended to speak French to get the job. That's really when the trouble started. I was certain

Madame . . . er, my employer, would eventually forgive me. Instead, things got worse."

"I'm so sorry to hear that." Mireille's expression softened and she lowered her voice. "What are you going to do now?"

"If all goes well, I'll study French at the institute for a few months."

"The *Institut d'Études Françaises* in Tours?" When I nodded, she continued. "It's a great school with an outstanding reputation. I'm sure you'll learn a great deal there."

"Yeah, I'm anxious to get started."

"But of course!" Mireille rifled through her purse and pulled out some lip balm. A hint of strawberries drifted my way as she applied it to her lips. "I just finished my first term exams at *Université François-Rabelais* in Tours. I'm going home for the holidays."

"Oh, so you don't live in Songais?"

"No, I was visiting my grandmother."

The door at the end of the coach opened and a train attendant announced the upcoming stop. *"Prochain arrêt, Cinq-Mars-la-Pile!"*

"Zut!" Mireille snorted and jumped to her feet. "This is my stop. It was nice to meet you, Linda. I hope you enjoy the rest of your stay in France."

"Thank you. Good luck with your studies."

As I watched her rush off the train, a heaviness hit me. Recounting my troubles at the *Château de Montclair* with Mireille left my emotions in turmoil. The nightmare was over, but uncertainty filled its place. Would I be able to find a decent room to rent in Tours on my meager budget? Was it realistic to think I could learn fluent French in two or three months? I was more determined than ever to become a flight attendant with World Airways, but I knew they wouldn't consider me for the position unless I spoke a second language.

I let my head relax against the seat and my thoughts turned to a more pleasant subject—my boyfriend, Adam. *I can't wait to see him at the station. Eight days,* I whispered to myself. *We'll have eight glorious days together before he flies to Morocco for the holidays.*

He had been my white knight throughout my ordeal at the château. Without a doubt, my excursions into Tours to study French and to meet with him, Lori and other friends had kept me sane. I couldn't have endured Madame Dubois's humiliation and abuse without them.

When the Songais train came to a stop at the *Saint-Pierre-des-Corps* station, I leapt up and grabbed my suitcase, determined to be one of the first people out of the coach. As I disembarked, my eyes linked with Adam's cocoa-colored eyes and my breath caught. *Damn, he's such a hunk.*

Thick dark hair framed his chiseled, handsome face, falling to rest on his collar. Strong square shoulders tapered to a narrow waist, suggesting a lean frame without excess bulk. His clothes, a dark navy wool coat over a cream ski sweater, showed excellent taste.

Adam's musky cologne drifted my way as he bent forward for a quick kiss. "It is so good to see you, *ma chérie*. Has anything changed since Tuesday?"

I love it when he calls me "dear." "No, not really. Évelyne loaned me fifty francs. I talked to my folks and they've agreed to send money. I had a wonderful time sightseeing with her yesterday. We visited two different châteaux in the Loire Valley."

His fingers skimmed my cheek and dimples appeared. "Ah, *oui*. I forgot about that. Why don't you tell me about it on the way to my apartment?"

Without waiting for a response, he picked up my bag, entwined his arm in mine and led me out of the station. We crossed the street and found our rhythm, strolling along the sidewalk toward *la Place Plumereau* in *le Vieux Tours*, the medieval old town.

"So, where did you go with Évelyne?"

A contented sigh escaped my lips. "We stopped at *Villandry* first. The gardens were incredible. They had rows and rows of hedges cut into patterns. And did you know that the family who purchased it in 1906 still owns the place?"

Adam shook his head and I continued. "We toured *Azay-le-Rideau* next. It's built on an island in the middle of a river. And one of the bedrooms had an original bedspread from the 17th century embroidered in real gold!"

He chuckled at my exuberance. "It sounds like you had fun."

"Yeah, I sure did."

Adam guided me into a doorway, released my bag and flexed his fingers. "Give me a minute."

"I'm sorry it's so heavy. I've always wished it had wheels."

"*J'imagine bien.*" I'll bet. He kissed me again and we continued down the sidewalk.

We passed by several retail establishments—a boutique, an art shop, and grocer—all of them housed in half-timbered medieval buildings recognizable by their dark contrasting crisscrossed beams on the second level. Rounding a corner, a bakery with a bright red awning came into view. Delectable aromas of baked bread and cinnamon wafted out the door.

"Let's stop in here for a moment," Adam said, ushering me inside.

We entered the fragrant shop and I inhaled deeply. "It smells wonderful. I've always loved bakeries."

"*Moi aussi.*" On the way to the display counter, Adam grabbed two baguettes. "Why don't you pick something for dessert?"

"Mmm . . ." I scanned the rows of cookies, Danish and strudels until an oblong delight caught my eye. "How about *éclairs*?"

"*Bien.*" Adam placed our order, paid for our items and we exited the bakery back onto the busy sidewalk.

"We have one last stop." He grinned. "There is a *Marchand de Vins* a few doors down."

Adam led us into a crowded wine store chockablock with bottles. Two small tables highlighted special vintages of local Loire Valley wines and Adam selected a bottle of red *Chinon* before turning to me. "I know you prefer a white wine. How about a *Touraine Blanc*?"

My face warmed with pleasure. *He's so considerate.* "Perfect."

Adam paid once again and we exited the shop laden with our packages. Five minutes later, when we arrived at his half-timbered building, a sudden thought froze me in place.

"What's wrong?" Adam's forehead creased with concern.

"How did Marc react when you told him I would be staying at the apartment?"

Adam grinned. "He said it was fine. I think I mentioned this before, but he spends a lot of time at Yvette's."

"Oh, that's right." *Good, we'll have the place mostly to ourselves. I can't wait.* "Maybe the four of us can plan a dinner together again one evening? I'd be happy to cook this time."

Leaning forward, Adam outlined my chin with his finger. "*D'accord*, but let's not make any plans yet. I have a feeling we'll be busy for a few days."

2

*H*e was right. We didn't leave his apartment for two days. In fact, we barely left the bed, except to prepare a quick meal, sharing bites of food or sips of wine between kisses. The only reason we emerged on day three was because I had plans with Évelyne in Songais.

Adam walked me to the train station and we clung to each other, his embrace so intoxicating it was difficult for me to leave his arms. "I'm not sure how long this will take."

"*Tant pis.* I'll be waiting for you." His lips traveled up my neck and, when they arrived at my earlobe, I couldn't suppress a giggle. Pulling away, I climbed the stairs, turning briefly to wave goodbye.

"*À tout à l'heure!*" Adam shouted as I slipped through the coach door.

Clutching my bag to my chest, dizzy with romance, I plopped into a window seat and closed my eyelids. Recent images swept through my mind—scenes so amorous, my insides quivered. How could anyone be so perfect? His musky smell, his compliments, and his caresses . . . definitely his caresses.

Regaining my composure, I opened my eyes and shifted in my seat. *I'm excited to see Évelyne, but I hope it doesn't take all day.* Impatient now to return to Adam's arms, I made a mental note to hurry things along whenever possible.

Two hours later, with my spirits surging, Évelyne and I hopped in her car and drove the short distance back to Tours. The money from my dad had arrived and I was eager to accomplish two important tasks: register at the *Institut d'Études Françaises* and find a room to rent.

My new friend, however, shook her head in dismay, her short brown hair swinging as she searched the rental selections. "I can't believe there are only three options right now. Normally, there are at least a dozen to choose from."

I shrugged. "I'm not that particular as long as the heat works."

"*Mais, oui!*" Évelyne blinked with confusion. "Was this a problem at the château?"

"Uh-huh. Madame Dubois didn't bother to heat the third floor. I had to sleep in three layers of clothing."

Her eyes widened and she recoiled. "That woman is vile! I am so glad you are away from that place." She reached over to pat my hand. "Don't worry. We'll find you somewhere decent."

"I'm sure we will."

"What about registration at the institute? Shall we go there after we look at rooms?"

"Yes, that would be great!" *I can't believe this is really happening.* A few weeks ago, I would've never imagined it was possible and now I was signing up for classes.

"*Bien.*"

Évelyne relaxed into the seat and fiddled with the radio. "This station plays French top 40 songs. I think you will enjoy it."

We zoomed along the highway, listening to 1979 *musique pop* while I stared out the window. One after the other, rustic farmhouses, grand châteaux, manor homes and glimpses of the Loire River streamed by like frames in a movie reel. *This valley is so lovely. Will I ever tire of these magnificent views? I doubt it.*

Thirty minutes later, we crossed the Woodrow Wilson Bridge into Tours and I sat up straight, my nerves jangling with anticipation. Évelyne checked her map, made a couple of turns and, a few moments, later we parked in front of a three-story structure on the outskirts of town.

Both of us peered out the window to assess the well-kept, three-story apartment building before we climbed out of the car.

"Where's the institute from here?" I looked right and then left.

Évelyne tapped her forefinger against her mouth and then pointed behind her. "I think it's about two kilometers that way."

A little over a mile. "That's a long walk if it's crummy weather."

"You're right. Let's see if it's worth the price."

Évelyne led the way up the narrow walkway to the entrance, we entered the building and she rang the doorbell to unit number seven. Priced at 650 francs per month, the large room with a bath and a hot plate was nice, but over budget and far away from the school.

"Let's move on," Évelyne pronounced.

We didn't even bother to climb out of the car to view the second room. It was even further away from the institute and located in a neighborhood with rough-looking characters hanging out on street corners.

The third room for rent was situated inside a family's home. It sat on a quiet road, nestled between two larger buildings, a little under a mile from the institute. The three-story, stone-white residence with its Juliet balconies was one of the prettiest on the block.

"This might work," Évelyne said, her tone hopeful as we approached the front door.

She knocked twice and we heard a dog bark. Seconds passed before a middle-aged woman, holding a light gray poodle, peeked around the door and waved us inside. Évelyne introduced us and explained my circumstances while Madame Martin, and her dog, eyeballed me with interest.

Eventually, we followed Madame Martin up the stairs to the third floor as she shared details of the room. "The rent is 400 francs per month and I require a 100-franc deposit. There is a sink in the room and it comes fully furnished with a bed, nightstand, desk, and dresser."

We reached the top landing and proceeded down the hallway, bunching up when Madame Martin paused at a closed door. "This is the toilet. If you want to take a shower, you can use the bathroom connected to my son's bedroom on the second floor."

My jaw dropped. *What!* Did I understand her correctly? Would I have to get permission to use the shower? This was even less convenient than my arrangement at the *Château de Montclair*.

Closing my mouth, I followed Madame Martin into the bedroom. It was just as she had described—nothing fancy, but compact and clean. There was a small dormer window on the north wall with a radiator beneath it. When I drew back the curtain, I noted the rooftop view. *It's warm and cozy, but that shower situation is a real bummer.*

Once we were back downstairs, Madame Martin invited us into the salon for a cup of tea. She livened up a bit and her tone turned friendly, sharing information about her family and some of the house rules.

"I have been married for twenty years and we have two boys.

Thomas, my oldest, is fifteen, and Frédéric is thirteen." She held up her dog and gave her a little smooch. "You've already met my little girl, Sophie."

Good. She doesn't appear to be another Madame Dubois.

The dog woofed and Madame Martin gently shushed her. "We have two rooms for rent in our house and I expect residents to keep them tidy. Tenants can come and go as they please, but I ask them to be especially careful about noise after ten o'clock at night. My husband works an early shift and he needs his rest. Currently, no one is in the second room."

Did she just mention a curfew? I glanced at Évelyne and raised my eyebrows. French numbers, especially when they were tied to the time of day, continued to baffle me.

"I'll fill you in on the details later, okay?" Évelyne said, taking a sip of her tea.

I returned my attention to Madame Martin, who rattled off several more sentences that were incomprehensible. Évelyne asked a few more questions, we finished our tea, and rose to leave.

On our way out, Madame Martin pointed to a telephone on the kitchen wall. "Occasionally, I allow tenants to use my phone. Not long distance, mind you, but local calls."

This was an interesting development. Lori's apartment was located on the other side of town. If I had access to a telephone, we would be able to communicate easier. I would also be able to leave a message at the number Adam gave me. This was great news considering there was no way I could afford to sign up for my own phone line.

We said our goodbyes and Madame Martin watched from her stoop as we walked to the Citroën and climbed in.

"Well, how did you like the place?" Évelyne asked, her voice filled with excitement as she released the parking brake and pulled out into the street.

Scratching my neck, I debated the pros and cons. "I wish I had my own bathroom, but Madame Martin seems nice, and I do like the room."

"Ah!" Évelyne exhaled in relief. "*Ça y est: C'est parti!*" That's it: We're good! "I think you'll be happy here. Do you have any specific questions?"

"Yes—do I have to be home at a certain hour?"

Her eyes twinkled. "No." She filled me on the details of her conversation with Madame Martin and I felt my body relax.

Everything was falling into place. Thanks to Évelyne, I'd enrolled at the institute and I'd found a place to rent. I was finally on my own in Tours, and I couldn't wait to hang out with my friends and check out the social scene.

My insides rippled as I switched my thoughts over to Adam. *He'll be so happy to hear my news. I can't wait to hold him in my arms.*

3

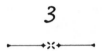

*A*dam rolled out of bed the next morning, unaware he had an audience. I watched him tug on his jeans, snatch a T-shirt off the floor and stretch it over his head, his lean muscles rippling with the movement. When he turned around, our eyes locked and his dimples materialized.

"I didn't mean to wake you." He walked over and sat on the edge of the bed.

"You didn't. I was just enjoying the view."

Adam laughed, a familiar, pleasing sound. With one swift movement, he gathered me in his arms. "*Je t'adore,*" he whispered in my ear, causing a million goose bumps to form on my skin.

I adored him too, but I knew this declaration would sound silly in English. *I'll show him instead.* I nuzzled his neck and then moved down his chest, leaving a trail of kisses behind.

He groaned and drew away, his demeanor suddenly turning serious as he dragged me to my feet. "We'll have to save that for later, *ma chérie.* Marc told me about another room for rent nearby on *rue Littre.* I think we should check it out."

My right eyebrow shot upward. "Huh? I told Évelyne I'd rent the room we found yesterday."

Adam let go of my fingers and shoved his hands in his pockets. "I don't like the shower arrangement at that place."

Ah, I see. I bit my lip to hide my amusement. He's worried about Madame Martin's son. I can't blame him. I wouldn't like it if our positions were reversed.

"Okay, but if this room doesn't work out, will you come with me to Madame Martin's so I can show you her room? You'll feel better after you see it."

"*D'accord.*" Adam glanced at his bedside clock and gestured to my clothes. "Hurry and get dressed. We can grab some breakfast along the way."

Four hours later, Adam and I retraced our steps back to his apartment; both of us contrasting the shabby, overpriced rental on *rue Littre* with my comfortable new room at Madame Martin's home.

"You were right." He steered me to the left to avoid a collision with a lamppost. "The room you found with Évelyne will work out fine. It's certainly a better choice than the other one."

"I'm so glad you agree." Glancing his way, I smiled and squeezed his fingers. "Oh, and thanks for helping me with the deposit and rental agreement. I would have been lost without you."

Adam brought my hand to his lips. "*Ce n'était rien, ma chérie.*" It was nothing, my dearest. My heart fluttered. He always seemed to know the perfect thing to say and his sexy French words were a never-ending source of pleasure. *I think I could get used to this. Will that be an option in the future?*

Now that an important issue was settled, our mood turned jubilant. We strolled down the sidewalk, conversing easily, our arms swinging as we maneuvered around passersby.

Across the street, a clothing boutique came into view, its pink neon sign flashing 'Hollywood Bazaar' every few seconds. Curious, I persuaded Adam to jaywalk to get a closer look. While he feigned interest, I peered in the window and wondered aloud about the garments on the manikins.

"Do you think these are the latest styles from Paris?"

He shrugged. "I have no idea."

"I've been meaning to ask. Why are there so few holiday decorations? Back home the stores go crazy, especially with their window displays."

"It is less common in France. There is a town . . . I think it's called Colmar. It is famous for its Christmas markets."

My words came out wistful. "I'd love to see that someday."

We resumed our promenade and stumbled upon an Angora tabby cat stretched out on a bench outside a bookstore. When we stopped to say "'hello," he jumped down to greet us, winding around our legs, purring loudly. Charmed, I bent down to stroke him and he rolled onto his back, exposing his tummy. When a car horn sounded, he jumped to his feet and scurried down the sidewalk.

Five minutes later, we arrived at *la Place Plumereau*. The unusually mild weather had lured tourists into the square. Many of them milled about, checking menus, trying to decide where to stop for a meal. Heavenly aromas drifted our way making my mouth water.

"Mmm, something smells delicious." I inhaled deeply.

Adam tilted his head. "Are you hungry? Do you want to stop and get something to eat?"

"Okay."

We sauntered along a row of restaurants until Adam turned to me, his expression changing from blasé to brilliant in an instant. "Hey, why don't we go to *Café Jacques*? He's asked about you a couple of times and I know he'd love to see us."

"Great idea! I wondered if we'd get a chance to see him before you left."

Adam's dimple materialized as he pulled me into his embrace. "We still have four more days before I leave. I don't mind sharing you tonight, but I don't think we should make any other plans after this."

My spirits soared. "Sounds good to me. When you return in January, we'll have plenty of time for our friends."

A muscle twitched in Adam's jaw and, for a split second, I wondered if he was keeping something from me. It disappeared swiftly, and when his lips covered mine, my thoughts muddled together and my concerns melted away.

*O*ver the next forty-eight hours, neither of us budged from the apartment, choosing instead to warm up *boeuf bourguignon* leftovers from our tasty dinner at *Café Jacques*. Caught up in our own world, we made love, played cards, listened to music and read books. Adam encouraged me to speak French and I felt my language skills improving.

"I think we need to go grocery shopping today," he announced the following morning as he rifled through the empty refrigerator.

"You're right. I can't cook you a fried chicken dinner until we do." On one of our first dates, I promised to cook Adam a typical American meal. Tonight was the night.

Feeling playful, I lifted my bare leg and twirled my foot to get his attention. "I guess that means I should get dressed?"

Adam's dimples appeared as he closed the refrigerator door and trapped me inside his embrace. "That would be a shame, because you look so cute in my shirt."

"Mmm, what a sweet thing to say." I reached up on my tiptoes and wrapped my fingers around his neck. "I've always thought that it looked better on you."

Adam swept me into his arms, his voice turning husky as he carried me to the bedroom. "Well, if that's the case, I think you should give it back to me immediately."

I met his gaze, my grin suggestive as I tried out a new French phrase. "*Avec plaisir, mon coeur.*" With pleasure, sweetheart.

An hour later, we walked out of the apartment building, the frigid temperature an unwelcome surprise.

"*Merde!* I wish the weather would stay consistent," Adam said, zipping up his jacket. "The grocer's isn't far. Let's hurry."

We picked up the pace and grabbed a cart outside the local grocer's, both of us heaving a sigh of relief once we felt the warmth inside the store. We leaned against each other, smiling as we discussed menus, gathered and purchased two bags of foodstuffs, including eggs, potatoes, fruit, cheese and green beans. There was no corn on the cob, even in the freezer. When we asked a clerk about it, he told us that the French considered it pig food.

Back on the cobbled sidewalk, we found a butcher shop, bought our chicken, and popped into the bakery for a couple of baguettes.

"What about wine?" I asked, glancing his way.

"Yes, let's stop at a shop on the way home. I think we should buy a white to go with the meal, don't you?"

"Perhaps a sauvignon blanc?"

Adam's eyes sparkled. "*Oui. Très bien.*"

We crossed at the next light, entered the wine store and, five minutes later, exited with four bottles of wine—two red and two white.

Continuing down the street, we passed by a tourist office. A question that I'd been trying to ignore came to mind. "What time does your train depart for Paris on the twentieth?"

Adam blanched. "I am not sure. Sometime around ten."

His strong reaction surprised me. I didn't realize how upset he was about leaving me behind. *Darn, why did I bring this up right now?* With our hands full of groceries, neither one of us could reach out and comfort the other.

Swallowing hard, I ventured, "I'll miss you. Thank goodness it's only two weeks. Will you write to me?"

Adam glanced my way. "*Bien sûr, ma chérie.*"

Don't push too hard, Linda. I couldn't stop myself.

"Do you promise?" My lips formed a smile as I eyed him with feigned suspicion.

There was only the slightest hesitation. "I promise."

Once we arrived back at the apartment, Adam helped me put away the groceries, and then rushed out again to run some errands while I prepared dinner. It felt good to have some time alone and I planned to use it wisely.

I flicked through the record collection, my mouth dropping when I spotted Rod Stewart's "Blondes Have More Fun." *Right on! Does this belong to Adam?* I had a strong suspicion it was part of Marc's collection.

Singing along to "Da Ya Think I'm Sexy," I cut the chicken into pieces, dipped them in egg and rolled them in flour. A little salt and pepper, and into the refrigerator they went. Next, I peeled and cut up the potatoes, leaving them submerged in water so they wouldn't brown. Grabbing a few beans at a time, I trimmed the ends, filled a pot with water and placed it on the burner. *Voilà*, the last of my food preparations were complete.

Anticipating a nice long shower, I undressed, entered the bathroom and pulled back the curtain. When I heard the front door slam, my head turned. "That didn't take long." I shouted, wrapping a towel around my body before entering the hallway.

"Marc!" I felt my eyes widen as I searched for the correct French words. "I didn't . . . I mean . . . I'm so sorry, but Adam is not here. He went to get his airline ticket. He should be back in an hour or so."

His bangs fell forward as he appraised me from top to bottom. When he spoke, his words were slurred. "*Eh bien.* I can wait for him. You don't mind, right?"

"No . . . Of course not," I lied. *I know this is his apartment, but this is so awkward.* I was pretty sure he'd been drinking and we were both too focused on my lack of attire. "If you'll excuse me, I'll go and put on some clothes."

I turned and headed for the bedroom until I heard Marc's footsteps right behind me.

"What are you doing?" I threw over my shoulder, alarm increasing the pitch of my voice.

He pushed his hands into his back pockets and his body swayed right, then left. "I thought you might like some help getting dressed."

My lips thinned as I narrowed my gaze. His behavior was totally inappropriate. "I think you should go."

He grabbed me by the wrist with surprising speed. I wrestled free and glared at him. "I mean it. Leave right now and I won't tell Adam about this." *Or your fiancée,* I thought silently.

He laughed as he wandered down the hall, slamming the front door. My knees almost buckled and I collapsed against the wall for support. *Oh my God! I can't believe that just happened.* Did he really think I would agree to such a thing? What a sleaze. Poor Yvette, he might be good looking, but he was definitely not a catch.

When Adam returned home, I didn't mention the incident with Marc. I knew it would throw a shadow over our special dinner alone. He had already warned me that a few of his friends would be stopping by the following day to say goodbye, so this was our last night together.

"Your dinner smells delicious." Adam joined me in the kitchen, smiling as he studied my face. *"Tu es très belle ce soir."* You're beautiful this evening.

My cheeks warmed. I had spent a bit more time on my appearance and I was pleased that he noticed.

"Thank you," I replied, reaching up to brush my bangs to the side. "Will you please open the wine while I dish up?"

"Bien sûr."

Once we were seated at the table, Adam poured the wine and we held up our glasses for a toast. "To us," he proposed before we both took a sip.

"What do you think of the sauvignon blanc?"

I let the wine rest on my tongue before swallowing. "Mmm, I like it very much." He gave me an approving nod and then focused on the food.

The wine disappeared swiftly while we ate, prompting us to uncork a second bottle. Sharing stories, offering each other bites of chicken or potato, giggling and touching, we enjoyed the moment.

Eventually, Adam relaxed in his chair and patted his abdomen. *"Très bon.* What a fabulous meal. I've never had anything quite like it."

I stretched my hand across the table to rest on top of his. "I'm so glad you enjoyed it."

Once we finished our wine, Adam cleared the table while I straightened up the kitchen. When the doorbell rang, both of us started.

"I wonder who that could be?" he said, placing our dishes in the sink.

Twisting the ring on my finger, I shadowed him into the foyer. *I doubt Marc would use the doorbell, but . . .*

When Adam pulled open the door, Albert and Lori stood there

holding two bottles of Syrah. It took us a few seconds to react, our embraces warm and welcoming once we recovered from the surprise.

"I know we weren't invited, but we wanted to see Adam before he left town," Lori explained, giving me a hug as she passed her bottle to Albert. "Maybe I missed my girlfriend too."

"*Naturellement*. We're glad you came." Adam collected their coats and draped them over a chair. "Albert, it looks like you need a corkscrew."

The husky Swede grinned. "I think you have it right."

We watched the guys walk into the kitchen. Once they were out of sight, Lori whispered, "Like I've said before, aren't we lucky girls." She pulled me into the living room, plopped down on the couch and patted the spot next to her.

"So, how are things going?" She examined my face, nodding with approval. "Hmm, I can see that you're happy, but I'd love to hear you say it just the same."

I sighed with contentment. "Yeah, we're getting along really well. Adam is wonderful . . . but you already know that. I just wish he didn't have to leave so soon. Thank goodness I'll have you around during the holidays."

Lori pushed out her bottom lip and my eyes widened in surprise. "Don't tell me that you're going home for Christmas too?"

"Yeah . . . I'm sorry. My parents bought me an airline ticket a few days ago. I leave on the twenty-third."

Competing thoughts swirled inside my head and my mouth went dry. I missed my family. I wished that I could go home for the holidays too, but there was no way my parents could afford to buy me a ticket. Heck, I was just thankful that they let me stay in France, so I'd just have to make the best of it. It wouldn't be easy without Adam and Lori.

Shaking my head, I offered her a tenuous smile. "I'm bummed that you won't be here, but of course I understand. When will you return?"

"December thirtieth. We'll celebrate New Year's Eve together, okay?"

Some of my tension melted away. "I'd like that."

Her face brightened. "So, did you find a place to live?"

"Yeah, I sure did." I shared some of the details of my new room.

A few minutes later, the guys entered and passed drinks to us. Adam sat on the floor next to me, his back propped against the sofa while Albert claimed the sole armchair.

"So . . . what have you two been up to?" Lori asked, targeting Adam as she took a sip of wine.

He scratched his head and searched the ceiling for an answer while I suppressed a giggle. This was a tricky question. We'd spent most of our time together tangled up in bed. "I took Linda to dinner at *Café Jacques* a few nights ago. Mostly we've stayed pretty close to home."

Lori's right eyebrow lifted. "Well, you guys really missed out. A group of us went to *Club Bonne Ville* last weekend." She glanced my way. "I'm pretty sure I told you about that place, right?"

"I think so."

"The DJ joined us on the dance floor and showed us some funky moves. It was so awesome . . ."

Over the next few hours, we recounted stories and played cards, our joviality increasing with each uncorked bottle of wine. When the clock struck two, our friends finally staggered to the door.

As we said our goodbyes, Lori lingered to whisper in my ear. "On Thursday, Albert and I will pick you up around ten o'clock. It's about time you experienced some Tours nightlife."

My chest tightened. "I doubt I'll be in the mood."

Lori harrumphed. "Come on, Linda. It'll be a great distraction. You don't want to spend your first night without Adam alone, do you?"

Maybe she's right. "Okay, you win. I'll see you on Thursday."

She patted my arm and followed Albert into the hallway, their heels clicking an irregular beat down the wooden stairs.

"What was that about?" Adam asked, drawing me close.

"Lori's determined to keep me busy after you leave . . . for a few days anyway." My words sounded heavier than I intended.

"What do you mean?"

"She's going home for Christmas too."

Adam's shoulders sagged. "*C'est nul*, I'm so sorry to hear this."

Standing on my tiptoes, I wrapped my arms around his neck and pressed the length of my body against his. We had only two days left together. I didn't want to waste time discussing things we couldn't change—especially not tonight. "Let's focus on something else, okay?"

Adam's eyes filled with mischief as he kissed me. His grip strengthened and our passion escalated until he broke away, leaving me gasping for air. I watched as he yanked off his shirt and then reached out and tugged mine over my head. With a firm hand, he drew me back into his embrace and a jolt of electricity surged through my body.

I swooned against him, my words almost a moan. "It's time for bed, don't you think?"

His breath felt hot against my cheek. "No, *ma chérie*. It's time for love."

5

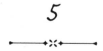

*T*he next day, I woke up in bed alone. Puzzled, I slipped into my robe and discovered Adam's note in the kitchen. *Ah, he's running a few errands. Did he tell me about this yesterday?* Oh well, it doesn't matter. He'll be back in a few hours.

Stifling a yawn, I pushed my hair behind my ears and filled the sink with soapy water. There were several dirty wine glasses around the apartment, so I collected and washed them before wiping down the counters.

While I worked, my mind filled with fantasies about a future with Adam. Would he be willing to stay in France after he finished college? *I wonder how his family would react if our relationship turned serious.*

Once this area was clean, I straightened the bedroom, dressed and settled at the table to write in my diary. A quick review of my recent entries warmed my insides—and my cheeks. Most of them centered on romance and today was no exception.

> *Adam held me in his arms all night long. I felt very close to him and I think I might be losing my heart to this special man.*

Time passed slowly. By midafternoon, I decided to get some fresh air and take a walk to the post office to phone my parents. Wrapping a knitted burgundy scarf around my neck, I descended into the frigid cold and picked my way along *rue de la Grandière,* shivers hurrying me toward my destination.

Soon the Tours Post Office came into sight. *I hope my French is good enough to place a collect call without Lori's help.* All of the booths were filled, so I waited until someone left before squeezing through the door. With great concentration, I inserted my money and asked the operator to place a collect call. After three rings, someone answered.

"Hello?"

Darn, I forgot about the time difference. It was around six o'clock in the morning in Seattle.

"Hi, Dad."

"Linda! It's so nice to hear from you. Is everything okay?"

"Yes . . . yes, I'm fine." I cleared my throat. "Did I wake you?"

I heard some rustling noises and I assumed he took a seat nearby. "No, not at all—I was up an hour ago. It sure surprised me when the phone rang, though. Are you still at Évelyne's?"

"No, I'm staying at a friend's apartment in Tours until I move into my new room around the first of January."

"Oh, good. So you found a place to rent?"

My lips slid into a smile. "Yes, yes I did."

Running my fingers up and down the metal phone cord, I described the highlights of my room and told him about my visit to the institute. I also gave him bank instructions on how to wire money to my account in Tours.

Dad didn't ask me who I was currently staying with, and I didn't enlighten him. Since I had shared very little about Adam in my letters, I didn't want him to come to the wrong conclusion: that I left the château to be with my boyfriend. There would be plenty of opportunities to discuss this later.

"So . . . it sounds like you're set for the time being. I'll send more money in a few days."

"Okay, that would be great." Sudden emotions surfaced and my vision blurred. "I miss you and Mom. It'll be strange not to be home for the holidays."

"Your mother was saying something about that yesterday."

Back home, Christmas was usually a simple affair with immediate family members. Occasionally, Mom's sister Josie and her husband Dusan would show up with a six-pack of beer and a *kielbasa*. Every year, Dad purchased a scrawny tree at Chubby and Tubby, and I'd do my best to "pretty it up," filling in the big gaps with ornaments and tinsel. For dinner, mom baked a ham while I prepared the mashed potatoes and gravy. A 'Slavic' salad, lettuce with oil and vinegar, rounded out the meal. All of us looked forward to Mom's delightful Croatian apple strudel for dessert.

"I suppose you'll be with your friends?" Dad's question brought me back to the present—in a cramped phone booth.

"Yeah, I'll probably spend the day with Évelyne." *At least I hope so.* I hadn't received an invitation from her yet, but I didn't want to worry him.

"That'll be nice."

"Yeah." I shifted from one foot to the other. "So, how are the rentals?"

"Oh, you know how it goes—it's always a struggle to keep them filled."

Poor Dad. He hates being a landlord. My parent's low-income rental properties supplied them with a meager living, but it was tough to find good tenants and there were constant repairs.

"I'm sorry to hear that." Then more intense, "I hope you know how much I appreciate you and Mom letting me stay in France."

"Yes, honey, we know."

There was a long silence. I knew my dad had exhausted his communication skills and it was time to end the conversation.

"Well . . . I guess I should get going. Give my love to Mom and Bud."

"I will. Be careful, and write to us as soon as you get a chance. You know how much we enjoy your letters."

When I returned home, Adam met me at the door. He wasn't alone.

"*Salut!*" Marc said, exiting his room, dragging a suitcase and backpack into the foyer. When he leaned in to greet me with a kiss, I resisted the urge to pull away. *Hmm, it looks like we're going to act like nothing happened. Fine by me.*

Marc glanced at his bags and shrugged his shoulders. "*Eh bien*, I think I'm all set. Yvette and I hope to be in Paris by early evening." He turned to me, "When do you move into your new place?"

"The first of January." I removed my coat and laid it on a chair.

"Okay, that should work out fine. We return home on the second."

Good, I thought silently. *I won't have to worry about unexpected visitors.*

Grinning, Marc raised his hand and whacked Adam on the back. "Why don't you help me get this luggage into the car?"

"*Bien sûr.*" Adam grabbed the backpack and they headed for the exit, Marc wishing me "Happy Holidays" over his shoulder as they walked out the door.

When Adam returned ten minutes later, I wrapped my arms around him. "I missed you," I said, smothering his face with kisses.

He frowned and pushed me away gently.

"What's wrong?"

There was a long pause and, when he finally spoke, his voice sounded strained. "I phoned my parents today. There are some—problems—I have to deal with, once I return home." Then, softer, "I'm sorry, *ma chérie*, but I won't be much fun tonight."

A cold chill ran up my spine as I recalled a previous incident with Adam. Shortly after we met, he cancelled a date because of a phone call from home. At that time, he was very upset about some "unresolved issues." Apparently, they had resurfaced.

"Maybe I can help? Let's sit down and talk it over."

He lowered his eyes and I felt his anguish. "There is nothing you can do. Can we drop it for now?" Adam rubbed the back of his neck and turned away. "I have to pack. Would you fix us something to eat?"

"Of course." I felt my shoulder's slump as he walked away. *What a bummer.* This was so unexpected. I could see that he was miserable, but I couldn't comfort him unless he told me what was wrong.

The rest of the day dragged on and on and on. Adam filled a suitcase and dealt with last-minute bills and correspondence, while I puttered around the apartment wishing for the umpteenth time that he had a television. Every once in a while our paths crossed and he would reach out and brush his hand against me. Each time he did this, my heart lurched. He'd shut down emotionally. *But why?*

Hoping to pass the time, I picked up my book and snuggled onto the couch, but I couldn't concentrate. After the third attempt at rereading the same paragraph, I laid it on the side table. I wanted Adam to tell me what was wrong. Was he afraid I'd judge him or his family? He couldn't have been further from the truth.

At seven o'clock, Théo and Sébastien, Adam's friends from college, showed up, each waving bottles of Bordeaux in the air. The wine flowed freely and, after several glassfuls, everyone's mood improved—except mine. I tried to participate, but I got lost in the French conversations and felt left out.

At around midnight, I pulled Adam aside in the kitchen and offered him a shaky smile. *Try not to sound needy, Linda.* "I'm sleepy. I think I'll go to bed."

He met my gaze and I thought I saw something hidden in his eyes. Regret? Or maybe sorrow?

"Adam—"

He placed his thumb against my lips. "Don't ask. Now is not the time. I'll join you after a while."

I swallowed my words, spun around and headed down the hall. *I wonder when he'll come to bed.* It was our last night together and I really needed some reassurances from him.

6

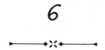

*W*hen I opened my eyes the following morning, Adam was gone. *Oh my God! Did he come to bed last night? I hope he hasn't left yet!* My nerves jumped and then calmed once I spotted his bag resting near the door. I tugged on my clothes, ran a brush through my hair and joined him in the kitchen.

"*Bonjour, ma chérie,*" he said, his face somber as he passed me a mug of coffee and then leaned against the stove.

Damn, this sudden distance is killing me. He was leaving soon and I still had no idea what was going on. I glanced at the clock on the wall—it was nine o'clock. *I wish we had more time.*

"It looks like you're ready to go," I said, trying to control the trembling in my voice. "I'd like to come with you to the train station."

"That's not necessary."

"I'd like to come," I repeated, holding back tears of frustration.

Adam wrapped his arms around me. "Okay, okay," he said, resting his chin on the top of my head. "Finish your coffee and then we'll go."

Fifteen minutes later, Adam slung the duffle on his back. We walked out of the apartment and headed toward the train station. Melancholy thoughts weighed down my shoulders and it seemed to affect Adam too as we walked along in silence.

"What time is your flight to Morocco?" I ventured.

"7:20 p.m." Grasping my upper arm, he guided me around a group of tourists.

"That's good. You'll have plenty of time to get to *Charles de Gaulle* once you arrive in Paris. Who's picking you up at the airport when you arrive home?"

"My father," Adam replied, his words curt . . . bitter?

"You don't sound thrilled about that."

"I'm not." His dark brown hair fell forward as he moved his duffle over to his other shoulder. "My father and I rarely see things the same way." Adam didn't elaborate, but I was now fairly certain that the "problems" he referred to yesterday revolved around his dad.

We entered the *Saint-Pierre-des-Corps* train station and walked onto the platform. Adam laid his bag aside as we said our goodbyes.

"*Je suis désolé,*" I'm sorry, he whispered into my hair. "I didn't mean to leave you this way."

I lifted my head, my chest pounding as my eyes filled with unshed tears. "I don't know what to say, Adam. Maybe you can explain it to me in a letter?"

"I'll try, *ma chérie.*" His kiss was perfunctory—not the kind I expected.

"*On embarque maintenant pour Paris!*" Boarding now for Paris!

The train attendant's announcement froze me. *I don't want him to go.* "You get back on January second, right?"

"Yes, although that could change. I'll contact you as soon as I

return." Adam pulled away and picked up his duffle. "I have to go."
He climbed the stairs, waved, and then slipped through the coach door.

Feeling weak in the knees, I leaned against the wall watching the train pull out of the station. *What just happened?* All week long I felt so close to Adam. *Maybe too close.* I'd even started to think about a life together. Now, he felt like a stranger. How could a family phone call change things so drastically?

Scowling, I tried to break my chain of dark thoughts. Hopefully, I would get some answers in the mail. He'd only be gone for two weeks.

I fell in behind a group of tourists and followed them outside and onto the sidewalk. Pausing, I glanced right and then left, wondering what to do next. The idea of returning to Adam's empty apartment felt depressing.

My stomach growled and a sudden realization lifted my spirits: *Today is Thursday. Maybe I can meet up with Adeela—I would love to see my "French tutor." It would be a great distraction.*

Fifteen minutes later, the *Café de l'Europe* came into view, its faded red paint and black-framed windows and doors a familiar sight. The place was packed with students, and it took me a while to locate my friend seated near the back of the room. As I approached, she glanced up from her textbook, her coffee-colored eyes widening with delight when she greeted me in French.

"Linda! What a pleasant surprise." Adeela rose to her feet and her spicy citrus scent filled my nose as she hugged me. "I have wondered what became of you many times."

The corners of my mouth lifted slightly and words tumbled out faster than I intended. "I'm sorry I didn't come sooner. There have been so many changes in my life recently."

"*Eh bien.* I didn't mean to scold you." Adeela waved her bejeweled hand at the empty chair, adjusting her lime-green scarf before sitting down. "I really am pleased to see you."

A waiter appeared, and I asked him about the lunch specials, choosing a *croque monsieur* sandwich and a *café au lait.* As soon as he left, Adeela sat back and folded her hands in her lap. "I'm impressed. Your French has improved since the last time we met."

Her kind words warmed my cheeks. "Thank you. I've been

working hard on it. Adam has been a big help."

"Excusez-moi, s'il vous plaît." Our waiter brought my order and asked if we needed anything else. We both shook our heads.

Adeela met my gaze. "So . . . are you still working as an *au pair* in Songais?"

"No. I gave notice at the château over a week ago."

Her right eyebrow lifted. "Start from the beginning and tell me the whole story. How did Madame react when you told her you were leaving?"

After taking a sip of my coffee, I sat back and recounted my dramatic tale once again—in French this time. I stumbled several times, searching for the right words. I felt thankful for Adeela's help. An hour flew by before I slipped in an inquiry of my own. "Are you finished with your studies at the university?"

A fragile smile came and went. "Almost. The term ends mid-January."

"That's wonderful," I exclaimed, sitting up straight. "What happens now? Will you remain in France?"

This time Adeela blanched, her words barely audible as she pushed some food around her plate. "I doubt it. My parents want me to stay in Tours, but they're running out of money."

Had she ever mentioned her hometown in Lebanon? Even if she had, my knowledge surrounding this war-torn country was limited. I didn't want to upset her, but I felt anxious about her welfare. "Is it safe for you to return home?"

Her gaze swept up to meet mine. "I think so. My family has stayed intact so far. At least that's something."

I flinched and my words came out wobbly. "I'm so sorry . . ."

She nodded. An uncomfortable silence ensued as I searched for something to say. *What a drag. It's still so difficult to communicate in French.*

Adeela glanced at her watch, her bangles clinking together as she reached for her coat. "I have to go. I have an appointment at two o'clock."

With a weighty sigh, I stood and circled the table to say goodbye. "Thank you, so much, for your friendship. I wish there was something I could do to help."

"Don't fret, Linda. I will be fine." She lifted her chin to emphasize her determination. "I'm not sure how much longer I'll be in town, but you'll find me here on Thursdays until I leave. Good luck with your French studies at the institute."

"Good luck to you too, Adeela."

As I watched her walk out of the café, feelings of sadness and humility flooded my mind, blurring my vision. Concerns surrounding my relationship with Adam were trivial compared to the dangers Adeela faced back in Lebanon. I was worried about a broken heart. She might lose her life.

After I returned to Adam's apartment, I stayed busy with household chores and letter writing. At eight o'clock, I climbed into the shower, my face flush with excitement as I anticipated hitting the clubs with my friends.

Thank goodness Lori talked me into going out. It would have been awful to spend my first night away from Adam alone. The last two days had drained me emotionally. Tonight, I wanted to push my worries aside and cut loose.

Sifting through my clothes, I settled on black corduroy jeans paired with a purple peasant top. Makeup came next—lots of black mascara, eyeliner and blue eye shadow—followed by an impulsive decision to let my hair dry naturally into waves. Now that I was free of Madame Dubois, I felt like I could be more adventurous. Silver drop earrings completed the look and finally, a dab of Tabu, my only perfume.

As promised, the doorbell rang at ten o'clock.

"Hi," Lori said, giving me a quick embrace. "Are you ready to go?"

"Yeah, I'll grab my coat."

I locked the door and we joined Albert waiting outside the building. He threw his cigarette on the ground and, arm in arm, the three of us strolled down the streets of Tours. Thirty minutes later, we reached our destination.

The trendy club I'd heard so much about was easily identifiable from a distance. Situated under a modern three-story building, a large lime-green neon sign above the entrance flashed *Club Bonne Ville* every few seconds. Music, with a deep-bass sound, flowed through the open double doors.

"This way," Albert said, guiding us into the short queue outside the club. "Don't worry, the line moves fast."

He was right. Moments later, we surged inside. It took a few minutes for our eyes to adjust to the lighting as we searched the room for an empty table.

"Over there." Albert pointed to the right.

Single file we maneuvered around throngs of people and sat in a booth near the window—Lori and Albert on one side and me on the other.

Grinning, Lori leaned across the table. "I still can't believe you're here. I've been stoked all day to show you this place."

I chuckled at her choice of verbs—one of my brother's favorites. "It's really cool, Lori. I'm so glad you convinced me to come."

Surveying the club, I noticed a large crowd at the bar and a few small groups on the dance floor. In the corner of the room, an energetic DJ placed a record on one of the two turntables in front of him. Grabbing his microphone, he flipped on a switch and announced, "Off The Wall," by Michael Jackson. All around us, people jumped up and scrambled onto the dance floor.

Turning to Lori, I shouted, "So, you don't need a partner in France?"

Lori shook her head. "Nope. If you want to dance, join the party."

This was fascinating. Back in Washington, I loved to frequent nightclubs with my friends. Carline, Cindy and I knew all the "Ladies' Nights" throughout the Seattle area. Depending on the day of the week, we frequented one club or another, taking advantage of the free cover charge and specialty drinks. Dressed up and ready for action, we'd flirt and entice guys onto the floor whenever we heard our favorite songs. Occasionally, we'd bring one of them home at the end of the evening.

"What would you girls like to drink?" Albert's question refocused my thoughts. "How about a couple of French 75s?"

"What's in them?"

Albert rattled off the ingredients. "Gin, champagne, lemon juice and . . . ?" His brow furrowed and he glanced at Lori.

"Sugar," she affirmed before giving me a nod, "I think you'll like it."

"Okay, sure."

I passed Albert some money and, as soon as he left, Lori squeezed in beside me. "Was it hard to say goodbye to Adam this morning?"

I clamped down on my lower lip to stop the tremble. "Yeah, it was terrible." *For more reasons than one.*

Lori slung her arm over my shoulder. "He won't be gone long, and you'll be so happy when he returns. It's hard to talk with the music so loud. You can tell me all about it tomorrow night, okay?"

I forced a smile, pleased that she'd offered me an excuse to drop the subject.

The DJ announced his next choice and Lori squealed with delight. "Come on! This is the new hit song from ABBA."

She pulled me onto floor and we wound our way around dancers, settling on a spot directly in front of the DJ's station. Smiling, Lori waved at him and he winked in our direction.

Getting my groove on, I moved to the beat of the music while a disco ball reflected light in multiple directions. *This is fun.* It felt good to be on the dance floor again. After months of being cooped up inside the château, I was finally experiencing and enjoying the club scene in Tours with people my own age. I could stay out as late as I wanted to and I didn't have to report to anyone the next day.

When the next song came on, Lori sidled up and lightly bumped her hip against mine. *Ah, the "bump."* Smiling with recognition, I twisted and banged my opposite hip against hers. This exchange continued to the beat of the music, Lori and I laughing as we lost ourselves to disco fever.

7

*T*he splitting headache I went to sleep with dogged me the next morning. *Damn.* Why did I let Albert talk me into that last French 75? I promised I'd visit Songais *Collège* today, but I wasn't sure I'd make it.

Holding my head with both hands, I tracked down two Tylenols, swallowed them with a big glass of water, and returned to bed.

Three hours later, when I finally boarded the one o'clock train, I felt a whole lot better. By the time I reached the school and walked through the double doors into the reception area, my headache disappeared.

"*Bonjour,* Linda!" Évelyne jumped up from her desk and embraced me warmly. "I was starting to worry about you."

"I'm sorry I'm late—I'll explain later."

"No problem. I'm just glad you're here now." Glancing at the clock, she grasped my elbow and led me down the hall, our shoes click clacking against the shiny linoleum floors. "Madame Bernard has been asking about you. Her students have something special prepared."

When we reached classroom fourteen, Évelyne rapped on the door, pushed it open, and stood aside for me to enter. "Have fun," she whispered.

Once recognition took hold, Madame Bernard smiled broadly and gestured me to the front of the class with her hand. "Ah, Mademoiselle Kovic. It's so nice to see you."

The noise level in the classroom rose as I joined her, so she raised her arm to gain control. "*Les enfants . . . calmez-vous.* Shall we start with a greeting in English?"

"Welcome back!" they shouted.

Nerves jumping, I took a deep breath. "Hello, everyone!"

Madame Bernard clasped her hands together and surveyed the room. "Who would like to tell Mademoiselle Kovic why we asked her here today?"

Several hands flew into the air. She chose Simone, one of my devoted fans from an earlier visit. Pushing her dark mane behind her back, Simone stood and glanced around the room at fellow students while she spoke. "Mademoiselle, because you were so kind and helped us with our English, we collected money and bought you some Christmas presents."

I pressed my palm to my chest and I spun toward Madame Bernard. "Presents? I don't know what to say. I really enjoyed spending time with all of you. This is completely unexpected."

Madame Bernard beamed. "Madeleine and Sylvie, why don't you

two fetch the gift."

Giggling with excitement, they retrieved a large beautifully wrapped box from the closet and handed it to me.

My throat swelled with emotion and I coughed to clear it. "How lovely. Shall I open it now?"

"Yes, please!" All eyes focused straight ahead as Madame Bernard brought a chair and encouraged me to sit down. My hands trembled as I gently tore open the red and green wrapping and peered inside. One by one, I pulled out chocolates from the town of Blois, a bottle of Grand Marnier, and a sleepy-eyed French souvenir doll from the Loire Valley.

Clutching them close, I choked out some earnest words. "Thank you, so much, for these wonderful presents. The doll is beautiful—I will treasure her always. And chocolates are my favorite candy. How did you all guess?"

"It wasn't a difficult assumption. Who doesn't like chocolates?" Madame Bernard placed her hand on my shoulder. "*Alors*, now that we've given Mademoiselle Kovic her gifts, perhaps she will tell us a bit more about her plans for the future?"

The noise level in the classroom rose once again and Madame Bernard clapped her hands until the children calmed down.

Over the next thirty minutes, I answered a series of questions from the students—so many that I felt like I was on a game show. Questions about my new room in Tours, questions about my enrollment at the institute, and loads of questions about my dream of becoming a flight attendant.

When the bell rang and Madame Bernard excused the children for recess, many of them approached to shake my hand and say goodbye. Simone and her friends lingered to share some holiday plans until their teacher insisted they move on.

We watched them walk out the door, and then Madame Bernard motioned for me to take a seat beside her desk. "The children were so excited to see you today."

"Hmm, I still can't believe they gave me these gifts." I shook my head. "It was such a surprise." Then with a grin I said, "I have a feeling you had something to do with this too."

"Maybe a little, but it was mostly their idea." She brushed a strawberry-blonde curl from her cheek. "So, things seem to be going well for you."

"Yeah, it feels good to be on my own."

Madame Bernard nodded. "I think you should know that Madame Dubois paid me a visit recently. She tried her best to defend her actions, claiming that you left her in a terrible predicament . . . and that she had no choice other than to act as she did. I told her that her behavior was inexcusable. I think it's safe to say that we'll never be friends."

My chest constricted with the mention of my former employer's name and feelings of guilt overcame me. "I'm sorry to hear that. I didn't mean to put you in that position. All of this trouble started with me. I'm the one who lied in the first place."

"Yes, that's true, but she took advantage of the situation and mistreated you, especially in the end." She shifted in her chair. "I also learned something else. You aren't the first girl to have trouble with her. Three years ago, her *au pair* left after only one month."

Emotions bubbled to the surface and my words came out crackly. "Really? That's awful. Well, I'm just glad the nightmare is over."

Madame Bernard patted my hand. "Yes, of course. We all are." Pursing her lips, she glanced at her wrist. "*Zut alors!* I have a few things to finish up before the students return. The school has an early dismissal today for the holidays."

"No problem. I think Évelyne made some plans for a late lunch."

"How nice." She handed me my box of goodies. "I'll walk you to the office, and you can tell me more about your new room along the way."

After Madame Bernard and I said our goodbyes, Évelyne drove us to a charming, picturesque restaurant called *Maison Henri* on the outskirts of Songais.

Breathtaking views of the green valley and a glimpse of the Loire River combined with the restaurant's casual elegance—mahogany tables and chairs, crystal chandeliers, and white tablecloths—to produce the perfect atmosphere for our special meal.

A waiter in a black apron ushered us to our seats, handing us menus before scurrying away. Évelyne translated a few dishes for me and, when he returned, she placed an order for two specials: roasted *turbot*—a popular flatfish—smothered in a *beurre blanc,* a butter and wine sauce. She ordered a bottle of *chenin blanc* to complement the fish.

The wine arrived almost immediately and, a short while later, our waiter delivered our *turbot*.

"It smells fantastic—don't you think?" Évelyne asked, inhaling the superb aroma.

"*Oui*, heavenly."

Communication wasn't easy, but we managed using a combination of broken English and stilted French. I told her about my new life in Tours and she talked about her job at the school. When our waiter returned to clear the table, Évelyne brought up a timely topic.

"You must be excited to spend Christmas with your friends this year. I can only imagine what the holidays would have been like for you if you'd stayed at the *Château de Montclair*?"

My body tensed, and I wiped my hands on my thighs. *I'm not going to tell her about my lack of plans yet. I don't want to put her on the spot.* "Yeah, Christmas with the Dubois family would have been miserable. What about you? Do you have plans?"

"I go home every year to Lyon to celebrate the holidays with my mother and younger brother's family. Nothing too special, but I really enjoy seeing my niece and nephew."

I shifted my gaze and hid my disappointment in a sip of wine. "Mmm . . . it sounds like fun." *Darn it. I'm happy for her, but it's not the answer I'd hoped for.* The waiter delivered the bill and Évelyne reached for her purse. "This lunch is a Christmas gift from me," she said with a wink.

Astonished by her generosity, it took me a few seconds to respond. "Thank you . . . Thank you, so much," I managed, my words rough with emotion. "I wish I could do something special for you. Maybe someday you'll come to the United States for a visit."

Évelyne smiled sweetly and dabbed her lips with a napkin. "*Peut-être.* I enjoy your company, Linda. I don't expect anything in return."

Ten minutes later, she dropped me off at the station and I caught the train back to Tours. On the ride home, I reflected on our lunch. She had such a big heart and was so easy to be around. I wished we could be together at Christmas. *Argh . . . there has to be somewhere I can go.*

A train traveling in the opposite direction brought me back to the present and I watched it flick past. When the view opened up, I released a long lingering sigh as the Loire countryside descended into darkness.

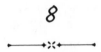

I walked out of the apartment into the cool, crisp air the following morning, and headed toward *Basilique Saint-Martin* to attend the eleven o'clock Sunday Mass. Only two days remained before Christmas and, even though I didn't go to church often, I enjoyed the songs and sermons during the holidays more than any other time of the year. It would feel good to be around people today—I definitely needed a change of scenery.

I glanced at my watch and flinched. Darn, I should have left the apartment fifteen minutes ago. *I don't want to be late.* Wrapping my scarf around my neck, I hurried along *rue des Halles* and arrived at the entrance with only a few minutes to spare. Panting, I climbed the stairs, pausing to catch my breath before entering the church. I kneeled, dipped my fingers into the holy water, made the sign of the cross and slid into a pew near the back.

Given the special time of year, the Catholic ceremony was even more elaborate than the Mass I had attended with the Dubois Family at *Cathédrale Saint-Gatien*. Christmas music filled the nave, decorated with holly and mistletoe, while scents of citrus and spices from the frankincense permeated the crowd. The priest's oration was in French, so I understood very little of what he said, but emotions clouded my eyes more than once as I bowed my head and thanked the Lord for his sacrifice and prayed for the safety of my family and friends.

I felt invigorated after the Mass, so I decided to explore a few of the side streets in *le Vieux Tours* on my way home. Veering left down a cobbled lane, I discovered *Le Café Vert*, a quaint restaurant, painted hunter green, tucked under a half-timbered building. A faint smell—perhaps vanilla—drifted through the open window and I closed my eyes, inhaling deeply. The café probably baked its own desserts. *Mmm . . . I'll bet they're good.*

There was a menu displayed in the window and, when I strolled closer to look, a big-bellied man with a large mustache and an apron tied around his waist appeared.

"*Bonjour, Mademoiselle. Vous voulez une table?*" Hello, Miss. A table?

I bit my lip. *Maybe just a cup of coffee.* After my spending sprees over the last few nights, I wasn't sure I could afford lunch. "*Oui, merci.*"

The waiter seated me near the back of the room and took my order. As soon as he left, I surveyed my surroundings.

Eight oak tables with lace tablecloths sat beneath low-hung glass chandeliers. A collage of black-and-white framed photographs of the Loire countryside, large and small, hung on the sky blue walls.

There was only one other person in the tiny restaurant and, when our eyes met, he nodded in my direction. The unexpected attention from a strange man tensed my jaw and I quickly looked away. *Oh dear, this could get awkward. What have I gotten myself into?*

The waiter swooped in with my *café au lait* and addressed the man nearby with mock frustration. "Where is everybody today, Michel? You need to tell more of your friends about this place."

Michel chuckled and crossed his arms. "Bruno, I've brought you plenty of business over the years. You should be glad I'm a regular."

"Perhaps you're right," Bruno mumbled, wandering toward the kitchen.

I watched with unease as the man, now identified as "Michel," stood and approached my table. "*Salut.* I hope you'll forgive me, but I hate to see a beautiful woman sitting alone in a restaurant. May I join you for an *espresso*?"

My stomach twisted as I contemplated his suggestion. How would Adam feel about this? *Maybe I should refuse. Why? It's only a cup of coffee.*

"*D'accord.*" I nodded.

As soon as Michel took his seat, Bruno magically reappeared and passed him a menu. "Just in case you'd like to order lunch."

While Michel perused the menu, I studied him with a critical eye. He was older than me, perhaps in his late twenties, with coffee-brown eyes, an angular face, and thick dark hair that fell to his shoulders. His body, wrapped in a charcoal gray sweater, was lean and compact. An average man—not handsome like Adam.

Once Michel placed his order, Bruno left us alone. *"Vous êtes américaine?"* Are you American?

"Yes. Do you speak English?"

He shook his head. "No, I'm sorry."

Hmm . . . then this won't be easy. "I guess we'll have to speak French. I have to warn you, I'm not very good at it."

Michel smiled and I noted his straight, white teeth. *"Alors,* you know my name, but I don't know yours."

"Linda . . . My name is Linda Kovic."

"What a pretty name." He reached into his coat pocket, pulled out a pack of *Gitanes,* and raised his eyebrows. "Smoke?"

"No, thank you."

He lit a cigarette and inhaled deep. "Tell me, Linda. What brought you to Tours? Are you a student?"

"Sort of." Trying to keep it simple, I told him about my desire to learn French and a few details surrounding my time as an *au pair.*

Because of the language barrier, the conversation stalled on more than one occasion, but Michel didn't seem to mind. He was helpful and tolerant with my French, articulating his questions in a slow, deliberate manner, often rephrasing his sentences so they were easier to understand.

"Why did you quit your job as an *au pair?* Did they mistreat you?"

"Yes," I said, meeting his gaze. "My employer wanted a maid and a nanny, but I wasn't hired to do both jobs."

Michel snorted, ground out his cigarette and ran his fingers through his hair. "The French *bourgeoisie* think they can walk all over people. You stood up for yourself. Good for you."

I blinked. *Did he just call Madame Dubois bourgeoisie?* I didn't know how to respond.

Bruno saved me the trouble when he returned with Michel's meal. *"Voilà, une tarte au chèvre et un espresso."* Goat's cheese quiche and espresso.

Scrumptious smells of hazelnut and nutmeg filled the air, making my mouth water. "Will you join me?" Michel gestured toward the dish with his fork.

"Yes, please."

He slipped half of the fragrant tartlet onto a side plate and passed it over to me.

"Mmm, this is delicious. Thank you."

While we ate, I asked a few questions of my own. "What about you? Are you a student too?"

"Not right now. I'm taking a break from my graduate studies in psychology so I can earn some money."

Ahh . . . psychology—that explained his good listening skills. He was exceptionally patient with my broken French. "Doing what?"

Michel shifted in his seat. "I translate French books into Arabic."

"Like textbooks?"

"All kinds of books."

"I see." Really, I didn't, but Michel's short answers didn't encourage elaboration. While he lit another cigarette, I tried a more personal approach. "Did you grow up in the Loire Valley?"

His expression mellowed along with his voice. "No. I was born in Lebanon, but my mother is French."

My sip of coffee went down the wrong pipe. I coughed and reached for a napkin. *That's crazy!* During my short stay in France, I'd met two different men with foreign fathers and French mothers. Was that a common thing? It would be rude to ask.

I pushed my hair behind my ears and took a bite of my tart. "I met a wonderful girl from Lebanon a few months ago. Her name is Adeela and she lives in the area. Perhaps you know her?"

"No, that name doesn't sound familiar." Michel relaxed in his chair and folded his arms across his chest. "What about you? What part of the United States are you from?"

"My home is on the west side of the country, in Washington State."

Over the next hour, we discussed everything from family to French culture. I learned that Michel's family—his mother, father and two sisters—still lived in Sidon, a large city in southern Lebanon along the Mediterranean coast. He left there in 1970 and never returned.

When he told me this, my mouth gaped. I couldn't imagine a ten-year stretch without seeing my parents or brother. "How sad. You must miss your family."

He nodded. "Yeah, I planned a visit shortly after I moved, but it didn't work out. Everything changed after the war broke out in 1975."

The conversation took a turn when Michel asked a personal question—one I had anticipated. "What about boyfriends? Did you leave someone behind? Or maybe you've met someone since you arrived in France?"

Ah . . . finally. It'll feel good to get this out in the open. "I have a boyfriend here in Tours. His name is Adam."

Michel held my gaze. "I'm not surprised. A bit disappointed, perhaps, but not surprised. What are your plans for Christmas?"

My face warmed and I looked away. "Adam left town yesterday to be with his family for the holidays."

"What about you? Where will you go?"

"I'm on my own," I said, amazed at how steady my voice sounded. "It seems that all of the people I know are heading home. That wasn't an option for me."

Michel gave me a long silent stare and I wondered what he was thinking. "Why don't you join me for Christmas? I'm dining with a few friends . . . nothing fancy."

My coffee cup hit the saucer with an unintentional thump. *What? I barely know him.* "It's nice of you to ask, but I wouldn't want to intrude."

"You would be welcome. Like I said, it's no big deal."

I glanced around the room, looking for Bruno. "Listen, it's getting late. I really should go."

Reaching in my purse, I pulled out some francs and placed them on the table. Michel pushed them back. "My treat this time."

"Thank you." We both stood as I slipped into my coat.

"I enjoyed meeting you today, Linda." Michel offered me his hand and I noted his long smooth fingers. *He's clearly not a man who works with his hands.* "If you change your mind about Christmas, you can find me here tomorrow around the same time."

"I'll think about it. I really do appreciate the offer."

Frowning, I walked out of the café and strolled toward Adam's apartment, contemplating Michel's generous invitation. Maybe he was just being nice. Now that he knew I had a boyfriend, would it be okay for me to join him? *He's interesting and it's good for me to practice my French.*

What about Adam? I was fairly certain he wouldn't want me to spend the holiday with Michel. *Argh . . . he wouldn't want me to spend it alone either.* I wished I knew what to do. *I could really use a friend right now.*

9

$\mathcal{T}$he overcast sky matched my mood the following morning as I gazed out the living room window. It sure didn't feel like Christmas Eve. I took a deep breath and exhaled long and lingering. *I wonder what Adam's doing right now. Is he missing me as much as I miss him?*

Stop it, Linda. I let the curtain drop, walked into the kitchen, and warmed up some leftover coffee. After a quick look-see inside the bare refrigerator, I pulled out jam and my last croissant. *Looks like I need to go shopping.*

Just after one o'clock, I left the apartment with a mission in mind: check my savings balance at the Tours bank. Depending on the outcome, I would purchase some groceries—baguettes, cheese and eggs—at the very least.

An hour later, shoulders slumped, I retraced my steps toward *la Place Plumereau*. My visit to the bank had been a keen disappointment—only 360 francs remained in my account and there were no signs of a *virement*, or Telex transfer, from my parents. That left me 300 for the balance of my rent and only sixty for everything else. I wondered what the holdup was. I gave Dad all the instructions and he told me he'd send it in a few days.

Trying to release some tension, I rolled my neck from side to side. *Maybe I'm stewing over nothing. My money will probably arrive after Christmas.* Until then, I would have to limit my expenses.

A deliveryman stopped my progress. I watched as he struggled with a stack of packages, his legs buckling under the weight. Maneuvering around him, I continued down the sidewalk, my thoughts turning to

Michel. *Should I or shouldn't I spend Christmas with him?*

A sudden recognition rolled my eyes. *This is ridiculous.* There was no good reason I shouldn't. He knew about Adam and there was nothing wrong with having male friends. Back home, I had lots of them.

Glancing at my watch, I picked up my pace. Michel had made it clear that I could find him at the restaurant around one o'clock, and I would hate to miss him now that I'd made up my mind to go. There would be plenty of time for me to purchase a few groceries after I confirmed our arrangements for Christmas Day.

10

*A*t ten o'clock on Christmas morning, I leapt out of bed, made myself a cup of coffee, and dashed to the bathroom for a quick shower. Once I dried off, I tugged on my black corduroy jeans and eased my lavender mohair sweater over my head. I wasn't sure if my clothes were fancy enough for the occasion, but I no longer possessed shoes I could wear with a skirt. When an image of my 'shortie' boots popped in my mind, I winced. *They would look great with this outfit. Too bad I had to leave them at the château.*

I secured my hair in an up-do, applied light makeup and lip gloss, and put on my favorite silver drop earrings. Turning from side to side in front of the closet mirror, I gave myself a nod of approval. *I think that'll do—nothing sexy. I don't want to give the wrong impression.*

An hour later, snug in my blue wool coat, I walked out into the frigid temperatures and headed toward *Le Café Vert*. The sidewalks were deserted and traffic was light, so I made good time, my shoes tapping a steady beat on the concrete sidewalk. I turned left at the next corner and, when Michel came into view, he smiled and waved me over. He looked distinctly "European," with his hair tied in a low ponytail, navy trench coat, beige slacks and brown brogues.

"*Bonjour,* Linda. *Ça va?*" He bent forward and I offered him my cheeks to kiss, three times, in the Loire Valley custom.

"I'm good," I replied in French—my only option. "And you?" Pulling away, I caught a whiff of his cologne. *Mmm . . . his scent is similar to Adam's, with a hint of spice.*

"*Eh bien.*" Michel's lips parted slightly as he assessed me. "You look beautiful today."

"Thank you." I averted my eyes and fussed with my burgundy scarf to hide my discomfort. It was nice of him to notice, but I didn't want to send any mixed messages.

Michel lit a cigarette and then motioned toward the right. "This way."

"Do your friends live nearby?" I said, shoving my hands deep in my pockets as we progressed down the narrow lane.

"Yes, only a few hundred meters."

"That's good. It's turned chilly again." Shivering, I tilted my head in his direction. "So . . . how do you know these people?"

"Francis and I met in college, about seven years ago." Michel blew smoke out of the side of his mouth, away from me. "His mother and stepfather invite me every year for Christmas dinner."

"That's kind of them . . . especially since you don't have any family nearby."

"*Exactement,*" Michel said, grinning. "But every year I have to endure a lecture about the benefits of religion."

"What do you mean by that?"

Michel threw his cigarette on the ground and crushed it with his foot. "I hate organized religion."

I stiffened and stared at him, my mouth agape. "But you do believe in God, right?"

Michel shook his head. "Not the way most people do."

I wondered what he meant by this. It would break my mother's heart if I refused to attend Mass with her. We circled around two elderly women and continued down the sidewalk.

Michel lowered his brows and glanced my way. "From your reaction, I gather that you are religious?"

"Yes," I replied, lifting my chin. "I don't go to church every Sunday, but I was raised Catholic and I still enjoy going to Mass, especially this time of year."

His lips thinned, but he didn't pursue the subject; both of us distracted as we crossed a busy intersection. Once we turned the corner, he pointed to a dark gray building with an ornate metal handrail. "There it is. Number 201."

Michel followed me up the short flight of stairs, reaching over my shoulder to knock. The door opened and, a man in his late twenties, with dark-rimmed glasses and a striped shirt grabbed Michel's hand, and pulled him into a warm, jovial embrace.

Once we stepped inside the foyer, Michel introduced me to Francis and his mother and stepfather, Madame and Monsieur Durand. The middle-aged couple, she in a simple blue shift and he in a button-up sweater vest, smiled broadly, as they stepped forward and welcomed me into their home.

Greetings clogged the entryway for several minutes until Monsieur Durand said, "Shall we move into the salon?"

Michel helped me with my coat, handing it to Madame Durand, and we entered a charming room filled with graceful antique furniture, collectibles and family portraits. Drinks were served and complex French discussions commenced. I was utterly lost in minutes. Michel tried to bring me into the conversations on three different occasions, but I didn't encourage him, choosing instead to sit back and enjoy my wine.

When our hosts excused themselves to make final lunch preparations, Michel lit a cigarette and leaned toward me with a whispered apology. "I'm sorry if you're feeling left out."

I shrugged and gave him a tentative smile. "It's not your fault. I'm the one with the communication problem. I just hope I'm not ruining your day."

Michel's coffee-brown eyes sparkled. "No, not at all."

When Madame Durand announced lunch, we filed into an intimate space softly lit by a standing lamp and pillar candles. In the middle of the room, a square oak table laden with fine china and silver, sat waiting for five guests. Holly, artfully arranged in a vase, scented the air. Unsure where to go, I wavered, until Michel directed me to the chair beside his friend. "Why don't you sit here?"

While Francis circled the table, refilling our wine glasses, Madame Durand brought out the *mousse du canard*, duck *pâté* with salad greens and grated beetroot.

Once she sat down, all eyes turned to the host at the head of the table. Monsieur Durand bowed his head and, while he recited the Lord's Prayer, I snuck a peek at Michel, curious to see his reaction. Our eyes met and, when he winked, I quickly lowered my gaze.

Silence, and then compliments, followed as everyone sampled the *pâté*. Before long, the second course arrived—rice and *fricassée de volaille à l'ancienne*, a chicken stew simmered with hearty vegetables in a rich white-wine sauce. Steam rose from the dish and delicious aromas filled the air. A cheese board came next, featuring goat cheeses from the Loire Valley.

When Madame Durand presented the final course, a log-shaped cake, "Oohs" erupted around the table. Trying to be discreet, I lowered my voice. "Michel, what is this dessert called?"

"*Bûche de Noël*. It's a traditional Christmas dessert flavored with chocolate and chestnuts. I think you'll enjoy it."

"Mmm . . . that sounds good."

Once everyone finished the exquisite dessert, Monsieur Durand raised his goblet in the air. "May I propose a toast to Solange? Thank you very much for the marvelous meal."

"*Merci*, Robert," Madame Durand said softly, a blush tinting her cheeks pink as glasses clinked all around the table.

After coffees, Monsieur Durand suggested everyone retire back into the salon for a *digestif*, an after-dinner liqueur. I hesitated when I spied Madame Durand picking up some dishes and heading toward the kitchen.

"You go on ahead. I'm going to help clean up," I whispered to Michel. He nodded and smiled his thanks as I gathered plates and followed my hostess into the adjoining room. Madame Durand passed me an apron and instructed me, with easy-to-understand French directions, on her dishwashing practice. Once the job was complete, we rejoined the others in the salon for a balloon of Cognac. An hour later, we all gathered at the front door to say our goodbyes.

Facing my hosts, I uttered a few rehearsed French accolades, saving my best one for Madame Durand. "Thank you for the wonderful dinner. I enjoyed myself. It was kind of you to invite me."

"*Je vous en prie*," she replied, her eyes twinkling as she grasped both of my hands in hers.

We walked out into the cool night air, choosing a familiar path toward Adam's apartment. After a while, Michel broke the silence.

"So . . . did you mean what you said to Madame Durand? Did you enjoy yourself?"

"Well, it was definitely better than spending Christmas alone." *Oops.* I covered my mouth.

He laughed. "I guess I deserved that. It was a stupid question."

I reached over and touched his arm. "No, I really did have a good time. The meal was delicious and the Durands were so kind. Thank you very much for inviting me."

"I'm glad you came." Michel said with a grin. "Without you, it would have been just another boring holiday meal."

11

*T*wo days later, biting my lip and trying not to cry in public, I marched out of the Tours bank and headed north on *rue Nationale.* There was still no sign of a Telex transfer from my parents, and I had only a few francs left. The money should have been here by now. *I need to call Dad and find out what's wrong.*

Once I arrived at the post office, I chose a phone booth in the back, hoping to gain a bit of privacy. *Wait . . . what time is it in Washington?* I checked my watch. *Good. It's around eight o'clock in the morning. Someone should be up.*

My hand trembled as I inserted coins into the slot. One franc dropped to the floor and I watched it roll to a stop before I retrieved it. When the operator came on, I asked her to help me place a call and, after five rings, my mom picked up the phone.

"Hello?"

"Will you accept a collect call from Linda Kovic?" the operator said.

There was a long pause before she responded. "Uh . . . who is dis?"

The operator raised her voice, repeated her question, and my mom finally agreed to the charges.

"Hi, Mom."

"Lindy?"

"Yes, it's me."

I heard familiar noises, scraping and then mumbling. "My hearing aid is buzzing, *Cekay malo* . . ." Seconds passed until she spoke again.

"*Yoy meni*, I'm so glad to talk to you. Is everything okay?"

"Yes . . . well . . . not so much. My money transfer hasn't arrived yet and I'm worried there's a problem." The instant I said this, my vision blurred and my voice turned gravelly. "I really want to talk with you, but can you go get Dad first?"

"George is not here right now. I'm not sure where he is . . . Maybe he took a walk. Bud's gone too."

A tear rolled down my face and I wiped it away with the back of my hand. I swallowed hard and enunciated every word with precision so she could understand. "Mom, I'm almost broke. Do you know if Dad's made the transfer to my bank account yet?"

There was a long silence and I wasn't sure if she understood me. "Mom, did you hear me?"

"Yes, I heard you. Things have been upside down. Your dad has depression again."

Alarms went off in my head and my chest constricted as childhood memories washed through me. My father struggled with bipolar disorder most of his life, triggered in part by a tragic accident that occurred when he was twelve. Unaware that the neighbor's gun in his hand was loaded he accidently shot and killed his younger brother, Harold. This agonizing event, followed by horrific experiences aboard the *USS Enterprise* during World War II, led him into alternating episodes of depression and mania.

During the summer months, when he was feeling good, he would stop taking his anti-depression medicine, and then, when winter set in, he would start back up again. This unfortunate mental roller coaster ride of "highs" and "lows" continued after he married and had children. It had become a familiar pattern throughout my life.

"So, Dad hasn't sent my money yet?"

"No, but I will tell him to do it today. I promise." I heard the concern in her voice. Given her severe hearing loss, she couldn't make the transfer herself. She needed Dad's help whenever things turned complicated.

"Good." I relaxed my shoulders and sat back in my seat. *I think she understands, but now she has to get Dad to the bank.*

Moving on to other subjects, I asked about her sister Josie and we talked briefly about Christmas. When I tried to tell her how I spent the holiday, she didn't respond and the conversation lagged. *I wish she could hear me better over the phone. It would be so nice to share some of my experiences with her. I sure miss talking with her.*

"Well, I should probably go. There are people waiting to use the phone."

"Da, da . . . When will you call again?"

"As soon as the money arrives," I replied, reaching up to rub the knot in my neck.

"When?"

I pressed the receiver closer to my lips. "I'll telephone you in a few days when my money arrives."

"Yah, yah, yah. You do dat. I'll be worried until you call back."

Fresh tears filled my eyes and I looked up, trying to control my emotions. "I love you, Mom. I'm sorry to be so much trouble right now. I know you have your hands full with Dad."

"It's okay. You are more straight with this than me. I love you too, honey."

After I hung up the phone, I sat still for a few seconds contemplating my situation. *I wonder how long a Telex transfer will take.* Why didn't I ask about that when I was at the bank today? I would guess no more than a day. The money would probably arrive in my account tomorrow morning.

12

——•✕•——

I was wrong. There was still no sign of a transfer the following day at noon. In an attempt to stay busy at the apartment, I tried to write a letter, but I only managed a few paragraphs, erased several sentences, and then put it aside. When I picked up my diary and reread my entry from the day before, my eyes filled with tears.

> *Until I receive more money from my parents, the days ahead shall be miserable. I don't even have enough money to wash my clothes. I feel like I will go mad from either boredom or worry.*

All of my entries sounded the same lately—I either moaned about missing Adam, whined about being bored, or complained about my lack of funds. Today's entry would be another depressing repeat. Why bother?

It had been a long time since I was dependent on others and I hated the way it made me feel: scared and vulnerable. I was used to taking care of myself. I acquired my first job as a bus girl when I was fourteen and I'd worked steady since then, even through college.

I shut my diary with a slap, stood, and paced the short distance between the stove and refrigerator. A sudden realization froze me in place. I hadn't eaten a decent meal since Christmas and I had very few groceries left—a couple of croissants, a chunk of Brie cheese and some jam. Tomorrow, I would be hungry.

What am I going to do? I closed my eyes and rested my forehead against the refrigerator door. *Think, think, think. Lori doesn't return until December thirtieth, but what about Évelyne? No, she's gone until the first of the year. I can't afford a train ticket anyway.* I raised my head and glanced out the window at the dark overcast sky. *I have to get out of this apartment. I don't care if it's raining.*

I grabbed my coat, an umbrella, and walked outside into a

cloudburst. Taking advantage of storefront awnings, rushing along familiar sidewalks, I tried and failed to avoid the downpour. Ten minutes later, when I arrived at *Le Café Vert*, I paused at the doorway to remove and shake my coat before entering.

I spotted Michel right away, at his regular table, absorbed in a book, his pens and papers lying beside him. He didn't notice me at first, but when our eyes met, his face lit up.

"*Bonjour*, Linda. *Ça va*? I wondered when I might see you again." He stood and kissed my cheeks. "Isn't the weather terrible? Please sit down."

I attempted a smile, draped my coat over the back of a chair and lowered myself into a seat.

"Would you like a *café au lait*?" Michel's dark eyebrows furrowed as he studied my face.

"Yes, please." An uncontrollable shiver prompted me to wrap my arms around myself for warmth.

Michel called Bruno over to place the order before returning his focus on me. "Is something wrong?"

"Yes." I drew in a breath and tried to steady my voice. "My parents are supposed to send money, but it hasn't arrived yet . . ."

He sat back, lit a cigarette and listened, uttering very few words while I rehashed my troubles. I struggled with my French more than once, but he encouraged me with a nod or a gentle correction. When the tears began to fall, he handed me a paper napkin off the table.

"I'm sorry," I blubbered, blowing my nose and dabbing at my face. "I had to talk to someone and I'm afraid that you're it right now."

Michel's eyebrow lifted. "That's not very flattering."

"Sorry." I grinned through the fog and blew my nose again. I felt better already. I was glad I came.

Bruno delivered my coffee and Michel watched me take a sip. "Are you hungry?"

"No, not really, but thanks for asking."

Michel avoided my gaze and picked up a teaspoon. He studied it as he turned it in his fingers. I watched, mesmerized by his actions, waiting for him to speak. "I can loan you some money, if you'll let me."

My heart rate increased as I contemplated his suggestion. *I was down to my last francs, but I hardly knew him. What would Adam say?*

"That's kind of you, but I'm still hoping my money will arrive later today."

"*D'accord.*" Michel combed his fingers through his hair. "If not, my offer will still stand tomorrow."

His words calmed my nerves and I rewarded him with a wide smile before excusing myself to use the restroom. I rinsed my face repeatedly with water, trying to soothe my puffy eyes. In the end, I shrugged at my reflection in the mirror and returned to the table.

Michel convinced me to have dinner with him and, over the next few hours, we sat in *Le Café Vert* exchanging stories from the past. His calm demeanor and sharp wit lifted my spirits and, for a little while, I set aside my money troubles. It was the best time I'd had in days.

The conversation turned serious after dessert, when Michel rocked back in his chair. "So . . . tell me about your boyfriend. Where did you meet him?"

I felt a flush creep across my face. *This doesn't need to be awkward, Linda.* It was nice of him to ask. "We met through my American friend, Lori. He's studying business at the *Université François-Rabelais* . . ."

Once we exhausted this subject, we moved on to other topics and an hour slipped by unnoticed. When I finally checked the time, it was five o'clock and dusk was approaching fast.

"I really should let you get back to your work." I stood and smoothed down my sweater. "Thank you so much, for everything. I feel so much better now than when I first arrived."

"*De rien.*" Michel replied, circling the table to help me into my coat. "I have an idea. Why don't we meet here again tomorrow and I'll take you to see a French film? Yves Montand is starring in *I . . . comme Icare* at a local theater. It's a thriller about the Kennedy assassination. I've wanted to see it for some time."

I didn't understand some of his words, so I asked Michel to repeat his invitation. "It sounds like fun," I said, "but I don't have any money to spare. You've done enough for me already." It almost sounded like a date anyway. I didn't want to lead him on.

Michel read my mind. "Listen, Linda, there are no expectations other than friendship. I'd really enjoy your company."

The corners of my lips lifted. "Okay, why not? Maybe someday, when I get this money thing figured out, I'll be able to return the favor."

Michel didn't miss a beat. "*Génial.* I'll look forward to that."

13

———◆╳◆———

*T*he following day, after another discouraging visit to the bank, I strolled toward *Le Café Vert*, my mind reeling. *I guess I'll have to accept Michel's loan after all. I have no choice. Thank goodness he offered.*

I rolled my eyes skyward. How did I get myself into this jam? Maybe I should have gone home when I had the chance.

The honk of a horn diverted my thoughts. No. I would have always wondered about Adam, and I can't leave France until I learn French. *Things will turn out okay. They have to.*

As soon as I turned the corner, I spotted Michel and Bruno absorbed in a conversation near the café entrance. Both men called out greetings as I approached.

"*Bonjour.*" I licked my lips nervously as I hovered beside Michel.

He widened his stance and crossed his arms. "I'm taking Linda to see *I . . . comme Icare.*"

Bruno tugged on the corner of his moustache. "Aha, I've heard that's a good film." He whacked Michel on the back. "Aren't you happy that I convinced this good-looking girl to come into my café?"

"*Mais oui.*" Michel shifted from one foot to the other and turned to me. "Shall we get going?"

After a quick goodbye, we proceeded down the lane. Once we were beyond earshot, he raised his eyebrows. "So, did your money arrive?"

I frowned and shook my head. "No, not yet."

He pulled me into a doorway, reached into his pocket and passed me forty francs. "If you need more, just ask."

Overwhelmed by his kindness, I gave him a quick hug. "Thank you, Michel. I'll pay you back as soon as I can."

His mouth twitched with amusement as he adjusted his coat. "I know you will. I'm not worried."

We continued down the sidewalk and, as we walked along *rue Nationale* toward the movie theater, Michel pointed out some of his favorite businesses. Even though I'd traveled this route many times, I hadn't noticed the unique shops and galleries until today.

"*Le Fromage* sells cheeses from around the world and pairs them with complementary wines. Someday, when we have more time, maybe we can go in and try some of their samples."

He spoke faster than normal, so I only caught a few French words, but his excitement was contagious. "*D'accord.*"

A few blocks down the street, Michel paused in front of another building. "Have you heard of Pierre Hamon?" I shook my head and he continued, his voice rising and falling with enthusiasm. "This art gallery is currently highlighting his work. He's a watercolor artist from the Loire Valley."

There was silence as we considered the artwork displayed in the window. "They're lovely . . . the colors are so . . . bright." I said, my brow creasing with uncertainty.

He gave me an approving nod and we continued on our way, arriving at the movie theatre with only ten minutes to spare before showtime. When we walked up to the cashier, Michel leaned forward as he purchased the tickets.

"Two for *I . . . comme Icare*, please. We'll be able to sit together, right?"

"Yes," the woman affirmed, counting back his change. "There's plenty of room."

"*Merci.*"

Moments later, we entered the theater and found our seats in the crowded auditorium.

After the movie, as we retraced our steps back toward *le Vieux Tours*, I bombarded Michel with questions about the plot. He answered them good-naturedly, but as we neared our destination, he finally threw up his arms, "*Zut alors!* Maybe we need to see the movie again. It'll be a lot more interesting for you the second time around."

I laughed aloud. "That won't be necessary. You've cleared up most of my confusion. The storyline makes a lot more sense to me now."

"*C'est bon.*"

We crossed the street, weaved our way across *la Place Plumereau* and arrived at the entrance to Adam's half-timbered building.

Michel glanced at the entrance. "Are you going to invite me in?"

My stomach lurched. "I don't think Adam would like that."

"You're probably right."

I kept my gaze on the ground and rubbed the twitch from my eye. "Thanks again for the money . . . and the movie."

"*De rien,*" Michel said, lighting a cigarette and taking a drag. "What are your plans for New Year's Eve?"

"My friend, Lori, gets back in town tomorrow and I think she has something in mind." A sudden image of Lori popped in my mind. *I can't wait to see her. I wonder how she'll react when I tell her about Michel. I'm anticipating a long lecture.*

"What about Adam? When does he get home?"

"Last I heard, January second." I cleared my throat. "I'll probably see you before then. As soon as my dad transfers the money, I'll come and find you at *Le Café Vert.*"

"All right." He stepped forward and kissed my cheeks, his lips lingering against my skin longer than necessary.

I pulled away and shook my head. "Michel . . ."

He held up his palm and smiled sheepishly. "Sorry. I can't help it if you smell good."

I watched him walk away and then entered the building, contemplating my evening with Michel. It had been a fun evening, but it was pretty clear that he had feelings for me. I'd been honest with him about Adam, but somehow it still felt like I was leading him on. *Why does everything have to be so difficult?*

14

*A*t seven o'clock the following evening, a knock on the door startled me. When I opened it, Lori threw her arms around me.

"Linda! It's so good to see you," she said, her voice rough with emotion. "Did you miss me?"

"I sure did." I giggled.

We broke apart and she removed her coat. "I came over as soon as I arrived home."

"I'm glad you did. I was hoping I would see you today." I directed her into the kitchen. "Do you want something to drink? I have some Vouvray."

"Yeah, that would be awesome."

After I poured the wine, we moved to the living room and I turned on some music. Once we settled on the couch, Lori gave me a look. "So . . . what's new? How was your Christmas?"

My face warmed and Lori's eyes widened. "What happened?" she demanded, curling her legs beneath her.

I rubbed the back of my neck. "I met a new friend at a café nearby. His name is Michel."

She groaned. "That sounds—"

I held up my hand and lifted my chin. "Before you scold me, why don't you listen to the whole story, okay?"

Lori nodded and sat back.

"First off, I was super sad while you were gone. Everyone I knew, including Évelyne, left town to be with their families for Christmas . . ." One after the other, words tumbled from my mouth as I recounted the past week since she left, placing special emphasis on my loneliness, lack of food, Michel's kindness and my dire financial situation.

Lori sipped her wine in silence and, when I finished, her voice was soft with understanding. "Okay, so I get why you spent Christmas with Michel, but I'm concerned about the loan. Have you paid him back yet?"

I looked away, my glass knocking the edge of the coffee table when I tried to set it down. "No, my transfer from home still hasn't arrived. I'm expecting it any day."

Lori's forehead creased. "Do you need some money? I don't have much to spare, but I can loan you a few francs."

I offered her a shaky smile. "Thanks, but I'm okay for now."

"What about Adam? Have you heard from him?"

I shook my head. "No, not a word. I've checked the mail daily. I expected to hear from him by now."

"That's odd." Lori narrowed her eyes. "Adam is usually so considerate. Luckily, he'll be home in a few days and you guys can work this all out. Family stuff is hard."

"You're probably right." Vivid memories of our lackluster goodbye at the train station washed over me and my jaw tensed. I couldn't wait to see Adam again, but I didn't know what to expect. Would there still be "unresolved issues" with his parents? Would he share them with me? This time, I wouldn't take no for an answer.

I glanced at her empty glass. "How about some more wine?"

"Sure . . . but I have something to tell you first." She laid her hand on my arm and I watched her face pale. "My parents are getting a divorce. I have to return home at the end of the month."

An ache gripped my heart and her face blurred for a second. *Nooooo, this can't be happening right now.* "I can't believe it. This is such terrible news." Then barely audible, I said, "Have you told Albert?"

"Yes. I saw him last night." Lori pulled a Kleenex from her purse and dabbed her nose. "He's really bummed. I convinced him to stay for another semester and now he's stuck."

"It's not your fault, Lori. I'm sure he understands that." *Poor Lori. Poor Albert. What will we do without her?*

"Yeah, he doesn't blame me, but it's still a drag." Lori held up her glass. "Okay, now I could really use that second drink."

Over the next few hours, Lori and I drained a bottle of wine while she recounted the family drama that occurred over Christmas. Eventually, we moved on to other subjects, firming up our plans for New Year's Eve. Since neither of us had much money, we decided to organize a small gathering at Adam's apartment.

"I'll invite Julie, if that's okay. Oh, and I think Albert mentioned a couple of his buddies too."

"All right, but let's keep it small. If everyone brings a bottle of wine, we should have plenty to drink." I chewed on my bottom lip and then shook my head. "I can't afford appetizers, though."

Lori's face brightened. "No worries. Leave that up to Julie and me. We'll tell everyone to come over around eight o'clock." She downed her last mouthful of wine and released a sigh. "Well, at least I get to ring in the New Year with all of my French friends."

I swallowed hard at the lump in my throat and raised my glass in a bittersweet toast: "To bringing in 1980 with a bang."

15

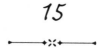

*W*e did, indeed, bring in the New Year with a "bang." The wine flowed all night while we listened and danced to songs like "Bad Girls" by Donna Summer and ABBA's "Gimme! Gimme! Gimme!" Just before midnight, Julie popped the cork on a bottle of champagne. When the clock struck twelve, we all hugged, kissed and cried as we wished each other *"Bonne Année."* As I watched Lori and Albert embrace, my thoughts turned to Adam and my chest tightened. *I wonder how he brought in the New Year. Did he think about me? I wish he were in my arms.*

When the party finally broke up at four o'clock in the morning, I invited Lori and Albert to crash on the couch, and we slept until noon. Empty wine bottles, loose record sleeves, dirty glasses and overflowing ashtrays greeted us on New Year's Day.

"What a mess," Lori said, surveying the room as she drank a glass of water.

Albert shook his head and pulled out the garbage can. "Yeah . . . well, the sooner we get started, the sooner this place will get cleaned up."

Lori and I joined in the effort, wiping down tables, washing dishes and moping the floor. Four hours later, we walked out of Adam's apartment with all of my belongings in tow.

"Ah, the fresh air feels good." Albert inhaled deeply as we exited the building and progressed toward my new home.

Lori scowled at him. "What's your secret, anyhow? How can you drink that much wine and not have a hangover?"

Albert puffed out his chest and slapped it like a gorilla. "It must be the Swedish blood."

"Well, whatever it is, I envy you," Lori said, rubbing her temples.

"How much farther is your new room?" Albert staggered, and then caught his balance, as he muscled my heavy suitcase down the sidewalk.

"It's just around the corner." I turned to hide my grin. "I'm sorry. I know my bag is cumbersome. Adam gave me a hard time about it too."

We made a left at the next intersection and passed several retail shops—a hair salon, a grocer, and a bakery—and moments later, my new home came into view.

"This is it, number nineteen," I said, licking my lips as I climbed the steps and rang the doorbell. We heard a dog bark and the door creaked open.

"Ah, there you are, Mademoiselle. I was wondering when you would arrive. I expected you earlier this morning." Madame Martin picked up Sophie and her eyes skimmed my companions as she ushered us into the foyer.

"Yes, well we got a late start." I reached into my purse and pulled out an envelope. "Here is the rest of the rent I owe you."

"*Merci.*"

She passed me a key and, after a quick introduction, Albert, Lori and I climbed the stairs to the third floor. As we proceeded down the hall, I pointed to my left. "Here's the toilet, and this is my room." We bunched up at my door. I unlocked it and everyone followed me into the small space.

"Well, what do you think?" I lifted my hands and glanced around the room. "I know it's bare, but once I get some knick-knacks and put up some posters, the place will warm up."

"It looks nice." Albert sat on the edge of my mattress and bounced a few times. "The bed is soft too."

Lori plopped down next to him and grinned at me. "It's perfect, Linda. I'm so happy for you."

Albert patted Lori's thigh to get her attention. "I'm going to use the toilet, and then we should go."

She nodded and we watched him exit. "When do your classes start at the institute?"

"January fourth, but I have orientation on Thursday. I can't wait to get started."

"Right on. I'm sure we'll talk before then. It's so cool that you'll have access to a phone."

Albert returned and Lori caught me in a hug. "Call me if your transfer doesn't arrive over the next few days. Maybe I can work something out."

She's a true friend, but I can't ask her for money. "That's sweet, Lori, but I'll be okay. Thanks for all your help today."

"Phfft. What are friends for?"

After Albert and Lori left, I unpacked my bag, hung up my clothes and organized my toiletries. When I stepped back to admire my handiwork, I realized that something was missing—bedding. *What am I going to do?*

A knock on the door turned my head.

"*Entrez!*" I called out.

There was a slight hesitation before Madame Martin pushed the door open with her hip and entered the room, her arms loaded with sheets, blankets, a pillow and towels. "I thought you could use these. I always have some extras around just in case."

"How wonderful." I reached out to help her. "I don't have the . . . I . . . er haven't had a chance to go shopping yet."

"Not a problem. You can use these as long as you like."

My spirits soared. This was fantastic news. "*Merci beaucoup.*"

She smiled and gave me a nod. "Well, I'll see you later then."

I kept my excitement under control until after she closed the door. Then I clasped my hands together and said a little prayer. This was good news. I wouldn't have to purchase my own bedding and towels. *What a relief.*

Once I made my bed, it looked so inviting I decided to take a nap.

I removed my shoes, curled onto my left side and yawned. *Albert's right. The mattress is super comfortable.*

Just before I drifted off to sleep, troublesome thoughts swirled inside my mind. If my Telex transfer didn't arrive tomorrow, I'd have to call home again. Would this be a pattern during the rest of my stay in France? *I sure hope not.*

16

*M*idafternoon the following day, I left the post office and headed north on *rue Nationale* toward home. There was still no sign of my bank transfer, and no one had answered the phone when I tried to place a collect call. Something was terribly wrong. My money should have arrived by now. *Dad must be going through a hard time.*

A memory—one I'd tried hard to forget—entered my mind. On a foggy ferry ride from Whidbey Island to Seattle, during one of my dad's major bouts with depression, he lifted his tear-stained face and told me: "Linda, I didn't mean to shoot Harold. How could this have happened to me?"

I remembered how my insides shook; how I tried to hide it, while I comforted him. "Dad, it wasn't your fault. You were only a boy. It was a terrible accident."

I remembered the shake of his head, and how I'd felt punched in the guts when he said, "I know . . . but I still wish I could crawl in a hole and die."

Even now, at twenty-one instead of seventeen, his words pierced me like a knife.

I stopped abruptly. Maybe Dad was in that dark place again. How terrible for him. If he was, Mom wouldn't be much help. She'd have her hands full trying to deal with his depression and the rental properties. Feelings of guilt filled my mind. *I should be there to help and here I am adding to their stress.*

My mouth went dry. *It's January second. Adam's supposed to return today, but I haven't heard from him yet. Maybe he's been delayed. I've only got a few francs left.* I glanced at my wristwatch. I hated to ask Michel for more money, but my options were limited. I gripped my purse, took a deep breath, and held it tight as I rushed toward *Le Café Vert* and my "unwanted savior."

17

*O*n Thursday morning, as I headed toward the *Institut d'Études Françaises* for my orientation, the marvelous aromas from a local *boulangerie-patisserie* drew me through the open door like a magnet. A big-boned, cheerful woman behind the counter offered me a sample of the freshly baked *pain au chocolat*. She watched me take a bite, her eyes wide with interest. When I nodded and licked my lips, she chuckled with delight.

"*Délicieux!* I'll take two, please."

Thanks to Michel, I had eighty francs hidden at home and twenty in my purse—more than enough to splurge on breakfast. I was grateful for his generosity, but I now owed him a whopping 140 francs.

To me, this was a considerable amount of money, seventy percent of my monthly budget after tuition and rent, but Michel waved off my concerns. "I know you'll pay me back once your transfer arrives, and I won't miss it until then."

He was right, of course. My dad's Telex would eventually appear, and in the meantime, I had one less thing to worry about. *I wonder what Adam will say when I fill him in on everything.*

Ten minutes later, I arrived at the institute. Amid a bustle of excitement, I followed a group of students through the massive double doors into the building. We congregated inside the foyer until members of the staff directed us into an adjoining room for the formal part of the orientation. We watched a short film on the history of the institute, listened to a lecture about the school's philosophy, and then broke into smaller groups for questions, answers, and a tour of the school.

Our cluster of thirteen people consisted of all ages, hailing from the Middle East, Asia, and parts of Europe. All of the communication was in French and our assigned leader, Madame Cohen, showed incredible patience, nodding as she repeated instructions and answered badly phrased questions.

"After the tour today, all of you will take a French placement exam. The results of this test will determine your grade level at the school." Madame Cohen paused and scanned the crowd. "Are there any more questions? No? Good. Then let's proceed with the tour."

Fourteen pairs of shoes tip-tapped up wooden stairs and hallways. We visited six classrooms on the second and third levels, where there was a mix of the "old"—iron radiators, white wainscoting and tall green shutters—and the "new"—white boards, sleek tables and chairs. Saving the best for last, Madame Cohen's pride was evident in her squared shoulders as she gestured with a manicured hand at the rooms designed for Audiovisual Learning and Phonetics.

"*Eh bien,* this concludes our tour." She glanced at her watch. "After a ten-minute break, return here to take your placement exam."

Two hours later, test complete, I followed the students from my group out the huge double doors into a gentle rain. That wasn't so bad. *It'll be interesting to hear the results tomorrow.*

I glanced back at the elegant two-story stone structure and smiled. I still couldn't believe this is actually happening. After five long months of struggling to learn the language, I was finally taking French classes at the institute. My dream came true. I couldn't wait to get started.

A raindrop hit my eyelid and I quickly opened my umbrella as I descended the stairs and turned left toward *Café de l'Europe.* I had to eat lunch somewhere, and I hoped to run into a few of my friends at my old hangout. *Maybe someone's heard from Adam.*

Fifteen minutes later, breathless from exertion and anticipation, I entered the café and surveyed the room for Adam, Adeela or Lori, but none of them were there.

Oh well, I guess I'll have to eat alone. I found a seat near the window, slipped off my coat and plopped into a chair. A waiter materialized, his foot tapping a nervous beat as I settled on my usual, a *croque monsieur* sandwich and *café au lait*.

As soon as he left, I reached into my purse and pulled out two French pamphlets from the orientation. I could only decipher a few words and, when my meal arrived, I gladly set them aside.

Inhaling the sublime aroma, I took a bite of my sandwich, savoring the salty layers of ham and *Gruyère* cheese. *Mmm, delicious.* A trickle of juice escaped the corner of my mouth and left a trail down my chin. I reached for my napkin and froze when I saw Marc walk through the café door.

Our eyes linked and he sauntered to my table, a leer glued to his handsome face. Ever since the incident at the apartment, the mere thought of him made my skin crawl. Today was no exception.

"*Salut*, Linda."

I stood, offering him a thin smile as he kissed my cheeks. "Salut."

"How was your Christmas?"

"It was okay." I shifted my weight from one foot to the other. "How was Paris?"

"Boring."

I felt my eyebrows lift, but I didn't pursue the subject. I really didn't care. "Have you heard from Adam?"

"Yeah. He'll be home late tomorrow evening."

My mouth fell open, but I quickly recovered. "Really? That's great." My voice betrayed me as my pitch climbed higher. "Did he mention me?"

Marc's mouth twitched and he rocked back on his heels. "No—it was a very short conversation."

I stiffened and a flush spread across my face. *That's so weird. Why didn't Adam give Marc a message for me?*

"Linda, it was no big deal. A short phone call to let me know his schedule."

I swallowed and steadied my voice. "Okay, so . . . can you ask him to meet me at the *Café Briand* at noon on Saturday?"

"Sure, I'll tell him." Marc glanced over his shoulder, nodding to a group of students as they passed by. "Well, I should probably get going."

"Yes, of course."

After Marc left, I watched him join friends at a table nearby and slowly lowered myself down into my chair. *Something doesn't feel right. Adam should have contacted me.*

I downed my last bit of coffee, took another bite of my sandwich and then shoved it away because it tasted like cardboard. My appetite was gone. I wiped my palms on my thighs, waved to my waiter and asked him to wrap my meal.

When I walked out of the café five minutes later, I resisted the urge to look at Marc. *I hope he remembers to deliver my message to Adam about Saturday. How will I get through the next two days?*

18

*T*he next morning, as I walked toward the institute, I pushed aside my apprehensions and gave myself a pep talk. *Don't worry about Adam right now. There's nothing you can do about the situation. Today you need to focus on school. That's why you're in France, remember?*

My stomach quivered as I smoothed back my hair and entered the *Institut d'Études Françaises.* I followed the "New Students" signs down the hallway and joined the line in front of the main desk.

When it was my turn, I stepped forward and waited for the receptionist to look up. "*Bonjour.* My name is Linda Kovic."

She thumbed through a file with her perfectly painted fuchsia nail and withdrew a note card. "Your test results placed you in Level Three French. Go up these stairs to the third floor, classroom eighteen, on the left."

My eyes followed her finger. "Okay, thank you." I was glad she pointed me in the right direction because all I heard was "eighteen."

I found my classroom, took a seat in the front row, and watched as twenty other students filed through the door. A thin, fashionably dressed woman, about forty years old, entered the room. She pushed a lock of brown hair from her face, laid a pile of papers on the desk, and smiled at the class.

"*Bonjour*, my name is Madame Caron. All of you are in Level Three French, correct?" She raised her eyebrows and paused. "Good. So, before we move on to dictation, I'd like to learn something about each of you."

Over the next hour, Madame Caron moved from one student to the next, listening as they answered a range of questions in French centered on background, goals and expectations. Next, she dictated several sentences in French.

She's speaking slowly, but this is tough. I frowned as I scribbled a few recognizable words on the paper. I was pretty sure most of my answers were wrong since I was spelling out the words just like they sounded.

Once class ended, I lingered, hoping to discuss my concerns with Madame Caron.

"What can I do for you, Mademoiselle?" She asked, perching on the edge of the desk.

"I think I might be in the wrong level. I've never taken any formal classes in French grammar. I couldn't complete a single sentence today during dictation."

"Ah, I see. You speak quite well, but maybe you need to drop back to Level Two French . . . at least for a while." She picked up her pen and jotted down a few notes. "I'll talk to the director and we'll find you a new class for tomorrow."

"Thank you." Relief swept through my body as I exited the room. *Thank goodness Madame Caron agreed.* If I wanted to speak French well, I needed to understand the basics first; never mind that I should have learned these long before I accepted a job in France.

On my way home, I stopped by the bank to check on my transfer. Fifteen minutes later, when I exited the building, disappointment slumped my shoulders once again. Veering along the now-familiar path to the Tours Post Office, I looked up and mumbled a little prayer, "Please let my Dad answer the phone."

Clutching my purse, I entered the crowded building, slipped into the only vacant phone booth and placed a collect call home. After seven long rings that felt like seven long years, someone finally picked up and accepted the charges.

"Linda?"

"Dad! I'm so relieved you're home. I've been trying to reach you."

"I know you have. Did you get the money?"

"No, I didn't." Saliva clogged my throat and I coughed. "When did you make the transfer?"

"Thursday afternoon." There was a protracted pause and I wondered if we had lost our connection. When he finally spoke again, his words came out scratchy. "I know I promised to send it to you a long time ago . . . but I just couldn't get it done until now. There's a little extra in there since it's so late."

My head cleared and I remembered to breath. "Thank you, Dad—that's such a relief. I really appreciate it. Did the bank tell you how long the transfer would take?"

"A few business days, but I think it goes to Paris first and then they route it to your account in Tours. I really feel bad about this."

I rolled my shoulders. *Good, the money is really on its way this time. I'll be able to pay Michel back.* "That's fine, Dad. Really it is. A friend loaned me 140 francs, so I'm okay for now."

"I'm glad to hear it."

Twisting the phone cord, I pushed out a difficult question. "Mom said you're having a hard time lately. Are you keeping up with your medicine?"

His long, drawn-out sigh spoke volumes. "I'm trying, but it doesn't seem to do much good."

It felt weird to talk to Dad about his depression over the phone. "I'm so sorry . . . I wish I could help. Have you seen much of Bud?"

"Yeah, he tries to come home from school every other weekend."

"Good. That makes me feel a bit better." There was another awkward silence, so I quickly filled the void with details about my new room, the Martin family, and my first day of school. When the conversation lagged for a second time, I knew it was time to end the call.

"Well, I should go. Thanks again for sending the money." My voice broke as tears surfaced. "I love you, Dad. Give Mom a hug. I'll write as soon as I get a chance."

"We'll look forward to it."

I hung up the receiver and stared at the wall. I was worried about Dad. He was in a bad way. *What a terrible time for me to be in France. Thankfully, Mom and Bud are there for him.*

19

$\mathcal{S}$aturday finally came; although it felt as if two years had passed, instead of two weeks, since I'd last seen Adam.

I wanted to make a good impression, so I brushed my hair until it shone, applied my makeup with precision, and dabbed perfume on my wrists and neck.

Discarded clothes lay in a heap on the bed, but after three outfit changes, I finally found the right combination. I stood in front of the mirror, turning from front to back, checking my appearance with pursed lips. The dark purple sweater complimented my green eyes, and I liked the way my faded jeans clung to my hips and thighs. *I can't wait to see Adam. I hope everything's okay.*

Shaky with apprehension, I glanced at my wristwatch once again. *Ten-thirty.* I still had an hour to go.

During the next sixty minutes, the hands on the clock moved in slow motion. I kept rechecking my lip gloss and fussing with my hair. I tried to write in my diary but I couldn't concentrate. Letter writing wasn't successful either. Finally, at 11:30, I grabbed my purse and slipped out the door.

With my nerves on high alert, I walked into *Café Briand.* Adam and I discovered each other at the same moment and, when our eyes locked, I felt my legs buckle. *He looks good . . . perhaps a little stressed.*

He stood to greet me and I sprinted into his arms, burying my face in his chest, savoring his familiar musky scent as it settled around me.

Adam's body stiffened. He gently pushed me away and peered into my eyes. "We need to talk. Why don't we take a walk?"

"Okay." Alarms sounded in my brain and my stomach tightened as

I watched him pull on his coat. *What's he going to tell me? Something is terribly wrong. Please let it be something we can work out.*

He steered me outside and gestured toward *la Place Plumereau*.

Trembling, I adjusted my purse on my shoulder. "What's going on, Adam?"

He pulled me into a doorway and his voice cracked with emotion. "Something happened after I returned home. It's hard to explain. There's no easy way to tell you."

"Just say the words."

Adam shoved his hands into his pockets, tipped his head back and closed his eyes for a few seconds. "Long ago, my family arranged a marriage for me. I've resisted for years, but I finally had to agree to the engagement."

My jaw dropped and I stepped back. I couldn't speak.

Adam reached for my arm. "I know this is a shock. I'm not in love with her, Linda. I had no choice—you have to believe me. We can still be together . . ."

I shook off his hand and my upper lip curled with disgust. "What! You can't be serious? There's no way I'd be with you now. How could you agree to something like this?"

"Please don't judge me. You can't imagine the family pressure I've been under."

I didn't stick around to hear the rest of his explanation. Without another word, I spun around and rushed for home, my eyes brimming with tears as I concentrated on placing one foot in front of the other to keep from falling.

The dam broke when Madame Martin's stoop came into view. Huge sobs racked my body as I unlocked the front door and ran up the stairs to my bedroom. Careful not to slam the door, I threw my things on the floor and collapsed on the bed.

I trusted Adam with my heart, but he deceived me. How could he have kept something like this from me? All along, his "unresolved family issue" was an arranged marriage. He should have told me about this long ago. If he cared about me, he would have.

I cried for hours. I cried myself dry. Eventually, I cried myself to sleep. When I woke, it was late afternoon and my room was dark except for a sliver of light shining through the window. *I still can't believe he's engaged. How could I have been such a poor judge of character? He wasn't my white knight after all.*

I groaned, turned on my lamp, threw my legs over the side of the bed and rubbed my swollen eyes. Disappointment and despair sat like weights on my neck and shoulders. I felt sick to my stomach.

How would I ever get through the night? I would give almost anything to be with my family and friends back in Seattle right now. Cindy and Carline were such good listeners—they would find ways to help me through my grief. My mom would hold me in her arms . . .

A whimper escaped as recognition took hold. I didn't get a chance to tell my parents about Adam . . . and now he's gone. *I can't believe it's over. I feel so alone.*

20

*A*t five o'clock, the following afternoon, a soft knock brought me to my feet. I swallowed hard, tried to gain control of my emotions, and opened the door. "Thanks for coming, Lori."

"Of course." She folded me in her arms. "You sounded terrible on phone."

I nodded into her shoulder. When we finally broke apart, she smiled and gently guided me to a seat on the bed. "I guess things didn't go well with Adam."

My chin quivered and my vision blurred. "It's over, Lori. Adam came back from Morocco engaged."

Her brow furrowed. "What?" She pulled a Kleenex out of a box nearby and passed it to me. "As in marriage?"

"Uh-huh." I dabbed my tears and blew my nose. "Apparently it was arranged by his family a long time ago."

"That's crazy. Really crazy." Lori shook her head a couple of times and sat on the edge of the bed. "Adam always seemed like such an honest guy. I'm shocked that he didn't tell you about this long ago."

"Me too." I blew my nose again and then tossed the sodden tissue in the garbage. "He certainly had lots of chances."

"I'm so sorry, Linda." Her forehead wrinkled. "Maybe he hoped it would all just go away one day."

"Well, it didn't, did it?"

Lori's sable brown eyes searched mine. "Listen, why don't you let me buy you dinner? There's this great pizza place nearby."

"I'm not in the mood . . ."

She cut me off. "Oh, come on. It'll be a great distraction." Her brows lifted and she made an attempt at levity. "We can plan our revenge."

I forced a smile, knew it was tenuous. Maybe she was right. I felt terrible, but it might help to get out of this room. "Okay."

"Great." Lori grabbed my hands. "I know things are rough right now, but Albert and I will help you get through this. I promise."

"I know you will."

My heart inched up into my throat as I grabbed my coat and purse. It wouldn't be easy, but starting Monday morning, I'd pour myself into my classes at the institute. I would spend most of my free time studying. And as soon as I learned French, I'd go home!

PART TWO

A Fresh Start

21

———◆✕◆———

*O*n Monday morning, I entered classroom number eight, took a seat in the second row, and pulled out my notebook and a pencil. As I waited for my new professor to arrive, I doodled on the page and my mind wandered. *I wonder what Adam is doing right now? Does he feel bad about his deception? I still can't believe it happened . . .*

Professor Toutain's booming voice brought me out of my reverie. *"Bonjour. Comment ça va aujourd'hui?"* How's it going today? Wearing a wide smile and sporting an impeccable beige suit, he marched into the room and set a handful of books on his desk.

Several students mumbled French greetings as he took his place in front of the class. He ran long fingers through graying hair and whipped off his glasses, scanning the room. His animated blue eyes eventually settled on me.

"Alors, I see that we have a new student. Mademoiselle, please tell us your name, where you are from, and why you are studying French."

I felt my face warm as all eyes turned toward me. Thank goodness I understood the question. "My name is Linda Kovic. I am American, and I want to learn French so that I can get a job as a flight attendant with World Airways."

"Well done, Mademoiselle." He handed me some papers and then addressed the class. "As we learned yesterday, people attend the institute for a variety of reasons, but most of you have a common goal—to learn French. So . . . let's get started."

Professor Toutain put on his glasses and pointed to the first sentence on the chalkboard. "The French alphabet has the same twenty-six letters as English and many other languages, but some of the letters are pronounced differently. Here is one example . . ."

All around me, students grabbed their pens and took notes; I wasn't far behind. Deep in concentration, I chewed on my bottom lip, bulleting important points and adding new vocabulary in the side margin of my notebook.

On four different occasions during Professor Toutain's lecture, I raised my hand and asked him to please repeat or clarify a particular point. Each time I did this, his face brightened and his voice rose in pitch and volume.

"Yes, of course I can repeat that, Mademoiselle. When you pronounce the French letter "I," it sounds like "ee" in the English word "free." Your name would be pronounced Leenda. Does that make sense now?"

"*Oui, merci.*" I scooted my chair closer to the table as I scribbled down his example.

Time passed quickly and, just before ten o'clock, Professor Toutain glanced at his wristwatch. "Why don't we take a short fifteen-minute break and then we'll try some dictation."

I rose with everyone else and followed two Asian girls down the hall to the bathroom. On the way back, I introduced myself.

"Hello, my name is Linda," I said in French, extending my hand.

They furrowed their brows, peered at me, and one of the girls accepted my handshake. "I'm Tomoko and this is my sister, Akiko."

"*Enchantée,*" I replied. "Do you speak English?"

Both girls shook their long dark manes.

"We speak very little English or French." Tomoko glanced at her sister. "I doubt you speak Japanese."

"You're right about that."

An awkward silence settled as I tried to think of something else to say. *Oh well, maybe we'll get to know each other once we learn more French.* "It was nice to meet you."

"Yes," Tomoko and Akiko said in unison.

It took all of my willpower not to imitate their bows.

After the break, Professor Toutain dictated ten simple sentences in a slow, deliberate manner similar to Madame Caron. I finished first and my confidence soared.

"Okay, now let's see how everyone did." Professor Toutain clasped his hands together. "Who wants to come up and write the first diction on the board?"

Several hands flew skyward and he pointed to a student in the front row. A handsome young man, perhaps German, jumped to his feet, and scribbled his sentence on the board.

When he stepped away and revealed his work, my jaw dropped. *What? That's not what I wrote.* My self-assurance plummeted as Professor Toutain congratulated him on his work. "Well done, Dieter."

All of my words, except two, were misspelled and the rest of my dictation followed a similar pattern. *I sure have a lot to learn. Oh well, that's why I'm here.*

Once class ended, the students filed past Professor Toutain and he singled me out. "Mademoiselle Kovic, you did very well today. I like your enthusiasm and I think you'll learn rapidly in my class."

"*Merci, Professeur.*" Warmed by his encouragement, a genuine smile slipped into place—the first since Adam shared his news.

At one o'clock, I entered *Café Moderne* and claimed the last remaining window seat. Situated a few doors down from the institute, the old restaurant with its faded red paint and blue-and-white-striped awnings, was a popular hangout for students.

A busy waiter dropped off a menu and I perused my choices until a familiar face outside the window caught my attention. Lori waved and I watched her walk through the entrance.

"You look a lot better today," she said, squeezing me harder than necessary. "How are you holding up?"

"I'm doing okay. Thanks again for hanging out yesterday."

"That's what friends are for." Lori looked around, wriggled out of her coat and slid into a seat. "This place is nice. I'm glad you suggested we meet here. It would be a drag to run into Adam at *Café de l'Europe.*"

My stomach tensed at the mention of his name. "Yeah, I plan to avoid that place for a while."

A waiter took our orders and, as soon as he left, Lori sat back and crossed her arms with a matronly air. "Just so you know, I didn't see Adam around this morning. When I do, he'll get a piece of my mind."

I frowned and folded my hands in my lap. "Well, I appreciate the support, but I'm just trying to move on."

Lori studied me for a few seconds and her voice mellowed. "Okay. Why don't we talk about something else? How did your class go today?"

"Much better. I think Level Two is a better fit."

"Good for you."

I shifted in my seat. "What about you? Have you heard from your folks?"

"I talked to my mom two days ago and she's super upset. I'm glad my brothers are there for her." She averted her eyes, fiddling with a ring on her finger. "Albert and I are spending as much time as we can together before I have to leave."

My lower lip trembled. "Of course. Good for you."

Our waiter delivered our food and we scrambled to make room on the table as he laid down our plates. While we ate, we chatted about other things, friends and recent events, the conversation light and easy until Lori brought up my finances.

"Did your money arrive yet?"

"Not yet, but it's on its way." *I hope it's on its way.* My eye twitched and I rubbed it. "My dad's been dealing with some health issues and he couldn't get to the bank until a few days ago."

"Well, that's good news—you'll be able to pay back Michel." Lori took a bite of her grilled cheese sandwich and wiped her hands on her napkin. "Have you seen him lately?"

"No, but I'm going to try and catch up with him at *Le Café Vert* tomorrow."

Lori's eyes rounded as she leaned forward. "Hey, I just thought of something. Now that Adam's out of the picture, would you go out with Michel? Is there any chemistry between you two?"

"I don't know." I shook my head and wrapped my hands around my coffee cup. "The whole time I've known Michel, I've been focused on Adam."

"Hmm . . . but now things have changed."

"I suppose they have." I checked my watch to hide my uneasiness. "Well, I guess I should go. My first Phonetics class starts at two o'clock."

Lori's forehead wrinkled and she reached for her coat. "Yeah, I've got a ton of homework."

Our waiter delivered the check, we paid him and left, pausing on the sidewalk to say goodbye.

"This was fun," Lori said, hugging me. "Listen, maybe we can check out some clubs this weekend?"

"I'd love to, but I can't afford it unless my money arrives. I'll call you on Saturday and we can talk about it."

"Okay, sounds good. See you later."

As I strolled back toward the institute, I contemplated Lori's question about Michel. Did I find him attractive? He was intelligent and interesting, but I wasn't sure about the physical part. I'd never thought about him that way.

Shaking my head, I moved my purse to my other shoulder and picked up my pace. *Don't be ridiculous, Linda. You need to focus on your French. The last thing you need right now is a new romance.*

22

I entered *Le Café Vert* midafternoon the following day and found Michel at his favorite table, hard at work on translations. We spotted each other at the same time and, as I approached, he smiled and stood.

"*Bonjour,* Linda. It's so nice to see you." He kissed my cheeks, helped me with my coat and waved me into the chair across from him. "Would you like a *café au lait?*"

"*Oui, merci.* I hope I'm not disturbing you."

"No, of course not, I'm overdue for a break." Michel placed my order and, after Bruno left, he pulled a cigarette out of his pack and struck a match. "So, what's new? Your classes started on Monday, right?"

"Yeah, I've been placed in Level Two with Professor Toutain. He's teaching us all about basic French grammar." I pushed my hair behind my ears. "Oh, and I talked to my dad on Thursday. He said he wired the money a few days ago."

"*Bien*. And what about your boyfriend? He must have returned by now."

Bruno arrived with my coffee and, after he left, I drew in a breath and wiped my sweaty palms on my thighs. *It'll feel good to get this over with*. "Yeah . . . well . . . we're not together anymore."

"Huh?" Michel sat up straight and his mouth dropped. "Why?"

My voice broke as I held back a flood of emotions. "He came back from Morocco engaged."

Michel's eyebrows furrowed. He shook his head and took a long drag on his cigarette. "*Merde*. That was a crummy thing to do."

I winced. "Yeah. I thought so too."

"Would you like to talk about it?" He looked down as he tapped his cigarette against the ashtray.

It was sweet of him to ask, but I knew I couldn't handle this discussion right now. "Maybe some other time. Let's focus on something else." I picked up my napkin and dabbed at my eyes.

"Of course." He stretched his legs beneath the table. "Why don't you tell me more about your classes?"

Michel listened while I described some of my classroom activities, nodding and asking questions as the conversation progressed. He seemed especially fascinated with my Phonetics and Audiovisual Learning labs.

"Many people say that French is a difficult language to pronounce accurately because the vowels have such a distinct sound. I'm glad to hear the institute gives you extra help with this."

"Can you repeat that, please?" My confusion must have been written on my face.

Michel smiled, repeating the words and a small dimple formed on his right cheek.

How strange that I've never noticed this charming facial feature before.

"Yeah, I'm thrilled to have additional help with pronunciation." I reached for my purse and pulled out my lip gloss. "I met another girl from the US in that class. She's a few years younger than me, but we seem to have a lot in common."

"How nice for you. What's her name?"

I looked up at the ceiling and contemplated his question. "Janet, no Janice . . . yeah, that's it. She's from Los Angeles, California."

"What brought her to the *Institut d'Études Françaises?*"

"She's starting college at University of Los Angeles in the fall as a French major. She's hoping that a few months at the institute will give her a head start with her studies."

He nodded. "She's probably right."

"Et alors," Bruno said checking back with us. "Would you like something else?"

Michel met my gaze. "Will you stay and have dinner with me?"

I nodded and his expression brightened as he perused the menu. "Do you like fish? Bruno's *sole meunière,* filleted fish in butter sauce, is delicious and we could have *kouign-amann,* caramelized cake for dessert."

"Sure, why not."

He placed our order and, a few moments later, Bruno returned with a bottle of wine. He bowed to offer Michel a view of the label, a *Sancerre.*

"Yes, that's the one," Michel affirmed.

Bruno opened the wine, poured, and left.

"To you," Michel said softly, raising his glass. We both took a sip and he raised his eyebrows. "What do you think?"

"It's delicious."

He beamed with satisfaction. *"C'est bon.* I felt certain you'd like it."

Our conversation continued. Bruno returned to fill our glasses and a short while later our dinners arrived.

"Merci, Bruno. This looks fantastic." Michel met his gaze. "All we need now is some bread."

"Of course."

Once Bruno left, I closed my eyes, inhaled, and placed a forkful of fish into my mouth. A moan escaped. When my lids opened, I caught Michel staring at my lips.

Without warning, my pulse quickened. *Where did these feelings come from?* "The sole is wonderful—it has a buttery, lemony flavor I love."

Michel smiled with satisfaction and settled back in his chair. "Yes, this dish is one of my favorites too. Wait until you taste the dessert."

We chatted amicably during the rest of the meal and the wine slowly disappeared. When discussions turned personal, I took advantage of the opportunity and asked Michel a question that deepened the lines in his forehead. "What about love? I assume you've had your share of relationships?"

Michel picked up his wine glass and averted his eyes while he swirled the contents. "Yes, I've met some interesting women, but the relationships didn't last long."

"Oh?" I waited for him to elaborate.

His eyes met mine. "Maybe I was waiting for the right woman to come along."

I couldn't come up with a single response and found myself fiddling with my hair instead. When Bruno returned to clear the table, I glanced at my watch.

"It's getting late. I really should get home. Professor Toutain gave us some homework and, unfortunately, my classes start early, 8:00 a.m."

"*Quel dommage.* I wish you could stay, but I do understand."

He helped me with my coat, looped his arm in mine and led me outside. When we turned to face each other, my stomach fluttered. *Oh dear, I feel so confused. I'm not sure I'm ready for this.*

"I had a good time. Thank you for the fabulous meal." I offered him my cheek and his spicy cologne filled my nose.

"You're welcome," he held my shoulders while his lips brushed my temple. Reacting to his touch, my body relaxed against him.

Michel noticed, and I felt his muscles tense. "When can I see you again? How about Friday? I'll cook you a Lebanese meal at my apartment." When I wavered, he reached for my hand. "Please come."

I took a slight step backwards. *Are we moving too fast? I don't care.* "Okay."

"*Très bien.* I'll meet you in front of *Le Café Vert* at five o'clock." Without breaking eye contact, Michel brought my trembling fingers to his mouth, and I slowly released my captive breath.

23

*T*he weather hovered around freezing on Friday afternoon, and although the sun shone bright, patches of ice patterned the ground. These frigid temperatures didn't diminish my spirits.

My Telex transfer from home had finally arrived, and after days of moping around feeling sad and unhappy about Adam, this bit of good news put a wide smile on my face. It put me in such a good mood that I almost skipped instead of strolled toward *Le Café Vert* to meet Michel for our date. *I'm so relieved to have money again. It'll feel so good to pay back my loan.*

Ten minutes later, I rounded a bend and spotted Michel waiting in front of the restaurant. I waved and he smiled.

"*Bonjour.*" Michel's brows lifted as he greeted me, a kiss on each cheek. "You look cheerful. What's up?"

My words came out in a rush. "I have some good news—my money finally arrived." I reached in my purse and handed him 140 francs. "Thanks again for helping me out."

"Ah . . . I see." Michel pulled out his wallet and put the money away. "I'm glad I was able to help." He lit a cigarette, linked his arm with mine, and guided me around a couple of tourists who had stopped to check out Bruno's menu outside the restaurant.

"Brrr, the temperature has dropped again, don't you think?" I tightened my burgundy scarf as we proceeded down the narrow lane.

"*Oui.* The newspapers have been talking about a cold front coming into this area."

"I think it's already arrived." I glanced in his direction. "Is your home nearby?"

Michel nodded. "Only a few hundred meters."

"That's good." A sudden thought halted my steps and I turned to face him. "Hey, is there a wine shop near here? Why don't I buy a bottle of wine to go with dinner? It's the least I can do."

Michel smiled and shook his head. "It's nice of you to offer, but I've already finished the shopping. Maybe next time, okay?"

"All right."

He threw his cigarette on the ground and grabbed my hand. "Come on, the light's about to change. If we hurry, we won't have to wait."

We crossed the street and, moments later, Michel stopped at the entrance to an old white stone building with a blue slate roof. "I have to warn you, my apartment is nothing special."

Michel waved me into the building, unlocked the first door on the right, and stood aside. "*Alors*, as you can see, there's not much to it."

The apartment was mostly bed, with a tiny kitchen and a table for two situated under a window. There were no pictures or decorative items anywhere, only a few ashtrays spread around the room. *How strange. Where are his personal possessions?*

"It's cozy." I took off my coat, handed it to Michel and he hung it on a hook near the door. "It doesn't look like you've lived here long."

"Only a few months." He ran his hands through his dark brown hair before folding up the cuffs on his shirt. "Please sit down. I'll pour us a drink."

I took a seat at the table and watched the muscles in his forearm ripple as he uncorked a bottle of wine. Unable to resist, I skimmed the rest of his body and felt a jolt of lust surge through my body. He had a lean, solid build—just the way I liked my men. *Argh . . . stop it, Linda.* I squirmed in my seat and quickly looked away.

"So, what are you making tonight?"

"Lebanese chicken and couscous," Michel said, placing a glass of white wine in front of me. "And since you liked the *Sancerre* at *Le Café Vert*, I bought something similar—sauvignon blanc—to go with the meal."

I took a sip. "It's nice. There's a hint of spice in the end."

He took a taste and smacked his lips. "Yes, I think you're right."

We chatted while Michel placed the chicken in a skillet with onion, garlic and butter. Incredible aromas filled the room and my mouth watered.

The couscous came next and when he reached for the final ingredients, I wandered over to get a better look. Standing close and peeking over his shoulder, I watched him sprinkle cinnamon and allspice onto the chicken. The last step was a drizzle of honey.

"*Voilà!*" Michel stepped back to admire his work.

"Mmm." I inhaled deeply. "It smells wonderful."

Michel cut a bite of meat and I laughed as he placed it into my mouth. "It's delicious."

"*C'est bon*," Michel said, dishing up the food. "Let's eat."

He opened another bottle of sauvignon blanc and refilled our glasses before we took our seats at the table. Throughout dinner, the wine loosened our minds and our tongues. We moved from one topic to another in French—family, friends, and our life experiences—until Michel asked a question that stiffened my jawline.

"Have you heard from Adam since he told you his news?"

"No. There's nothing left to say. It's over." I grabbed my glass and took a big gulp. "I still can't believe he came back engaged."

"I'm sorry he did this to you." Michel's gaze locked with mine. "If you belonged to me, I'd never let you go."

My adrenaline surged as he rose out of his chair, grabbed my arm and gently lifted me to my feet.

Without another word, he tilted my head back and pressed his lips against mine. It was a passionate first kiss that lasted a long time, and when he drew back, I felt dizzy with longing.

Just like that, any lingering reservations about a romantic relationship with Michel disappeared. *I want him.*

"Mmm, you taste good," he whispered into my ear.

"*Toi aussi.*" My voice was barely audible.

Once again, his mouth covered mine. He led me to the edge of the bed and we sat down. Meeting my gaze, Michel stroked my cheek lightly with the back of his hand. "I have to warn you, I'm insatiable."

His words sent an electrical current through my body and my face heated with anticipation. "Oh . . ."

Shivers migrated down my spine as he pulled off my sweater, unhooked my bra, lifted my hair and leaned forward to kiss the base of my neck. When his focus moved lower, I closed my eyes and moaned with pleasure as his lips left a trail of sparks behind.

24

When I opened my lids the following morning, I found Michel on his side, propped up on his elbow, watching me. "*Bonjour, ma belle.*"

I grinned at his endearment and covered a yawn with the back of my hand. "*Bonjour.* What time is it?"

"Almost noon," Michel grinned, rolling out of bed and heading for the bathroom. "If you consider what time we actually went to sleep, that's pretty good."

He was right. We finally fell asleep a few hours after dawn, entangled in each other's arms. Michel was an excellent lover—his long drawn-out kisses, his slow, sensual caresses, and his willingness to please—left me exhausted . . . and satiated.

Closing my eyes, I sighed with pleasure as I recalled a particularly amorous moment enhanced by sexy French whispers in my ear.

Michel returned from the bathroom and perched beside me on the edge of the bed, running his finger along my jawline. "Are you hungry?"

I nodded. "What I really want is coffee."

He regarded me in what appeared to be an amused silence. "There's a café around the corner. Why don't you get dressed and we'll get some breakfast."

"All right." I threw my legs over the side of the bed and as I walked past, he slapped my behind, making me squeal and scurry into the bathroom.

Although Michel's apartment lacked a shower, I was thankful for the private sink and toilet. There was another low basin attached to the floor, but I had no idea what it was called and only a slight notion about its function.

On the way out of the building, I asked, "What's that extra porcelain basin in the bathroom for?"

"It's called a *bidet*." He paused, pulled out a *Gitanes*, and lit it. "It's there in case you want to freshen up after you use the toilet."

"Hmm . . . I see." I didn't really, but I was too embarrassed to ask for clarification.

"Is it for women or men?"

"Both." The corners of Michel's mouth twitched. "Actually, bidet is an old word for pony. The notion is that you ride a bidet, like you ride a pony."

"Where did you learn that?" I asked, grinning at the mental image.

"I'm not sure. I remember reading it somewhere. I've always been interested in a lot of different subjects."

Michel's knowledge of French culture and language was indeed remarkable. I learned at least five new things every time we got together and, since French was our only option, my language skills improved rapidly. Now that he'd proved himself to be a good lover, I was even more impressed.

I peered at Michel and my heart swelled. *He looks handsome in his blue shirt. I'm glad he's by my side.* I had a lot to learn—about France, about the language, about love—but at that moment, I was happy to be with my man.

Michel met my gaze and his eyes sparkled with mutual admiration. Smiling, he draped his arm around my shoulders. "Are you okay?"

"*Oui. Très bien.*" I grinned, hooking my thumb in his belt loop as we sauntered down the lane.

Two hours later, I returned to my room in the Martin family home and laid my packages on my desk. On the way home from Michel's, I stopped at the grocer's and bought a baguette, cheese, salami, apples, juice, a paring knife, a small cutting board, napkins, a basket and a pack of paper cups.

Since I had no refrigerator, I took advantage of the cold weather to preserve my foodstuffs. I put everything, except the baguette, in the basket and placed it outside on my windowsill.

A lone pigeon on the roof sidled toward my food and we stared at each other for a few seconds. *What if he gets into my stuff? Oh well, I'll just have to take that chance.*

Next, I focused my attention on my other purchase—a new book Professor Toutain recommended. On Friday, when I filed past his desk to leave the classroom, he called me over and made a suggestion.

"Linda, you speak French quite well, but I think you could benefit from more reading."

"What do you have in mind?" I asked.

"Here's a list of some French classics. *Le Petit Prince* would be my first choice. Why don't you pick up a copy and work your way through it. You'll learn some new vocabulary and you'll get used to seeing correct French sentence structures."

"Okay," I said with a nod. "I'll give it a try."

With my limited knowledge of the language, I knew it would be a challenge, but I couldn't wait to get started.

Clutching my new book, I turned to the beginning of *Le Petit Prince* and spent the next hour translating the first page of the story. Whenever I discovered a word I didn't understand, I looked it up in my dictionary and penciled the English word above the French. After I completed one full page, I reread it and then set it aside. *Not so bad—only ninety-five more pages to go.*

I got up, stretched, opened the window and fetched a drink from my "fridge." When I sat back down at my desk, my diary caught my eye, so I opened it and read my recent entry.

Hmm . . . what about today? After last night, I was pretty sure that today's entry would be a juicy one. I picked up my pen and began to write . . .

> *I'm afraid that I'm becoming very involved with Michel. We are very compatible both in and out of bed and I no longer wish to slow or limit my relationship with him . . .*

A knock on the door broke my concentration. "Come in."

Madame Martin peeked around the door. "Mademoiselle, a girl named Lori wants to speak with you on the phone."

"*Merci.*" I followed her down the stairs to the kitchen.

"Hello?"

"Hi. Did I catch you at a bad time?"

I shook my head, even though Lori couldn't see me. "Not really, I'm glad you called."

"Good. How are things going?"

"Okay . . ." I bit my lip and wrapped the cord around my finger. "I have some big news."

"What happened? Does this have something to do with Michel?"

"Yes," I said, moving the receiver to my other ear. "But I can't talk about it right now."

"Okay, but we're still getting together, right?"

"Sure, what's the plan?"

"There's this French girl, Paulette, who lives next door. She offered to drive Albert and me to a disco outside Tours tonight. She said you can come, too, and she'll pick you up along the way."

My volume increased with excitement. "It sounds like fun. What time?"

"Nine o'clock," she confirmed.

"Okay, I'll be ready. Thanks, Lori."

I replaced the receiver on the wall and returned to my room. Along the way, a series of yawns convinced me it would be a good idea to take a nap. I was fairly sure we'd be out late and I didn't want to burn out early.

I woke an hour later, famished, so I fetched my basket of food from outside the window, broke off chunks of bread and fashioned a makeshift dinner of salami and cheese. After I straightened up the room, I decided to take a shower.

Uncomfortable with the strange arrangement, I grabbed a bath towel, shampoo, and soap and descended the stairs to the second floor to knock on Madame Martin's eldest son's door. I heard shuffling noises and, a few seconds later, he stood in the doorway.

"Good evening, Thomas. Can I use the shower?"

"*Mais oui.* Come in." A slow blush climbed his neck and covered his face as the awkward fifteen-year-old waved me toward the bathroom.

"Thank you." I closed the door, secured the lock, and took my time. Given the circumstances, I planned to enjoy the experience to the fullest every chance I got. Twenty minutes later, with a towel wrapped around my head, I exited the bathroom and discovered Thomas lying on his bed reading a book.

"Sorry for the intrusion."

"*Pas de problème.*" He moved his novel aside as he checked me out.

I edged past him and slipped through the door. *Poor Thomas.* I was fairly certain he considered my showers an invasion of his privacy. Or maybe he didn't. It might be cool for a fifteen-year-old boy to have a young American girl using his bathroom. Oh well, either way, it couldn't be helped.

As promised, Paulette, Lori and Albert picked me up at nine o'clock and we drove a short distance outside Tours to the *Métropolitain* disco. There was a long line of people waiting outside the building, so Paulette dropped Lori and Albert off at the entrance while we parked the car. The lot was full, but we lucked out, found a place quickly and then joined our friends in line.

"Awesome place, right?" Paulette said, fishing through her purse.

"Yeah, it's huge." Lori peered toward the entrance around a group of giggling girls. "The stereo system sounds good."

Paulette nodded and reapplied lip gloss. "Wait until you get inside."

Moments later, we entered a large room with low ceilings, mirrored walls and an oval dance floor. The place was packed, but Albert found a table close to the bar and, as soon as we sat down, a server showed up to take our orders. She returned immediately "as if by magic" with our French 75s, which we sipped as we people watched.

When the DJ announced the next song "Locomotion" by Ritz— Lori and Paulette pulled Albert and me onto the dance floor.

As the evening progressed, the DJ played a great selection of music from all the current artists—Michael Jackson, ABBA, KISS— to name a few. We danced the night away, just like the Van Halen song suggested.

Lori and I didn't get a chance to talk privately until well into the evening. By then, she had already downed four drinks—too many for her small frame. "So, what's going on with you and Michel?" Her words came out thick and sticky.

She leaned too far forward and I reached out to steady her. "Last night, he cooked me this fabulous dinner at his apartment and . . . well . . . let's just say that we're no longer simply friends."

Her brow furrowed, and it took a moment before she understood my meaning. "Ah . . . that's cool." She nodded. "I'm glad you moved on. Adam doesn't deserve you."

"I knew you'd understand."

Lori continued to drink heavily and, at midnight, Albert and I both warned her to stop, but she wouldn't listen.

"She's going to feel bad in the morning." Albert shook his head.

I glanced at Lori on the dance floor and my lips twitched with amusement. Her head flung back, she was laughing as she shook her booty.

"I think you're right."

At four o'clock, when Paulette and Albert dropped me home, Lori was sound asleep in the back seat.

25

———◆×◆———

I didn't wake until one on Sunday afternoon. After two late nights, it felt good to get some extra sleep. *I'm so glad I didn't overdo it last night. I can only imagine how Lori feels today.*

Tossing the covers aside, I slipped out of bed, freshened up at the sink and got dressed. When my stomach growled, I opened the drapes and looked outside.

Ominous gray and white clouds filled the sky and there was a layer of ice on the roof. It looked cold outside. Thank goodness I was here and not in that garret at the *Château de Montclair*. I shivered and wrapped my arms around my body. *Maybe I'll take a walk to buy a coffee and a croissant.* I'd have plenty of time to study my French when I returned.

I grabbed my coat and descended the stairs. When I walked past the kitchen door, Madame Martin called out to me.

"*Bonjour,* Linda." She passed me an envelope. "A man left this for you last night."

I blinked, and warmth spread through my body as I pushed the envelope into my purse. *Who's the letter from? I can't wait to open it.* "*Merci.*"

As soon as I slipped through the door, a chilly gust of wind blew my collar open. I stopped to secure the buttons and rushed toward my destination—a small local restaurant around the corner called *Café Americano.*

I entered the fragrant café, took a seat near the window, and opened the sealed envelope. My hand trembled as I examined the three note cards signed by Michel. *His writing is so nice. No mistakes or crossed out words.*

"*Bonjour,* Linda. Would you like *un café au lait*?"

I jumped, startled from my thoughts by a familiar voice. Now that *Café Americano* had turned into a regular hangout for me, the waiter and I were on a first name basis. "*Bonjour,* Christophe. Yes, and a croissant, please."

After he left, I tried to decipher the first sentence, but I only got a few words. *Darn it. I need my French-English dictionary. I'll have to wait until I get home.* I frowned and put the cards away.

"It's chilly out there today." Christophe said, delivering my order. "I hope you didn't walk far."

"No." I took a sip of my coffee. "I live around the corner."

"Ah, that's good news." His blue eyes twinkled, and his mouth formed a sly smile as he scratched his neatly trimmed beard. "I live nearby as well, so maybe we can share a meal sometime."

"*Peut-être.*"

I smiled as he walked away. It was flattering to have a handsome French man flirt with me, but his offer didn't distract me for long. I was anxious to get back home and find out what the letter said.

When I returned home, I rushed up the stairs, flung my coat across the bed, and grabbed my French-English dictionary. Line by line, I translated Michel's mysterious letter.

Linda,

Lorsque je t'ai vu pour la première fois . . .

When I saw you for the first time I felt a magnetic force that pushed me toward you. So, I spoke to you and then I got to know you.

Something happened inside me, a feeling of tenderness, joy and beauty . . .

Now, having just left you, in my head there is a perfume, green and light, it is surely the *image of your fresh smile and your infinitely affectionate eyes.*

A mysterious thread ties me to you, but I am afraid, afraid as when I was a child and saw the moon for the first time.

Linda, don't take too much notice of what I say or write . . . the important thing is the silence, this white beach that you find between my words and my gaze. There where the clear blue sky joins the sea blue oceans, there are millions and millions of rose petals that form an island, an island that resembles a hand, it is this warm hand that I extend toward you.

Michel

I reread it twice and swallowed hard against the lump in my throat. No one had ever written anything like this to me before. I was flattered, but this was crazy. It was . . . it was a love letter and we hardly knew each other.

I got up from the desk and paced the small space in my room. *I'll show it to Lori.* Maybe parts of my translations were off. It would be interesting to hear her take on it.

Just after six o'clock, a knock on the door disrupted my French studies. *Who could this be?* When I opened it, Évelyne stood smiling in the doorway.

"*Bonjour!* It's good to see you!" My hug was so enthusiastic; I heard her "ooof" before I released her. "Please come in."

"I hope I'm not disturbing you." She glanced around the room, her sable-brown eyes settling on the papers on my desk. "I had some shopping to do in Tours, so I thought I'd stop in for a short visit."

"I'm so glad you did. Please sit down." I waved her toward the only chair in the room. "Are you thirsty? I have some juice on my windowsill."

"*Quoi?*" She glanced out my window. "Ah, I see. Yes please."

I poured two drinks and perched on the bed. "So, how was your holiday with your family?"

"Wonderful. My niece and nephew are growing up so fast. I wish I could see them more often," she sighed. "What about you? What did you do for Christmas?"

I pushed my hair behind ears. "I spent it with a new . . . friend."

"Oh? How did you two meet?"

"Well, a few days before Christmas I stumbled upon this café . . ."

Évelyne took a sip of her apple juice and sat back while I recapped the recent events of the past twenty-one days—my money issues, Adam's deception and my blossoming romance with Michel. Every so often, she mumbled "tsk, tsk" under her breath or asked for clarification.

When I finished my story, she laid her hand on my arm. "I'm so glad everything turned out okay. Thank goodness you met Michel."

I hesitated and Évelyne's brow furrowed. "What's wrong?"

"Well . . . there's just this one thing. Michel dropped off a letter yesterday and it . . . well . . . it seems . . . a bit much." I reached for the note cards and my stomach did a flip-flop. "Will you take a look at it?"

"*Mais oui.*"

Her eyes widened as she skimmed the cards. "This is lovely. He really cares for you. I'm not sure how men behave in the United States, but most French men aren't afraid to show their emotions."

She was right. The guys back home would think the letter was lame. "*Bien.* I'm glad I asked." It would take some time for me to get used to this kind of attention.

Our conversation moved on to other subjects—recent events at Songais *Collège,* my classes at the institute, our families—and an hour later, Évelyne checked her watch and slipped into her coat.

"*Alors,* before I go, I have to tell you how impressed I am with your French. The improvement is remarkable. You must be pleased?"

"Yes. I feel more confident every day, but I'm still struggling with reading and writing."

Évelyne kissed my cheeks and winked her reassurance. "Don't worry, now that you're at the institute, you'll see progress there too."

"I suppose you're right. Thanks again for stopping by. Please say hello to Director Moreau and Madame Bernard."

"I will." She wound her lilac-patterned silk scarf around her neck. "Now that I have your phone number, we'll be able to make plans easier in the future."

My face glowed with happiness. "I'd like that, Évelyne."

26

Four days later, I returned home from school, and as usual, Madame Martin and I exchanged "*bonjours*" in the hallway. When I heard the phone ring, a premonition paused me at the bottom of the stairs. *Is it for me?*

"Linda, Michel wants to talk to you."

My legs felt weak as I walked over and took the receiver in my trembling hand. "*Merci*, Madame."

"Michel?"

"*Bonjour.* I've missed you."

I glanced over my shoulder and verified Madame Martin had left the room. "Me too."

"Are you busy tonight? I'm dining with some friends at a Tunisian restaurant near *la Place Plumereau*. I wish you'd join us."

My words came out faster than I intended. "Yes, of course. What time?"

"Seven o'clock?"

"*D'accord.* I'll be waiting at the front door."

I returned to my room and checked my clock. Good—it was only 4:30, so I'd have plenty of time to study and get ready for my date. Humming a tune, I sat down at my desk and pulled out my homework.

Just before seven o'clock, I hovered in the foyer. When I heard a rap, I yanked open the door.

"It's so good to see you," Michel said, in his sexy French accent. When he pulled me into his embrace, his warm breath against my ear sent a jolt of electricity through my body. "Did you get my letter?"

"Yes. It was charming."

Our eyes met, and he touched his lips lightly against mine. "I meant every word."

Oh dear. Attention like this left me tongue-tied. What was I supposed to say to that?

We descended the steps and found a comfortable rhythm, conversing about things in common, as we strolled down the sidewalk. Occasionally, we'd stop to peer into store windows. Soon, Michel pointed to a restaurant and we jaywalked across the street, laughing as we dodged a bicycle.

Chez Zayd's gold-and-black color scheme distinguished it from other restaurants on the block, but it was the Arabic script and domed windows that added allure and intrigue. Cumin, nutmeg and other exotic spices drifted out the door.

"It's interesting and something smells good." I glanced at Michel, my voice filled with enthusiasm.

"I hope you like the food. It can be an acquired taste."

He opened the door and waved me inside the darkened room. It took a few seconds for our eyes to adjust.

"*Michel! Salut!*"

I heard his low chuckle, then he walked up to his friends and bear-hugged them. They exchanged a few pleasantries before Michel stepped aside. "This is Linda."

"*Enchanté.*" Pascal and Amir bowed, then took turns shaking my hand.

After Michel helped me with my coat, he guided me to a chair and ordered a bottle of red wine. The waiter circled the table, filling glasses while trying not to interfere with the conversations. My head whipped back and forth, as I attempted to follow the fast flowing French around me, but I couldn't keep up. Once again, I felt lost and left out.

Memories of dinners with the Dubois family and Christmas lunch at the Durands flooded my mind. *How disappointing. I guess I still have a lot to learn.*

When our food arrived, Amir and Pascal broke off in a private discussion and I leaned toward Michel. "What's this dish called again?"

"*Brika.* It's a deep-fried dough filled with raw egg, chicken and garnishes."

I nodded and took a bite, savoring the strange flavors. "It's tasty."

Michel smiled. "There's a Tunisian tradition surrounding *brika*. The bride's mother makes the dish for the groom and, if he eats it without spilling the raw egg, the nuptials can move forward."

I didn't understand a few of his words, so I asked him to repeat his anecdote.

"Aha! That's great." I laughed. "It's a messy dish, so that wouldn't be easy."

Emboldened by the wine, less concerned about mistakes or judgments, I participated in the conversations as we ate our meal. After we finished our dinners, all three men relaxed and lit cigarettes.

I watched for a few seconds as the smoke drifted and then dissipated around them. "Can I have one?"

Michel's eyes widened. "Are you sure?"

I hesitated. It wasn't easy to quit last year after a four-year habit. "Yes."

He shrugged and pulled out his pack of *Gitanes*.

"Perhaps you'd prefer a filtered cigarette?" Pascal said, his voice filled with concern. "I smoke Marlboro Lights."

"Yes, I think I would," I said, reaching across the table toward Pascal. "*Merci.*"

Michel lit my cigarette and, while the conversations swirled around me, I puffed on my smoke, feeling independent and rebellious. *This tastes good, especially with the red wine.*

Twenty minutes later, we all gathered outside the entrance and said our goodbyes.

Once we were alone, I snuggled up to Michel. "Thank you so much for dinner. What now?"

He pulled me close, his grin filled with mischief. "Why don't we go to my apartment?"

"I'm not sure that's a good idea," I teased, feeling light-headed from the wine. "It's a school night."

Michel brushed his lips against mine and his voice turned rough. "That's true, but we could go to bed early."

My veins pulsed with excitement as I met his gaze. "Okay."

Grasping my elbow, he led me forward at a pace far more brisk than our comfortable stroll to the restaurant. I couldn't help but smile—he was so obvious, so funny. When we reached his apartment, I laughed with delight as he whisked me inside.

27

*T*he next morning, Friday, when the alarm sounded at seven o'clock, Michel clicked it off, reached over and pulled me into his arms. I moaned and he strengthened his grip.

"You're not making this any easier."

"Of course not. I don't want you to go." Michel nuzzled my neck. "Why don't you skip school today? Come on, it's Friday. We can spend the day together and I'll help you with your French later."

I wavered. "It sounds tempting, but I don't want you to become a bad influence on me." I pouted to emphasize my point. "You know how important my classes are to me."

"Don't worry, *ma belle*. I only want the best for you."

Michel's right hand moved lower and my body tensed. *Ooh . . . he knows exactly how to please me.* It didn't take him long to figure it out. When my breath caught in my throat, I closed my eyes and pushed aside any remaining concerns about my pesky French class.

28

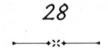

*M*idafternoon, the following day, I returned to the Martin's home to take a shower and to collect fresh clothing, toiletries, and makeup. Michel had suggested I spend the weekend with him, and I agreed, but not without reiterating my reservations about the bathing options at his apartment.

Images of the filthy bathroom popped into my mind and I shuddered. Last night, while Michel shopped for dinner, I grabbed soap, shampoo, and a bath towel and headed down the hall. The toilet was stained and stank, and the shower had a layer of mold growing on the walls and floor. Holding my hand over my mouth, I spun around and rushed back to his apartment.

When Michel returned home, he got an earful of my complaints. This bathroom might be useable to him, but I would never set foot in it again.

A soft knock brought me back to the present, but before I could respond, the door opened.

"Oh! *Je suis désolée*," Madame Martin sputtered. "I didn't realize that you had returned. I was going to vacuum your room."

"No problem, I was just leaving again."

She tilted her head and glanced at my bag. "You're spending another night away?"

"Yes. I'm meeting Michel."

"I see." She fiddled with her apron. "You've sure been spending a lot of time at his place."

"Have I?" I squeaked.

She met my gaze. "I've been meaning to ask you about him. What is his nationality? He doesn't look French."

What an odd question. A nervous giggle escaped. "Well, actually, his mother was French, but he grew up in Lebanon."

Her mouth tightened with disapproval. "And what kind of work does he do?"

"Michel translates French books into Arabic." Then with a defensive tone, "He's taking a break from his studies in psychology."

"Psychology . . . Mmm."

I switched my bag to my other shoulder and worked hard to keep the irritation out of my voice. "Well, I guess I better get going. See you later."

Once outside, I pondered our conversation. Even though my landlady hadn't mentioned her reservations aloud, her body language came across loud and clear. She didn't like my boyfriend. *How unfair. If she knew him better, I'm sure she'd change her mind.*

29

*M*onday morning, I woke with a start and glanced at the clock. *Damn! It's eleven o'clock. I slept through the alarm!*

Rubbing my eyes, I looked around the room. *Where's Michel? Oh, that's right, he told me he had some sort of business meeting at ten.*

I stifled a yawn, dressed and headed for the restroom. On the way, I spotted my homework on the table and my chest compressed with guilt. I couldn't believe I missed class again. Dad and Mom would be so disappointed in me. *Hell, I'm disappointed in me.*

As I washed my hands in front of the mirror, my reflection frowned back at me. My hair was dirty and I needed a shower, but there was no way I'd use the one down the hall. Pursing my lips, I grabbed a comb out of my bag, pulled my hair back into a low ponytail and exited the cramped room.

What now? I suppose I should try to study. I lit a cigarette, warmed up some coffee and pulled out my grammar lessons from Thursday.

Michel returned home an hour later, and as he pulled off his coat, I noticed tension in his jaw. "How was the meeting?" I shoved my papers aside.

He walked over to kiss me. "Fine."

I searched his face and then shook my head. "I can tell that something's wrong, Michel. You never want to talk about your work, but I'm not blind. You haven't pulled out your books or papers for days."

He reached up, combed his fingers through his dark brown hair and sat down. "That's because I've completed all the projects available right now."

"So what does this mean exactly? When will you get another one?"

Michel gave me a long look before he pulled a cigarette out and lit it. "Amir believes he'll have another project for me next week. Until then, I'll have to budget my money."

"Okay." *I'm glad he told me this. Communication is so important.* I walked around the table, climbed onto his lap, and laid my head on his shoulder. "At least you know that there are jobs coming, right?"

There was a slight hesitation. "Yes, in a few weeks at most."

"Good." I sat up straight. "I'd like to talk to you about something else that's on my mind, okay?"

"Of course."

"I've missed two French classes in one week and I feel really bad about it." I chewed on my lower lip. "I'm not taking care of myself either. I haven't showered in days and I wore the same outfit out two nights in a row. That's not like me . . ."

"So, what do you suggest?"

"I think that I should spend weeknights in my own bed." There, I said it. How would he react?

His body sagged and he pulled me close. "What can I say? You're right, of course."

Good. What a relief. He gets it.

We sat like that, holding each other in silence for several seconds. Then Michel ventured, "Do you want some help with your French? Isn't that paper describing your favorite holiday due tomorrow? I'd be happy to look it over."

My heart fluttered. I was surprised he remembered. "Yes, I'd like that very much."

He brushed his lips against my temple. "After that, we'll get a bite to eat and then I'll walk you home."

30

Shortly after one o'clock, two days later, I entered *Café de l'Europe* hoping to meet up with Albert or Lori. I paused at the entrance to scan the room. When I spotted my friends at a table nearby, I broke into a wide smile.

Lori leapt up to hug me. "It's great to see you. How are things?"

"Good. Really good."

"I'm so glad to hear that."

"*Salut*, Linda." Albert smiled as he greeted me, three kisses on the cheeks.

"Come sit next to me." Lori pulled me into the chair next to hers. "Look what Albert gave me." Her eyes sparkled as she leaned forward to show me her necklace.

I peered closely at the dainty heart-shaped gold pendant embossed with the swirly word "France."

"He gave it to me yesterday after class. It was such a surprise." Lori gave Albert an adoring glance and then she turned the pendant over. "It has 1980 engraved on the back so 'I won't forget him.'"

My stomach pitched. I couldn't believe she was leaving in only eight days. *I wish I had something to give her. I'm going to miss her so much.*

"It's lovely, Lori." I turned to Albert with a thumbs-up. "Good job."

Albert's face reddened and he picked at his frayed jeans. "Yeah, well, sometimes I get things right."

"That's for sure." Lori gave him a glowing smile and a quick kiss. "So, what have you been up to? Are you seeing a lot of Michel?"

"Yeah, we've been hanging out quite a bit," I shimmied out of my coat. "He took me to this awesome club on Saturday night. I think it's called *Le Baron*. Have you heard of it?"

"Maybe. Is it near *la Place Plumereau*?"

My forehead wrinkled. "Sort of, further south."

A waiter arrived to take my order and, after he left, we moved on to a new topic.

"Lori says to me that your French classes are going well. What's the latest?" Albert asked, lighting a cigarette and stretching his legs beneath the table.

"Well . . . Professor Toutain handed back our French composition papers today and I got a B+. Can you believe it?" I paused. "Oh, and after class, he told me that he thinks I should be in Level Three French."

"Are you moving up then?" Lori asked.

"No. I told him how happy I am in his class and he agreed to let me stay."

"That's great, Linda. I knew everything would work out."

Over the next thirty minutes, we chatted while I ate—Lori and Albert sharing a bit about mutual friends while I filled them in on my birthday plans for January twenty-sixth. Once I finished my meal, I reached over and pulled a Marlboro Light out of my purse. *Lori's going to have a cow. Wait for it.*

"Huh? Since when do you smoke?" A frown slid into place as she watched me strike a match.

"Since last week."

I didn't hear her response.

"Hi guys." Adam's arrival startled us all.

My adrenaline surged as I swiveled around and met his gaze. *Damn.* I was afraid that we might run into each other here. *How awkward.*

Lori and Albert managed a couple of weak hellos and then Adam leaned over, his words urgent in my ear. "We need to talk. Will you take a walk with me?"

I wanted to say no, but instead I heard myself mumble "okay" as I ground out my cigarette. How could I refuse? Maybe, just maybe, he'd explain the situation better to me this time.

With shaky hands, I pulled on my coat and laid some money on the table. Albert hugged me goodbye and then Lori stepped forward. "Don't let him talk you into anything you'll regret later," she whispered, her voice filled with concern.

My response came out solid. "Not a chance."

Once we were outside, we walked along the sidewalk in silence, our hands shoved deep in our pockets. Finally, I glanced at him. "So . . . what's up, Adam?"

Our eyes linked and he rubbed the back of his neck. "I felt bad about our last meeting. It was wrong . . . what I did to you. I realize now that I should have told you about my situation a long time ago. Can you ever forgive me?"

My lip trembled and I gripped my purse tighter. "Why does it matter? I've moved on. You should too."

He winced and pulled me under an awning. "That's just it, Linda. I don't want to move on."

"What does that mean?"

"I miss you. Can't we still be together?" He reached out to caress my face and I brushed his hand aside.

"I can't believe that you'd say that to me. You really don't know me at all, do you?" I shook my head in disbelief. "I wouldn't be with you now under any circumstances. You're engaged for crying out loud!"

"But I still want you."

"That's your problem." *And hers.* I took a deep breath. "Anyway, I've met someone else."

His shoulders slumped and a scowl emerged. "What's his name?"

"It doesn't concern you, Adam." I shifted from one foot to the other. "Listen, I have to get going."

Adam studied his shoes. "Well, then, I guess this is goodbye."

"It sure is."

I turned and walked away, feeling my resolve strengthen with each step. *It's over. Really over this time.* There was nothing left to say.

31

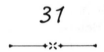

I turned twenty-two years old on Saturday, January 26, 1980. Since neither Michel nor I could afford a night out, he arranged a small party at Pascal's and his girlfriend, Monique's, apartment. I smiled as I recalled our phone conversation of two nights earlier.

"I wish I could take you somewhere special for your birthday." Michel's voice sounded wistful. "You deserve so much more."

"Aww . . . what a sweet thing to say. I'm just glad we'll be together."

"*Évidemment.*" Michel agreed. "Have you invited your friends?"

"Yes." I fiddled with the phone cord. "Lori, Albert and maybe Julie, are coming. Oh, and I've invited my new friend, Janice, from the institute."

I hope everyone gets along. Why wouldn't they? Michel was awesome and I had a cool group of friends.

"Good, I'm really looking forward to meeting them."

"They're anxious to meet you too."

Now that the big day had arrived, I couldn't decide what to wear, as usual. I tugged on my snug, stonewashed denim jeans and paired them with a loose-fitting navy cowl. When I checked my appearance in the mirror, I shook my head and changed into a clingy emerald sweater that emphasized my small waist. *That's better. The color makes my green eyes pop.*

I dabbed on perfume and brushed my hair until it fell in waves around my shoulders. A hint of pink blush, some lip gloss and my drop earrings completed the look.

A few minutes after seven, there was a knock on the front door. When I opened it, Michel caught me in an embrace.

"*Joyeux anniversaire, ma belle.* I've missed you." His mouth covered mine. "Mmm . . . you look beautiful and smell delicious."

I flushed with happiness. "*Merci.*"

A dog barked, and when I glanced behind me, Madame Martin scooped Sophie into her arms. "*Bonsoir*, Linda."

"*Bonsoir*, Madame." Stumbling over my words, I introduced Michel and after a short, polite conversation, we left.

Once we reached the sidewalk, Michel offered me a Marlboro Light from his pack. Ever since I'd restarted the habit, he'd switched over to my preferred brand.

"So that's your landlady. What do you think of her?" he asked.

"She's nice." I put the cigarette to my lips and paused while he lit it. "The other night, she invited me to watch TV with her family. There was this variety show on . . ." My eyes met his and I continued. "You know with singers and dancers. I really enjoyed it."

Michel shook his head. "Hmm . . . not my thing, but it was nice of her to include you."

"I thought so too." I took a drag and blew out the smoke. "Who else will be at the party tonight?"

"Amir. Oh, and Francis might come too. I've ordered pizza, and there'll be plenty of wine."

I grabbed his hand. "Thanks for arranging this for me."

Michel's expression relaxed and he brought my fingers to his lips. "*Tout le plaisir est pour moi.*"

Fifteen minutes later, we stopped in front of a three-story stone building topped with gray slate tiles. Michel led me up three flights of stairs and rapped on the door to apartment 337.

A black-haired, curvy girl with flawless skin answered. Her long black hair swished around her shoulders as she motioned us inside. *"Bonjour,* Michel."

He kissed her cheeks and then stepped aside. "Monique, this is my girlfriend, Linda."

Her dark-fringed eyes appraised me from top to bottom. *"Salut. Enchantée."*

Pascal and Amir joined us, but another knock caught everyone's attention. When Monique opened the door, Lori, Albert and Julie stood smiling in the entrance.

My spirits soared as I hugged everyone. "Hi guys. Thanks for coming."

Introductions and birthday wishes clogged the entryway for quite a while until Pascal offered to take our coats. "Please make yourself at home. There's wine and snacks in the kitchen."

I moved forward with the group until Lori beckoned me with a jerk of her chin.

"Michel, you go ahead. I'd like to talk with Lori and Julie for a while."

"D'accord. Have fun."

I joined my circle of friends and we switched to English. "Hey guys, I'm so happy you're here tonight."

We all high-fived and laughed, and then Lori's smile disappeared and her expression turned serious. "I'm just glad your birthday is in January so I could celebrate with you."

My heart thumped. "Me too."

Julie snorted. "Come on you two. We agreed not to discuss this tonight, remember?"

"You're right." Lori shook off her melancholy words. "Tonight we're celebrating a happy occasion." She got up on her tiptoes and peeked over Julie's shoulder. "So that's your Michel? He seems nice."

"Yeah, things are good," I sighed with contentment. *Really good.*

"He has a mysterious look about him." Julie's lips slid into a sly smile as she met my gaze. "I love his ponytail."

"You do?" I chuckled. "I'm not going to tell him you said that because I think he needs a haircut, or at least some layering."

When I heard the doorbell, I swiveled around to see the new arrival. "Hey, my friend Janice is here."

I watched while Janice greeted Pascal and Monique. Petite, a little under five foot five, she stood posture perfect, her shoulders thrown back, as she answered a battery of polite questions. Given her confident nature, no one in the room would have guessed that she was barely eighteen.

"Hi, Janice." I kissed her cheeks three times. "I'm glad you could make it."

Her face lit up and we continued in French. "Thanks for inviting me."

She looked around, her short brown curls brushing her cheeks as she turned to Monique. "This is such a cool apartment."

A green overstuffed couch, matching chair and coffee table anchored one end of the room, while a cabinet with a modern stereo filled the space on the opposite wall. Intricate wrought iron lamps supplied soft lighting and colorful modern art posters added points of interest.

"Yeah, we're lucky to have it." Monique turned to Pascal. "These girls need a glass of wine, don't you think? It's time to get this party started!"

After Pascal poured our drinks, we joined the group in the salon. When Michel caught my eye, I slid into a seat on the couch between him and Monique.

"*Ça va?*" he asked, giving me a quick kiss. I nodded, and he resumed his conversation with Albert.

"So, tell me, how did you and Michel meet?" Monique brushed her hair aside and took a sip of wine.

The corners of my mouth lifted. "We met at a small restaurant near Old Town."

"*Le Café Vert?*"

"Yes, that's it." I blinked. "How did you know? Have you been there?"

"No . . . no I haven't, but Pascal tells me that Michel hangs out there quite a bit."

"Yes. It's his favorite place to work on his translations."

Monique nodded and I saw indecision flick across her face. "Hmm . . . I think he met his last girlfriend there."

Her answer puzzled me. *What girlfriend?* I opened my mouth to ask her for an explanation, but she moved on to a new topic and my question got lost in the conversation.

The evening progressed—all of us mingling together, laughing and talking as soft rock music played in the background. *I'm so glad everyone is getting along so well.*

When it was time to eat, we followed Michel into the kitchen. "Please, everyone, *bon appétit!*" he announced, turning to open more wine while everyone dished up the pizza.

"It smells delicious." Inhaling, I detected hints of bacon and onion.

"Yes, I think you'll like this one. It's pizza *à la crème fraiche.*"

"Mmm . . . I can't wait. I've never eaten a pizza made with cream instead of tomato sauce before."

After dinner, when Michel brought out a chocolate mousse tart filled with candles, my hand flew to my mouth. "Aww . . . it's magnificent."

Sopranos and baritones mixed as everyone sang "*Joyeux anniversaire.*" When the song ended, I inhaled and blew out my candles. *It's so cool that I'm celebrating my twenty-second birthday in Tours. I wish Bud, Carline and Cindy could be here too.*

There were cheers around the kitchen and, once the room quieted, I cleared my throat. "I'm so glad you're all here tonight. I'd like to thank Monique and Pascal for hosting the party . . . and Michel for putting it together." I beamed at him. "Now, I need a knife so I can cut the tart."

After we ate dessert, the girls helped Monique straighten the kitchen, and then we rejoined the guys in the living room. Pascal put on some fantastic music—Sheila B. Devotion, Michael Jackson, and Freddie James—and this got everyone off the couch and onto their feet. Michel and I even attempted disco, eventually mastering a twirl or two.

"You're getting good," I told him after a flamboyant dip.

"Yeah, a regular John Travolta."

"No, not quite." I grinned.

When the party broke up at two o'clock, I pulled Monique aside and thanked her once again for a fabulous time. We all stumbled down the stairs and out of the building. Tipsy from the wine, our goodbyes were loud and boisterous.

"Don't worry, Linda, we'll make sure that your friend gets home okay." Lori slurred while she and Julie propped up Janice.

Michel and I laughed at the comical scene in front of us. "Good. I'm glad you have Albert along for added support."

"Yes!" Puffing out his chest, Albert gave me a thumbs-up.

"Thanks for including me tonight, Linda." Janice broke free for a wobbly hug. "I had a great time . . . one of the best since I arrived in France."

"I'm glad. Next time maybe we can check out some the local clubs." *She's sweet. I'm glad I met her.*

"What about me?" Lori's pout was obviously a fake.

I hugged her close. "Aww, Lori, you know that you're my favorite," I whispered.

"I think you're awesome too. I'll call you and we'll get together over the next few days."

"Okay, good."

As Michel and I walked back to his apartment in the cool, crisp morning air, I contemplated the evening. *I had fun tonight. It wasn't as big a deal as turning twenty-one, but I was glad I got to spend it with my French friends—and Michel—of course.*

32

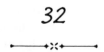

*T*hree days later, with a bounce in my step, I exited the bank and headed north on *rue Nationale* toward my apartment. Another Telex transfer had arrived from home and I was flush with money. Even after I paid rent, I'd have 700 francs left in my account.

I slowed my pace as an idea formed in my mind. *Maybe I'll invite Michel out for dinner.* Even though it was a school night, I couldn't resist.

When I arrived at *Le Café Vert*, there was no sign of Michel. *How odd. He's always here at this time.*

"*Bonjour,* Mademoiselle. *Une table?*" Bruno asked, motioning with his hand.

I bit my lip. *Maybe just a coffee in case Michel shows up.* "*Oui, merci.*"

Bruno showed me to a seat near the window and took my order. Moments later, he returned with my *café au lait.*

"Have you seen Michel today?"

He shook his head. "No. I haven't seen him for a couple of days."

"*Hmm . . . merci.*" My brow furrowed as I contemplated his answer. Michel must still be out of work. *I hope something turns up soon.*

After I finished my coffee, I paid my bill and returned home. When I walked past the kitchen door, Madame Martin called my name.

"*Bonjour*, Linda." Her gaze narrowed as she spoke. "Michel called a moment ago and asked me to pass on a message. He said for you to meet him at his apartment."

My pulse rate accelerated. "*Merci*, Madame."

I wanted to dash through the door, but I held myself back until I got outside. Madame Martin's inquiries about Michel the previous week left me feeling self-conscious about my relationship. I didn't want her to think I'd lost control of my sensibilities.

The cold air stung my face and I pulled my coat tighter around my neck as I hurried to my destination. I couldn't wait to see him.

Ten minutes later, Michel opened his door and pulled me into his arms. "*Bonjour, ma belle.* It's so good to see you. I'm sorry I missed you today at *Le Café Vert.* I'm waiting to hear about that translation job, so I've been hanging out around here instead."

"Well, that makes sense." I raised my eyebrows expectantly. "My Telex transfer arrived at the bank today and I wanted to ask you out for dinner."

Michel smiled and kissed me gently. "I'm touched that you thought of me, but I've already planned a meal. I know it's a school night, but I hope you'll say yes."

"Of course." I laid my coat over a chair. "What are we having?"

"*Coq au vin.*"

"Sounds delicious. What can I do to help?"

Michel reached into a drawer and handed me the corkscrew. "Why don't you open a bottle of sauvignon and set the table?"

We chatted while he cooked and, thirty minutes later, we sat down at the table. Rich, savory smells filled our nostrils as Michel lifted his wine glass into the air. "To us."

"To us," I echoed, taking a sip.

I placed a forkful of chicken into my mouth and he watched my lips as I chewed. "What do you think?"

"Mmm . . . it's delicious," I purred. "You're spoiling me." I meant it.

We took our time with dinner, sharing recent events and stories while we ate. The *coq au vin* came out so tender it fell apart on my plate, and with each bite the rich wine sauce, butter and onion flavors burst in my mouth.

After we finished, Michel refilled our glasses and relaxed in his chair. "I was wondering about something the other day." He paused and cleared his throat, twice. "Would you ever consider moving to France?"

Wine caught in my windpipe and I coughed into my napkin. "Permanently?"

"Yes." His dimple came and went. "Who knows, one day you might fall in love with me."

"Oh . . ." I couldn't find a breath to finish the sentence. This was heavy stuff. A life in France with Michel wasn't even on my radar. I enjoyed his company and I was very fond of him, but these thoughts hadn't entered my mind.

Sensing my discomfort, Michel reached forward and placed his hand over mine. "Don't worry, Linda, I'm not pressuring you. I was wondering how you felt about the idea of living abroad."

"I'm not opposed to the notion, Michel." I picked up my wine glass and examined its contents. *Darn, it's still not easy to express my feelings in French.* "I think I rushed into my relationship with Adam and I got hurt. This time I want to take it slow, okay?"

"*D'accord.*" Michel averted his eyes and pulled a cigarette from his pack. "Why don't we focus on something else? We'll have plenty of time to talk about these things in the future."

33

After class ended on the last day of January, I gazed out one of the institute's single-paned windows. Frowning, I watched as large droplets of rain fell on the stone balcony below. *Darn, it's a terrible day for traveling. Poor Lori.* I couldn't believe that she was gone. We hadn't spent a lot of time together, but she seemed to really "get me," and I knew that I would miss her friendly face.

Our goodbye the previous day was emotional. We both promised to write, but I had a feeling we'd never see each other again, and this added to my misery. A sudden gust of wind hit the windowpane, startling me, and I pulled my coat tighter.

"*Mon Dieu!* What a miserable rainy day," Professor Toutain said behind me in French. "I hope you remembered your umbrella."

I turned, and my lips formed a slight smile. "Unfortunately, I left it in my room."

"*Hmm . . . Tant pis.*" Professor Toutain scratched his scalp. "So, tell me, how is your translation of *Le Petit Prince* coming along?"

I was pleased he asked. "I've finished the first three chapters."

"Aha. Good for you. At this rate, you'll be done in no time." He paused and his eyebrows lifted. "Are you enjoying the story so far?"

"Yes . . . especially the part about the sheep. The Prince is quite a character."

Professor Toutain chuckled and pushed his glasses further up his nose. "Yes, he is. Just wait until you get further into the story."

I looked at my watch and then glanced out the window one last time. "I should go. I'm meeting a friend for coffee."

"*Eh bien.* Enjoy your weekend, Mademoiselle."

"Thank you." I grabbed my burgundy scarf and purse, and after a final wave goodbye over my shoulder, I slipped through the door.

When I walked into *Café Moderne*, Michel was waiting for me at a table near the window. Our eyes locked and my pulse quickened as he stood to greet me. *It's so strange to see him here instead of Le Café Vert. I wonder what's on his mind.*

He kissed me, waving me into the chair across from him. "*Bonjour. Ça va?*"

"No, not really. Lori left today."

Michel winced. "Oh, I forgot about that. *Quel dommage.*"

I paused and lifted my chin. "But on a positive note, thanks to Professor Toutain, I can conjugate most of the important irregular French verbs."

He grinned, and his dimple emerged as he watched me shrug off my damp coat. "*Bien.* That's quite an accomplishment."

"Yeah, when you consider there are over a hundred of them."

When our waiter arrived, Michel ordered an espresso for himself and a *café au lait* for me.

"So, what's up?" I folded my hands in my lap and met his gaze. "You sounded so mysterious over the phone."

A muscle worked in his jaw. "I hate to ask you, *ma belle*, especially today, but I need to borrow some money."

My adrenaline rate increased. *Wow!* I didn't see this coming. "How much?"

Our waiter delivered our coffees; Michel plopped in his usual two sugars and stirred. "Three hundred francs."

I flinched and wrapped my hands around my coffee cup as competing thoughts entered my brain: He was there for me when I needed him, but that's a lot of money. He wouldn't ask unless he was in a real jam. "Okay."

"That's a relief." Michel sighed, offering me a cigarette.

I leaned forward as he lit it. "When do you think you'll be able to pay me back? You know that I'm on a tight budget."

"I know you are." He reached for my hand and strands of dark hair fell onto his face. "I should have . . . I wish I would have . . . put more money away. My work was so steady for so long that I didn't give it much thought . . ." He paused for a moment and rubbed his jaw. "Amir knows someone who may have some translation work for me in Paris. I'll know more tomorrow, but I may need to go away for a while."

"Paris?" I couldn't keep the disappointment out of my voice as I took a sip of coffee. "How long would you be gone?"

"I'm not sure—a couple of weeks. Like I said, I'll know more tomorrow."

I stared out the window, holding back tears and retreating into my own thoughts. This day kept getting worse and worse and worse. I was already sad about Lori, and now Michel wanted to borrow money just before departing for Paris. Why couldn't he find work in Tours? Why did things always have to be so difficult?

Once our cups were empty, Michel reached in his pocket and laid some coins on the table. "Let's get out of here." He helped me with my coat, hooked his elbow through mine and led me out of the café.

Out on the sidewalk, he raised his eyebrows. "Can we stop at the bank on the way back to your apartment?"

I hesitated. *He wants the money right now. Things are happening so fast.* "Okay."

Michel opened his umbrella and we clung together underneath it as we hurried to our destination. Ten minutes later, we exited the bank, slipped under the umbrella once again and picked our way along the sidewalk, until we reached the entrance to the Martin residence.

At the stoop, I turned to say goodbye and feelings of insecurity surfaced. "Will I see you tomorrow?"

"Yes. Why don't you meet me at *Le Café Vert* around five o'clock and we'll make dinner together at my place."

"Okay. I'm meeting Évelyne in Songais for lunch, but I should be back by then."

Michel wrapped me in the muscular curve of his arms. "Thank you for the loan—it means the world to me. I'll pay you back as soon as I can." He broke away and his voice turned urgent. "You trust me, right?"

I looked deep into his coffee-brown eyes and searched my heart. *He's been good to me. There's no reason to doubt him now.* "Yes, of course I do."

After a final kiss, I ducked under the umbrella's edge, hurried up the stairs and slipped inside the building.

34

*T*he following day, after I returned home from Songais, I settled at my desk, lit a cigarette, and let my mind wander. It was so good to see Évelyne and what a nice surprise to meet her sister, Valérie, and her niece, Isabelle. I had no idea that Évelyne was such a fabulous cook—her *homard en croûte*, lobster pot pie, was a tasty treat.

A knock on the door brought me back to the present.

"*Entrez!*" I shouted.

The door pushed open and Thomas's boyish face appeared. "The postman delivered a package for you."

"Oh, how nice. Thank you."

He laid it in my outstretched arms. "You're welcome." He smiled shyly and closed the door.

Hmm, I wonder who it's from. The return address was smudged, but I finally made it out. *Carline and Cindy!* I grabbed some scissors, cut the tape along the seam and then pulled out the funny card. Chuckling, I moved on to the box that contained a gold chain with a tiny letter 'L' attached. *Aww . . . this is special.* I clasped the necklace around my neck.

While I gazed in the mirror, sudden feelings of sadness washed over me and my smile faded. I missed my friends back home. I wished I could talk to them about some of my concerns with Michel—especially his money issues. I was far away from the *Château de Montclair*, but I still felt isolated. Phone calls were expensive and letters were time-consuming. *Oh well, for now it's all I have.*

I returned to my desk and picked up a piece of paper and a pencil.

Hi guys. Your birthday package arrived today. It was such a wonderful surprise . . .

Three hours later, snug in my blue wool coat, I exited my apartment into the cold afternoon and headed toward *Le Café Vert*. The streets were busy for a Saturday, and I had to weave my way around groups of tourists clogging the sidewalks.

How odd—I no longer thought of myself as a tourist. I was familiar with most of the main streets through town and many of the people—bakers, grocers, waiters—in the shops and cafés nearby, addressed me by my name. After five months in the Loire Valley, I was finally starting to feel like a local.

As I turned onto a familiar cobbled lane, Michel came into view.

"*Bonjour.*" He bent forward and his lips barely brushed my cheeks as he steered me toward his apartment. "How's your friend . . . Évelyne?"

How could Michel forget her name? He seemed distracted. "She's great. It was so good to see her." I noticed a muscle jump in his jaw. "Is something wrong?"

Michel scratched his day-old beard. "I have to go to Paris even sooner than I thought—maybe tomorrow. It looks like that job I talked about is going to come through."

My stomach dropped.

"Oh, and I'll need to borrow another two hundred francs."

What! I stopped our progress and gawked at him. "That won't leave me much money to live on. Are you certain you'll be able to pay . . . ?"

Michel cut me off. "I already said that I would pay you back as quickly as I can." He narrowed his eyes and strengthened his grip around my arm.

I knew he was under a lot of stress, but I didn't like the way he was treating me. Five hundred francs was a lot of money. I had every right to be concerned.

We stood staring at each other for a few seconds and then Michel released my arm. "I'm sorry." He brushed his hair back and looked at the sky. "The last thing I want is to start a fight with you. Everything will work out if you'll give me some more time."

I heard the anguish in his voice and fought hard to gain control of my own emotions. I felt trapped, but how could I say no? I'd be in real trouble if he didn't pay me back. *What am I going to do?* "Maybe Amir or Pascal can loan you the money?"

"No, I've already asked."

I swallowed the lump of fear in my throat. *I'll have to trust him. I hope I'm not sorry later.* "Okay, Michel."

He gave me an approving nod and, after a quick kiss, we changed course toward the bank, conveniently open until seven o'clock.

An hour later, we returned to Michel's apartment and warmed up leftovers for dinner. There was a heavy, unhappy feeling in the air and we barely talked as we ate. Once we finished, I cleaned up the kitchen while he packed a suitcase and placed it near the door.

"Come on. Let's have a glass of wine." Michel's arms circled my waist as I placed the last dish in the rack.

At least he was trying to lighten the mood. I laid down my dishtowel. "All right."

I watched him rummage through a couple of empty cupboards until he found a bottle. "I'm sorry, but all I have is red."

"That's okay."

Michel filled a couple of glasses. With each sip, our spirits improved and the damage from our earlier incident dissipated.

"Would you like me to tell you a story?"

I relaxed in my chair. "Sure."

Michel was a good narrator, and I sat captivated for an hour, asking only for minimal clarification, as he shared a remarkable tale about kings, queens, and war in the Middle East.

"That was incredible," I said once he finished. "You have such a way with words."

"I'm glad you enjoyed it." Michel's coffee-brown eyes darkened as he grabbed my hand and led me to the bed. His lips skimmed mine and then he slowly lifted my sweater over my head, kissing the hollow areas around my neck and collarbone.

"Why don't you lie back and relax . . . ," he teased. "And I'll give you the royal treatment."

I giggled and tried to pull him with me. He resisted and his smile turned naughty. "*Non, ma belle.*"

Apparently, he meant what he said. Holding my arms over my head, he placed his mouth over mine and explored it with a passionate French kiss. Eventually, he released me and his focus moved lower. I heard myself moan. I tried to move. I wanted to move, but he wouldn't let me. With each caress, each stroke, the tension mounted until I tumbled into bliss.

35

I heard a door slam and sat up in bed like a shot. *Am I dreaming?* I checked the clock. *Oh my god, it's six o'clock in the morning! What's going on? Who's that man next to the bed?* Panic set in and my body started to shake as I pulled the covers up under my chin.

"Pack your bags and get out!" the man shouted, his huge hands forming fists at his sides.

Michel leapt from the bed shielding his face defensively. "Okay, okay. We'll leave. Can you give us five minutes?" He grabbed his pants off the chair and glanced at me while he tugged them on.

"No," the man barked, staring at me. "You're out of time."

"Come on, man. My girlfriend needs to get dressed."

The strange man met my gaze and I felt my face heat as he scowled in my direction. "Okay, you have five minutes."

I can't believe this is happening. I'm mortified. As soon as he left, I jumped up and pulled on my clothes. While my lungs pumped riotous in my chest, I ran into the bathroom and tossed my toiletries into a bag. Then I slipped on my coat and watched as Michel hurled a few more items into his suitcase and zipped it.

Both of us flinched when the man burst through the door. "Now, get out!"

We dashed passed him and, once we stood on the sidewalk, I turned and glared at Michel. *I feel sick. I hope I don't throw up.* "What just happened?"

Michel grasped my elbow in one hand and his bag with the other as he propelled me down the sidewalk. "My landlord's an ass. He wouldn't listen when I told him I needed more time to pay my rent."

My eyes filled with tears. "This is craziness, Michel. I can't believe we were thrown out of your apartment like that. I'm still shaking."

He pulled me under a doorway and laid down his suitcase. "I know . . . I'm really, really sorry. I had no idea he'd react that way so soon. I'm only two weeks late . . ." He drew in a breath and released it slowly. "Please don't overreact. Everything will be okay once I get this new job."

Given the early hour, there were very few people on the street, but we happened to block the entrance to an apartment building.

"*Pardonnez-moi, s'il vous plaît.*" Both Michel and I blinked at the man exiting with his dog.

"Of course." Michel led me back onto the street.

Unhappiness weighed down my body as we walked in silence; both of us mulling over gloomy thoughts. How did Michel let things get so out of hand? What had I gotten myself into? I needed some time to think.

I licked my lips and glanced at him. "You can't stay with me at Madame Martin's."

He paused and lit a cigarette. "I know that."

"Where will you go?"

Smoke filled the air and then dissipated. "To Paris."

My eyes widened. "Today? Right now?"

"Yes. I think it's best, don't you?"

"I suppose you're right." I was angry and upset with Michel, but everything was happening too fast. *I hate this kind of goodbye. And what about my money? Oh well, there's nothing I can do about it now.*

Ten minutes later, we entered the *Saint-Pierre-des-Corps* station and Michel purchased a ticket on the 7:03 a.m. train to Paris. Once we reached the platform, he put his suitcase down, pulled me into a firm embrace and buried his face in my hair.

"You mean the world to me. I'm sorry I let you down, *ma belle.* Can you forgive me?" His words were rough with emotion.

"I'll try, Michel." My tear-filled eyes met his. "Hopefully, this job will work out and things will get back to normal." *Whatever that is.*

"*On embarque maintenant pour Paris,*" the train attendant shouted, breaking us apart. Boarding now for Paris!

Michel wrapped his hands around my face, kissed me and then grabbed his bag. "I'll contact you once I get settled."

"Okay."

When he reached the top of the stairs, he turned and mouthed, "*À bientôt,*" before disappearing from view.

Feeling dejected and stunned by this sudden turn of events,

I watched the train leave the station and a sob escaped. The next couple of weeks would be hell. I'd be worried about Michel . . . and my money. *Will he be able to pay me back? He has to.* Why did my life in France have to be so complicated?

36

———◆⟩⟨◆———

*F*our days later, when I returned home from school, Madame Martin stopped me in the hallway. "*Bonjour*, Linda. *Un moment, s'il te plaît.*"

I transferred my purse from one shoulder to the other. *Hmm . . . I wonder what's up.* "*Oui*, Madame."

"Your friend Janice telephoned. She wants you to call her at this number." She handed me a piece of paper.

"*Merci*, Madame." My brief smile turned into a frown as I followed her into the kitchen. Thank goodness Janice called. *I can't hide in my room forever.* I needed to talk to someone about Michel, and it would feel good to get it out in the open.

I watched Madame Martin exit the room, and then I picked up the receiver and dialed Janice's number.

After a few rings, someone answered. "Hello?"

"Hi, it's Linda."

"Hey, how are you?"

Her voice sounded so warm and friendly. "Not so good."

"What? I had a feeling something was wrong when you missed the last Phonetics class."

"Yeah, I think I've gotten myself in a jam." My words sounded heavier than I intended.

"With Michel?"

I cleared my throat. "Uh-huh."

There was a pause. "Listen, I've got a paper to finish tonight, but do you want some company tomorrow?"

"That would be great." I heard my voice crack and pressed my fingers to my lips.

"What time?"

Fighting tears, I looked up at the ceiling. "Around four-thirty?"

"All right. See you then."

"Thanks. I really appreciate it."

I hung up the receiver and slumped back up the stairs to my room. My life in France had become a continuous series of ups and downs, like waves on the ocean. One day, things seemed to be going well. The next day things were all screwed up. I missed my family, and wished more than anything that I could walk over to Mom's tiny yellow kitchen to talk to her and Dad. I was certain that would cheer me up. It always did in the past.

As I reached my room, a sudden realization, one that had been fermenting for a while, froze me in place. If I became a flight attendant for World Airways, I'd be traveling and living in countries all around the world. Most of my time would be spent away from home. I'd lose touch with my friends and miss out on holidays and family events.

My heart compressed as I walked over and curled up on the bed. Was I cut out for that kind of lifestyle? I was no longer certain.

37

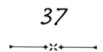

*J*ust before five o'clock the following afternoon, I heard Janice greet someone in the hallway outside my room. I jumped to my feet, opened the door and gave her a big hug.

"Hey, sorry I'm late. I had to finish my French assignment."

"That's okay. I'm just glad you're here," I replied, waving her inside.

Janice laid her coat on my bed and turned to me with wide hazel eyes. "So, what's going on?"

"Hold on a minute. First, would you like some white wine? It's the cheap stuff from the corner store, but that's all I can afford right now."

Her expression softened. "Yeah, that would be awesome."

"Great." I held up two paper cups. "Sorry, but all I have are these."

"I don't mind." While I poured the wine, she took a seat on my desk chair.

I handed her a cup, made myself comfortable on the bed, and lit a cigarette. "Michel started a new translation job in Paris."

"He's there right now?" She asked, taking a sip of wine.

"Yeah, he left last Saturday."

Her eyes narrowed. "Okay, start from the beginning."

"Well, he met me at *Café Moderne* about a week ago . . ."

Janice listened quietly while the words tumbled from my mouth. When I got to the part where Michel and I got thrown out of his apartment, she sat upright and her jaw dropped.

"That's crazy! And how did you react to that?"

"I got mad, of course. Then I walked him to the train station and we said goodbye."

Janice rose to her feet and paced the small room. "Well, five hundred francs is a lot of money, but Michel has never given you any reason to doubt his honesty, right?"

"No, he's been good to me. More than generous." I slid off the bed, grabbed the bottle of wine and refilled our cups.

"Well then, let's not jump to conclusions." Janice's forehead creased. "It sounds like he's fallen on some hard times and maybe you need to cut him some slack. Two weeks isn't unreasonable."

"That was my conclusion too."

"But do you need money? I can loan you some, if you're broke."

"Thanks, but I'm okay for now." *Janice is so considerate. I'm glad she's here.* Since Lori had left, we'd spent more time together and our friendship had flourished.

Attempting a smile, I reached over and laid my hand on her arm. "Thanks for coming over and listening to me. I really needed to talk this out with someone."

She brightened. "I'm glad I was able to help."

We hung out for a few hours, sharing stories and making plans for the following evening, Saturday night. Since neither of us had much money, I suggested we meet at eight o'clock at my place for some wine before going to *Club Bonne Ville*.

"Do you think your friend Julie would like to come?"

"Maybe. I'll ask her—but she's got to understand that we're on a strict budget."

Janice's face brightened. "Do you realize that this will be my first time at a club in France? Heck, it'll be my first time at a club ever!"

Her excitement was contagious, and I laughed aloud. "Well then, we'll just have to make sure you have a good time."

38

*T*he following evening, at 8:30 p.m., I heard a knock on my door. *"Entrez!"* I shouted, wiping my hands on a towel near the sink.

"Sorry we're late," Julie said passing me a bottle of sauvignon blanc. "We stopped for a quick bite to eat."

"No problem. It's good to see you."

We swapped hugs. "Hmm . . . you smell nice, like lilies," I said to Janice, inhaling her flowery perfume.

"Thanks. I just bought it this afternoon. It's called Anaïs Anaïs."

"Mmm, it's yummy." I grabbed my corkscrew and opened the wine. "Sorry, but all I have are paper cups."

Julie shrugged. "That'll do."

While I poured, Julie told Janice about *Club Bonne Ville.* "The dance floor is wood and there's this disco ball . . ."

This conversation led to a general discussion about the nightclubs Julie and I'd experienced back home, and an hour later, two bottles of sauvignon blanc sat empty on the desk.

"Well, what do you girls think?" I asked, downing my last gulp of wine before reaching for my coat. "Shall we get going?"

Janice and Julie nodded in unison and we headed out the door.

"I hope that cute DJ's at the club tonight." Julie's joviality was contagious as we strolled down the sidewalk.

"Yeah, I know the one. He plays the best dance songs." My mind flooded with memories of my first night at the club with Lori and

Albert. *I wish she were here. I miss her . . . and Michel.*

Twenty minutes later, the lime-green neon sign flashing, *Club Bonne Ville*, came into view. There was a long queue of people waiting outside the building, but the line moved quickly. It wasn't long before we entered the building.

Julie led the way to the crowded bar and we joined a group of people waiting to order drinks.

"Cool place, right?" Julie shouted, encouraging us forward so we didn't lose our place. "Don't you love that deep bass? I can feel the vibration through the floorboards."

"Yeah, the music's awesome." Janice glanced around the dimly lit room. "It's so much bigger than I imagined."

The bartender's voice startled us. "What would you ladies like to drink?"

"Three French 75s, please." Julie leaned forward so he could hear her.

"Coming right up."

We watched him make our drinks. Julie paid the bill and then passed the cocktails to us, one by one.

"Hey! There's a table. Follow me." She took the lead once again, weaving us around groups of people, holding her elbow to the side as she tried not to spill her drink. Once we arrived, we pulled off our coats and scooted into our seats.

Sipping our cocktails, we watched the DJ, the same one we'd discussed en route, grab his microphone and announce his next song from KISS. All around us throngs of people poured onto the dance floor.

Janice shouted. "So, in France, guys don't ask you to dance?"

I smiled, recalling a similar question I asked Lori the first time I came to *Club Bonne Ville*. Was that only two months ago? So much had happened since then. "No. If you like a song, you can just head out onto the dance floor."

"What a great idea." Janice grinned.

When the DJ revealed his next choice, "Video Killed the Radio Star," by the Buggles, Janice spun toward me, her voice filled with excitement. "I love this song. Will you guys come dance with me?"

I glanced at Julie. She nodded, and we made our way to an empty area to the left of the DJ's station. Laughing, we moved our hips and swayed as the music's catchy rhythm took hold. Our fun-loving attitude didn't go unnoticed. When the next song came on, two guys sidled up to us.

"*Salut.* I'm Luc. What's your name?"

"Linda," I replied without enthusiasm. Luc was handsome enough, tall with sandy blond hair, but I didn't want to encourage him. My failed relationship with Adam, and worries surrounding Michel, left me feeling bruised and cynical.

When I turned my back to him, Luc got the message and redirected his attentions to Julie, a much more willing target. *Good. They seem to be a perfect match.*

Throughout the evening, several more men approached me, offering me compliments and drinks, but I kept my distance, choosing instead to party with Julie, Janice and their newfound boyfriends. At three in the morning, the rowdy group walked me home, and I watched them stagger down the street. Tipsy from the wine and cocktails, I crept up the stairs to my room.

I was glad I went out with my friends, but it would have been more fun if Michel had been there. The pick-up scene at clubs—the games, the small talk, the expectation of casual sex—no longer interested me. I was looking for something different; something more rewarding. Maybe I was finally growing up.

39

*O*n Monday morning, I woke with a start and gasped when I looked at my bedside clock. *My alarm should have gone off at 6:30!*

I tossed off the covers, hurried to the sink and chastised my reflection while I brushed my teeth. *What's wrong with you? Why can't you make it to class on time? What is this, the tenth time you'll be late for school?*

Rushing now, at speeds that would impress a firefighter, I threw on clothes, combed my hair, grabbed my things and rushed down the stairs. The instant I closed the front door and stepped into the fresh air, my spirits improved.

The mild temperatures over the last few days provided a welcome change from January's cold weather. Bare beech trees lining the streets of Tours swayed in the breeze as I walked along the sidewalk. A couple of sparrows hopped down onto the pavement and flew away once they heard the click of my heels.

Continuing along *rue Nationale*, I spotted Pascal at a bus stop, absorbed in a book. As I approached, he looked up, his hazel eyes widening as recognition set in.

"*Bonjour*, Linda. What a pleasant surprise," he said swapping cheek kisses. "I hope you're well."

"Yes I'm good. And you?" Wind gusted and I pushed hair away from my face.

"Not too bad for a Monday."

I smiled and stepped aside so a woman with a stroller could pass. "Hey, have you heard from Michel? You know he's in Paris, right?"

Pascal pursed his lips and crossed his arms. "As a matter of fact, I saw him last night."

What! Panic closed my throat and I nodded mechanically. *Why didn't he contact me?* "So he's in back in Tours?"

"Yeah, but he seemed focused on his work. I don't think he planned to stay long." He avoided eye contact and seemed relieved when a noise drew his attention elsewhere. "Ah . . . here's my bus. By the way, Monique's been asking about you. Why don't you visit her sometime at the Hollywood Bazaar?"

"Tell her I'll try to stop in this week."

After a rushed goodbye, Pascal climbed on the bus and I continued down the street, my mind racing. Was Michel avoiding me? No, he wouldn't do that. *He'll probably contact me later today. I'll feel so much better once I talk to him.*

By the time I arrived at the institute, it was eight-thirty and I was a half hour late. I took the stairs two at a time, rushed down the hall and paused in front of classroom number eight to catch my breath. Clutching my purse, I pushed open the door.

"*Eh bien*, I have some good news for you—" Professor Toutain paused and brushed the chalk off his hands as he watched me slink across the room. "I'm glad you decided to join us today, Mademoiselle."

"I'm sorry I'm late," I replied. "For some reason, my alarm clock failed again this morning."

His lips turned down, but amusement touched his voice. "Well then, maybe it is time to purchase a new one."

"*Je veux bien,*" I agreed. Thank goodness he had a sense of humor. I certainly couldn't afford to buy a new alarm clock right now.

Refocusing on the class, Professor Toutain perched on the front of his desk. "As I was saying, I have some good news. I would like to celebrate the halfway mark of the quarter on February fifteenth."

A cheer erupted from the students.

Professor Toutain laughed. "There is one condition. I'll bring food and wine, if you agree to supply the entertainment, whatever you like."

There was a second, louder chorus of approval.

"Students, students, quiet down . . ." Professor Toutain held up his hands. "I'll give you more details later, but now it's time to get busy. Why don't you open up your French packets to page thirty-three? Today we're going to learn a few more verb tenses and then we'll practice using them in sentences."

Throughout Professor Toutain's lecture, I fretted over the reasons behind Michel's return to Tours. Why didn't he contact me? Maybe he had some loose ends to take care of regarding his apartment. Or maybe Amir had come through with some additional work. *Argh . . . I wish I had some answers.*

When Professor Toutain dismissed the class for a midmorning break, he motioned for me to approach him. "Is something wrong? You seem distracted lately."

"I know, and I'm sorry. I've been dealing with some . . . personal problems."

Professor Toutain peered more closely. "Can I help?"

"No." I shook my head and looked down. "Hopefully, things will work themselves out in a week or two."

"Okay, Mademoiselle. Just remember, I'm here if you need me."

I rushed home after my Phonetics class, burst through the front door and down the hall. In my haste, I ran headlong into Madame Martin exiting the kitchen.

"Oops . . . I'm so sorry," I exclaimed.

She smiled and brushed at a spot on her skirt. "*Pas de problème.*" Sophie woofed and she picked her up.

"Are there any messages for me?"

Madame Martin shook her head. "No."

How can that be? Why was Michel keeping me in the dark? I couldn't understand why he would treat me this way. "*Eh bien, merci.*" I couldn't keep the disappointment from my voice as I turned to walk away.

"There's a good western on TV tonight at eight o'clock. Why don't you join us?" Madame Martin asked.

I met her gaze and noted her pinched expression as she twisted her apron in her hands. *She looks concerned. I don't want to worry her.* "Okay, I'd like that."

Once I returned to my room, I settled at my desk and pulled out my homework, but I couldn't concentrate. I shoved it aside and picked up my diary while feelings of melancholy washed over me. With a sigh, I picked up my pen.

> *I find myself longing for home more and more with each passing day. It's surely not the right frame of mind for a girl who had worked so hard to leave it.*

40

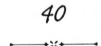

*D*ogged with anxiety, two days later, I entered *Café Americano* and found a seat near the entrance.

A busy waiter dropped off a menu and I frowned as I perused my choices. I hated to spend money on a meal at a restaurant, but I had to eat something for dinner. *A cup of soup won't cost much.* Nine days had passed since I left Michel at the train station and he still hadn't contacted me. Only fifty francs remained in my bank account.

"*Bonjour*, Linda."

A familiar voice caught my attention, and I swiveled to see Christophe approaching my table. I didn't recognize him at first because he was wearing street clothes rather than his waiter's uniform and an apron. "*Salut*. Aren't you working today?"

"Yes, but I had the early shift."

I set down the menu. "Oh, I see."

He shoved his hands in his pockets and his face brightened. "Hey, I've got an idea. Why don't you join me for dinner? There's a little Italian restaurant down the road."

I bit my lip. *He seems like a nice guy. I'd like to go, but I don't want to lead him on.* "I'm not sure . . ."

"Aww, come on," he pressed. "I hate to eat alone. It'll be my treat."

My hesitation turned into a smile. "Okay, why not."

"*Bien.*"

Christophe helped me into my coat and we exited the café, chatting about his job as we strolled leisurely along the sidewalk.

"So, have you worked at *Café Americano* long?"

Christophe scratched his beard. "No, just under a year. The family who owns it are friends of my parents."

"That's convenient."

"Yeah, it's worked out well so far."

Moments later, we arrived at the quaint, aromatic *Ristorante Italiano*. There was a red awning over the large black-paned windows. A planter filled with budding tulips rested near the door.

When we entered, a waiter appeared around the corner. "*Bonsoir, pour deux?*"

"*Oui, merci.*"

He ushered us to our seats and handed us menus, rattling off the specials before disappearing around a corner.

I glanced at Christophe and raised my eyebrows. "What do you recommend?"

"The pizzas here are fabulous." He pointed out a bottom section of the menu. "My favorite is chorizo and mushroom. We can share if you like."

"That sounds fine. I'll let you decide."

Christophe placed an order for a large pizza and paired it with a bottle of Italian red table wine. The server returned immediately and, with practiced expertise, he popped the cork and filled two glasses.

"*Santé.*" Christophe lifted his glass. We both took a sip.

"Mmm . . . it's good."

"*Ouais.*" He sat back in his chair and studied my face. "So, I think you mentioned you are at the *Institut d'Études Françaises.*"

"Yeah, for about a month now."

"I hope you're not one of those starving students I hear so much about?" he teased.

I laughed aloud. He had no idea how close to the truth he was. "I'm not starving yet, but I might be real soon."

"What do you mean?"

I looked away and swirled the wine in my glass. "Well, it's kind of a long story, but I've loaned money to this guy that I've been dating. Now, I'm wondering if he'll ever pay me back."

"Hmm . . ." Christophe's brow furrowed and he shook his head. "I hope it's not the same guy my cousin told me about yesterday."

My breath stopped. "What do you mean?"

"Well, I guess there's this man in Tours who asks his girlfriends for money and then he never pays them back. He usually targets foreign women."

My hand trembled as I set my glass down. "Do you know his name?"

"I think he said Michel."

Waves of dizziness overcame me, and Christophe's face blurred. When my vision cleared, his eyes were wide with concern.

"Is that the name of the man you loaned money to?"

"Yes," I whispered, unable to say more.

I inhaled and exhaled, trying not to hyperventilate or faint. *This is unreal.* There had to be another explanation. Michel wouldn't take advantage of me like this. Or would he?

"Linda, I had no idea . . ."

"Of course you didn't, Christophe. How could you have known?" My eyes clouded and I dabbed at them with my napkin. It was no use—the evening was ruined. I needed time to think. "I'm sorry, but I'm super upset right now. I can't stay."

Christophe rose in consternation. "*Quel dommage.* I won't deny that I'm disappointed. I was looking forward to spending time with you."

"Maybe we can try again another time." I attempted a smile, grabbed my coat and fled the restaurant.

Somehow I held myself together until I reached the Martins' house. Pausing, in the hallway to my room, I crumbled against the wall as tears of despair streamed down my face. Michel really seemed to care for me. He had been so convincing with his note and talk about the future. *Why do these things keep happening to me?*

41

———•✕•———

*T*he next day, I didn't attend school. Christophe's revelation at dinner kept me tossing and turning most of the night, as my mind filled with worry and dread.

I finally climbed out of bed at eleven o'clock and made my way to the sink. As soon as I gazed into the mirror, a frown formed. My hair was a tangled mess and yesterday's makeup was smudged around my eyes. *You look terrible, Linda.*

I washed my face and brushed my hair into a ponytail. *That's better.*

When my stomach growled, I opened the window, reached for my basket and brought it inside. After I poured myself a cup of juice, I tore off a hunk of stale baguette, paired it with a slice of cheese and sat down at my desk.

Today, I needed to figure some things out. How could I contact Michel? I had no idea where he was. Hell, I didn't know if he was in Tours or in Paris. Amir would know, but I didn't have his address. Should I try to contact Pascal?

After a weighty sigh, I brushed the breadcrumbs from my desk into my hand, and dumped them into the garbage.

It had been days since I wrote in my diary, and suddenly I felt an overwhelming urge to document my troubles. I picked up a pen, wrote a sentence, crossed it out and then wrote another.

I have more or less given up hope that I shall see Michel or that he will give me the money back I have lent him . . .

I paused, reread my entry and swallowed back tears. This wasn't helping. I closed my diary with a slap. I needed to talk to Janice. It was lunchtime and, if I hurried, I might run into her at *Café Moderne*. I'd love to hear her take on the situation. She was such a levelheaded girl.

At twelve-thirty, I exited Madame Martin's home into a gentle rain and paused outside the door to open my umbrella. It felt good to get out of the house and, for once, the wet weather offered a welcome distraction.

As I made my way along *rue Marceau*, I noticed a woman in front of me with a vaguely familiar gait. How did I know her? Was she a professor at the university?

I searched my mind, but just couldn't place her. When she finally turned around, my lungs froze. *Madame Dubois from the Château de Montclair!* My hand flew to my mouth, and I quickly ducked underneath a store awning.

Did she see me? Of course she did. She opened her mouth to speak, and then she seemed to have second thoughts, and closed it. Lifting her chin, she squinted and sniffed, before turning on her well-polished heel.

Once she was out of sight, I unclenched my jaw and continued toward my destination. *Whew!* I knew I would run into her one day. Now I hoped it wouldn't become a regular occurrence.

Two hours later, disappointment slumped my shoulders as I retraced my steps toward home. I was bummed I didn't see Janice. *I'll call her and see if she can meet me for lunch tomorrow. If I can afford to eat!*

When I reached the Martins', I shook my umbrella on the stoop and stepped inside. As I passed the kitchen door, Madame Martin called out a greeting.

"*Bonjour,* Linda." Her eyes sparkled with excitement as she reached around the corner and shoved a purple violet plant into my hands. "Your friend Janice left this for you."

My jaw dropped and my voice faltered. "Aww . . . what a wonderful surprise." *We must have just missed each other.*

"And here's your mail," she said, smiling.

"*Merci*, Madame."

I rushed up the stairs to my bedroom and set the plant down on my dresser. With anxious fingers, I opened Janice's card and a wide smile crossed my face. I had completely forgotten that it was Valentine's Day. *Leave it to my special friend to brighten my day.*

After I hung up my coat, I thumbed through the mail and watched as a letter fluttered to the carpet. I reached down and picked it up.

Oh my God—it's from Michel!

While my heart hammered out of control, I ripped it open and translated the words aloud. "I miss you. I'm coming to Tours on Friday, the twenty-second, and I want to take you out for dinner. I have so many things to explain to you. Be ready at seven."

I twirled around the room clutching the paper to my chest, light-headed with relief and happiness. Everything was going to be okay. I would see Michel a week from tomorrow. *I'm sure he'll pay back the loan.*

We still had some serious issues to discuss—his lack of communication and his previous interactions with 'foreign' women—but now that I'd heard from him, I felt like the worst was over.

Returning to the letter, I read the last sentence, "*Je rêve de toi.*" Unsure about the meaning, I peeked inside my French-English dictionary. *Mmm . . . he's dreaming of me. I can't wait to see him!*

42

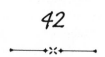

*T*he following morning, after one of the most restful nights of sleep in weeks, I arrived at the institute a few minutes early. Two at a time, I climbed the stairs and entered classroom eight. *I'm so glad I heard from Michel. Now I can enjoy the class party today.*

"*Bonjour*, Mademoiselle Kovic. It's good to see you." Professor Toutain rose and folded my hand in his. "I was a bit worried when I didn't see you in class yesterday. Did you get a chance to practice your song with the Clarks last night?"

"Yes." A smile formed and stuck like glue. "I think we're ready." John and Mary Clark, a handsome young couple from Kansas, and I made up the American contingent. Their two young children, Lauren and David, were joining us for the special event.

"*Très bien.*" Professor Toutain's eyes narrowed with suspicion. "I can see that something has changed. You're all smiles this morning."

"*Oui, c'est vrai.*" I laid my bag on my desk and brushed some stray hairs off my face. "A major problem worked itself out yesterday."

"Good for you."

Several students entered the classroom and we glanced their way. "Mademoiselle, I meant to ask, could you help with party preparations later?"

"Yes, of course," I replied, taking my seat.

Professor Toutain watched his students file through the door, greeting each of them in turn. After a quick head count, he clasped his hands together at the front of the class.

"*Eh bien.*" He rounded his eyes. "I'm sure you're all looking forward to our celebration, but we have some verb tenses to review first."

Two hours later, during midmorning break, Professor Toutain set up his portable record player, while I arranged the food, utensils and napkins on a folding table. There was a large selection of appetizers, including *tapenade noir aux figues*, a fig-olive spread, and *pissaladières*, onion and anchovy tarts, which I had never tasted before.

"Did you make these, Professor?"

His face reddened and he laughed aloud. "No, my wife made them. I wouldn't even know where to begin."

I spread some *tapenade* onto a *cracotte*, cracker, and popped it into my mouth. "Mmm, they're delicious."

"Yes, she's an excellent cook." Professor Toutain sounded distracted as he pulled a second bottle of red wine from the bag.

I watched him arrange the wine as contradictory thoughts entered my mind. *I can't believe he's serving us alcohol at school. This would never happen back home. Well, why not—it's a party, after all.*

When the students filed back into class, everyone crowded around the snack table. There were "oohs" and "aahs" while the students sampled the delicious French cuisine and wine.

Professor Toutain clapped his hands to gain everyone's attention. "I think it's time for some performances. Do I have any volunteers?"

Akiko and Tomoko stepped forward in unison and bowed toward Professor Toutain. "We can begin, if you'd like."

All eyes watched as Akiko handed Professor Toutain a record album and joined her sister at the front of the classroom. The girls opened their fans and Tomoko signaled Professor Toutain. The record dropped and the dance began.

With slow, deliberate motions, the girls dipped, bowed and turned while a *shamisen*, or three-stringed lute, played in the background. Opening, closing and twirling their fans, they mimicked delicate birds.

When the performance ended, everyone clapped and congratulated them. The sisters bobbed their heads before scrambling back to their seats.

"Who's next?" Professor Toutain asked.

"We'll go." John stood and met my gaze.

Adrenaline instantly flooded my body. *Darn this stage fright.* I took my place next to the Clark family and after a couple of guitar strums, John nodded in my direction.

With a slight hesitation, I stepped forward. "Today, we're going to sing an American song called 'Home on the Range.' I hope you like it."

As soon as the music started, we all chimed in and sang the familiar words, "Oh, give me a home where the buffalo roam . . ."

Mary's clear soprano contrasted nicely with John's deep baritone, while my voice faded into the background—but that was fine with me. When we finished our song, we received raucous applause as we bowed and grinned.

The rest of the performances continued until the bell rang and Monsieur Toutain excused us for the weekend. As they walked out, many students shook his hand and he beamed with pleasure as they thanked him for an enjoyable party. I was the last the leave.

"Can I help you clean up?" I said, gathering my things.

Professor Toutain chuckled. "No, that won't be necessary." Then with gentle pat on my shoulder, he added. "I'm glad you're feeling better."

"Me too." I smiled.

He pushed his glasses up his nose. "*Alors*, have a nice weekend and I'll see you on Monday."

43

———— ✦✕✦ ————

*J*anice loaned me 200 francs, and the weekend came and went in a whirlwind of activities—a get-together at Julie's house on Saturday night and a matinee movie called *C'était demain*, Time After Time, on Sunday.

A hectic Monday morning set the pace for the rest of the week. I kept busy with my French studies, translations of *Le Petit Prince*, entries in my diary and letter writing.

On Thursday morning, the day before my big date with Michel, struggles with my hair prompted curses at my reflection in the mirror. A quick glance at my watch confirmed I had just enough time to track down Madame Martin before I left for school.

"*Bonjour*, Madame," I called from the kitchen entrance. "Can I speak to you for a moment?"

She looked over her shoulder. "*Ah . . . bonjour*, Mademoiselle. Yes, of course."

"I was wondering if you could do something for me." I cleared my throat. "I can't afford a haircut, and I desperately need someone to trim my hair and bangs. Would you have time this afternoon?"

The corners of her mouth crinkled with delight. "But of course. I would be happy to help."

Pleased with her response, I reached out and gave her a quick hug. "Thank you so much."

"Good, then," she confirmed, adjusting her apron. "I'll see you after you return home from school."

44

When Friday finally came, my stomach was a tight ball of nervous energy.

Given the special occasion, I spent extra time on my appearance. At five o'clock, I showered, dried my hair, and put on light makeup. As usual, I vacillated over what to wear.

I tugged on my black corduroy pants and tried a few different tops, but none of them felt right. When I pulled on a cream short-sleeved sweater and looked in the mirror, a grin formed. *Yeah, that's it.* I reached up and fluffed my bangs. My hair looked much better after Madame Martin's handy scissor work the day before.

Once I was ready, time moved at a snail's pace. In an attempt to relieve some tension, I tried to write a letter. Every few minutes, I glanced at the clock and rubbed my sweaty palms on my thighs.

A few minutes before seven, I gathered my things and raced down the stairs. The house was so quiet, for a moment I wondered where everyone had gone. *Oh, that's right. Monsieur Martin said they had a family gathering in Tours tonight.*

I peered through the peephole in the front door, my body trembling with anticipation while I waited for Michel to arrive. When he finally came into view, my pulse rate went into overdrive. I moved back, waited for his knock, and threw open the door.

Our eyes linked and my mouth went desert dry.

Damn—he looks good. His new, layered hairstyle framed his face, softened the angles of his jaw, and highlighted his coffee-brown eyes. A teal-blue, collared shirt peeked out from under a black leather jacket that he'd paired with light gray slacks.

"You look beautiful, *ma belle*. It's so good to see you." Michel stepped forward, wrapped his arms around me and buried his head in my hair. "I'm really sorry . . . about so many things," he whispered.

I relaxed in his arms, but emotions roughed up my voice. "It's good to see you too, Michel, but we really need to talk."

We stood there for a long time holding each other and then he broke away and grabbed my hands. "I'll explain everything over dinner, okay?"

"All right." *I'll feel better once we clear up a few things.*

He led me through the door, paused on the sidewalk and pulled out a pack of Marlboro Lights. "Would you like one?"

"Sure, thanks."

Michel lit my cigarette and we progressed down the street. "So, I hope you're hungry."

"As a matter of fact, I am," I replied. "Where are you taking me?"

"Somewhere special," he said, draping his arm around my shoulders. "We haven't explored this part of Tours together, but the restaurant is located in the *Hôtel des Rois*, in the city center."

"Hmm . . . the name sounds vaguely familiar."

"There are some great specialty shops and boutiques in that area. Years ago, when I first arrived in Tours, I worked in one of the wine shops stocking the shelves."

My brow furrowed. "That's the first time you've mentioned anything about your past jobs. One of these days, I'd love to hear the rest of the story."

Michel grinned. "*Bien*, but we may not get to it tonight."

Twenty minutes later, when Michel paused in front of a grand hotel a few blocks from the train station, I shook my head with dismay. "We're eating here? I'm not dressed for it, Michel."

He brought my hand to his lips. "Don't worry. You'll fit in just fine."

The elegant, three-story, white stone building filled one entire block. Outdoor lighting, cleverly placed low, drew my eyes skyward, highlighting the lofty paned windows. High above the entrance, molded into a gable and framed with marble, was an enormous clock.

Michel gently nudged me through the entrance and, once we stood inside, I paused to admire the soaring ceilings, grand staircase and twelve-foot arched entryways—some with massive French doors—leading into banquet or meeting rooms. Period furniture mixed with modern art gave the place a stylish, eclectic feel, while large, colorful flower arrangements well placed around the room, added elegance and charm.

"This place in amazing."

"Yeah, it's one of my favorite hotels in Tours," Michel said, hastening me along. When I slowed to admire a particularly interesting painting, he took my elbow and gently encouraged me forward. "Come on or we'll be late for our reservation."

We walked through an arched doorway into an intimate, pale yellow room filled with palm plants and distressed, cream-colored tables and chairs. White tablecloths and billowy beige curtains gave the room a dressy feel, while orange handblown glass centerpieces added a splash of color.

A well-dressed man with a painted-on smile showed us to a table. He pulled out our chairs, passed us menus and offered a *bon appétit* before he disappeared with our coats.

After he left, I listened while Michel translated a few dishes for me. Our server reappeared, rattling off several complicated specials and Michel glanced at me with interest. "Do you like scallops?"

"I don't know. I've never tried them."

"Well then, tonight's the night." Michel turned to the waiter. "Two orders of *coquilles Saint-Jacques* please."

"*Ah, très bien.* Would you like to pair that with a *sauvignon blanc*, Monsieur, perhaps a *Pouilly-Fumé*?" He pointed to a selection on the wine menu.

"Yes, perfect."

The waiter brought our wine immediately. He bowed as he presented the bottle to Michel and offered a taste for his approval. At Michel's nod, he filled two glasses and left.

"To you," he raised his wine and we both took a sip. "It's good, don't you think?"

"Yes, delicious."

Michel stared at me for a few seconds and then reached inside his jacket. "Here's your five hundred francs." His hand trembled as he passed me an envelope. "I'm sorry . . . so very sorry . . . that I didn't contact you earlier. The simple truth is that I didn't want to see you, or talk to you, until I could repay the money I owed you. I let my pride get in the way. I know it was wrong . . . can you forgive me?"

I put the envelope in my purse. "I suppose I should be mad at you, but instead I'm just relieved you're back." Then with an exaggerated frown, "Will you promise me that you'll never do anything like that again?"

"Never . . ." Michel placed his hand on mine. "Never again."

My throat tensed. "I'd like to ask you about something else."

He stiffened and leaned back in his seat. "*D'accord.*"

"While you were gone . . ." *Shoot! This is hard, but I have no choice.* "I heard a terrible rumor about a man named 'Michel' who lived in Tours."

"What kind of rumor?"

"I was told that he takes advantage of foreign women. They loan him money and he doesn't pay them back." *There. I said it.*

Michel paled, and I watched as he reached for his pack of Marlboro Lights and passed one to me. "Well, I can imagine how much that must have upset you, but there's more to the story."

He lit my cigarette and then his. The familiar smell of smoke filled the air.

"I dated a woman a few years ago and she . . . well . . . she enjoyed my company more than I enjoyed her company. She invited me out several times, and she paid for a couple of weekend getaways. When I refused to date her anymore, she insisted I pay her back the money she spent. I refused."

"What happened after that?"

He downed his glass of wine. "She spread lies across town."

Our waiter's sudden appearance refocused our attention. "*Voilà,* your scallops." Savory aromas wafted our way. "Can I bring you anything else?"

We both shook our heads, so he refilled our glasses, bowed and slipped away.

Michel met my gaze. "Linda, I'm far from perfect, but I don't take advantage of women for their money. I'm not sure who told you this tale, but you just have to trust me once again."

I let his words settle in. He seemed sincere and he paid back the loan. *Mmm . . . and he looks so good.* "Okay, Michel. I had to ask. I feel much better now."

"*Alors,* taste the scallops before they get cold."

Michel watched me take a bite. "It's tender and . . . flavorful. Is that

Gruyère cheese?"

He grinned and my insides fluttered. "Yes."

"It's wonderful—my new favorite dish."

"I knew you'd like it."

While we ate, Michel filled me in on his current accommodations near *place de la Bastille* in Paris. "I'm staying with my friend, Jordan, and his wife Mada. The apartment is small, but I'm thrilled they agreed to let me stay with them for a few weeks."

"Do you have your own room?"

"Yes." Michel dabbed at his mouth with his napkin. "Otherwise I'd never be able to get my work done. Mada is quite the talker."

His comment made me smile. "So, you'll return to Paris on Sunday?"

"Yes." Michel nodded. "My current translation job will last a few more weeks, but I have another one lined up after that."

"Good for you." *I'm glad he's found more work.*

The wine disappeared and, when our server returned to clear the table, Michel asked him about a specific champagne.

"Do you have *Taittinger Brut La Française* on the menu?"

"*Oui*, Monsieur. Shall I fetch a bottle?"

"Yes, please. With two *tarte tatins*."

The waiter returned with flutes, poured our drinks and then brought our dessert. Laughing, we exchanged bites of apple pie and washed them down with the sweet bubbly wine.

Once we finished, Michel lifted the champagne bottle to refill our glasses, but I shook my head and covered my glass. "No, thank you. I think I've had enough."

"*Bien*." Michel signaled to the waiter. "Can you cork this so we can take it with us?" He handed over the bottle. "And the check, please."

I wiped my mouth with my napkin and laid it on the table. "I'll be right back." I stood and my eyes searched the room. "Do you see any signs pointing to the bathroom . . . oh, never mind, I see it."

As I wound my way around the tables to the hallway, I contemplated our fabulous meal. *What a treat.* It was the first time I'd eaten at a fancy restaurant in France, and I felt certain this kind of sophistication came at a steep price. Why wasn't Michel budgeting his money? His new projects must pay well, but still . . .

I returned to the table and we exited the dining room into the lobby. When Michel grasped my hand and pulled me toward the grand staircase, I met his gaze with wide eyes. "Where are we going now?"

His eyes sparkled with excitement. "I've booked a room for the night."

I paused mid-step. "Michel, are you sure you can afford this? Two weeks ago, you were broke and now . . . this?" I glanced around the room and lifted my arms.

"It's not as expensive as you think, *ma belle*. The hotel was offering a special price for dinner and a room. After my awful treatment of you, I wanted to do something special."

"Oh . . ." I closed my mouth. "I don't know what to say. I can't believe we're going to spend the night here."

"Come on. I'm excited to show you the room." He pulled me up the stairs to the third floor and we paused at room thirty-one. Michel opened the door and stood aside.

A large bed with a cherry headboard, matching nightstands, and snow-white duvet dominated the room. On the opposite wall, there was a built-in closet and mirrored dressing table. Elegant floor-length burgundy drapes framed the lofty six-foot tall window, and two graceful armchairs rested nearby.

I turned and threw my arms around Michel. "It's wonderful! What a fantastic surprise."

"I'm so glad you're pleased," he sputtered. "Here, give me your coat and I'll pour you a glass of champagne."

I handed it to him and wandered over to the window. "What a pretty view. The train station is all lit up."

"Yes, it's quite lovely at night." Michel handed me a flute and I took a drink. "Mmm . . . this really is delicious."

"Yes, it is." Michel's gaze locked with mine and a jolt of electricity surged through my body.

Frozen, I watched his eyes darken as he took the glass from my hand and placed it on a nearby table. "I'm sorry, *ma belle*, but I've changed my mind. The champagne will have to wait."

Michel pinned me against the wall as he explored my mouth with his tongue. "I've missed your passion, your scent . . ."

"I've missed you too," I moaned against his lips, intoxicated with his kisses.

He released me and we pulled off our clothes, hurling them onto the floor. Sparks flew as we reunited in a sizzling embrace.

"*Je t'ai dans la peau*," Michel whispered, his breath hot against my cheek.

I didn't respond, but as he led me to the bed, I let his words settle in my mind. *I'm really into you, too. Really, really, really.*

45

At nine o'clock the following morning, Michel and I descended the stairs, hand in hand, and entered the hotel dining room for breakfast. We chose a seat near the window, and a server appeared almost immediately.

"*Un café au lait, s'il vous plaît*," I said smoothly.

"An *espresso* for me. Oh, and bring some croissants, please."

I placed my napkin in my lap and met his gaze. "So, how often will you return to Tours?"

"As often as you like. Every weekend, I hope." Michel grinned and I felt my face warm.

He's sooo sexy. I'm glad we're back together.

He pulled a cigarette from his pack. I held up my palm when he offered one to me. "Amir has agreed to let me stay with him whenever I visit Tours."

"That's nice of him." When the waiter returned with our order, I moved my purse to make room on the table. "*Voulez-vous autre chose?*"

I shook my head. "*Non, merci.*"

Michel plopped two sugar cubes into his cup. "Linda, I'm impressed. Your French has improved dramatically in the short time I've been gone."

I was glad he noticed. "Do you really think so?"

He nodded. "Uh-huh. I'm fairly certain even World Airways

would be impressed with your language skills now."

My throat compressed and I looked at my lap. "Hmm . . . you could be right, but . . . well . . . I'm no longer sure that it matters."

When Michel's coffee cup hit the saucer, I met his startled gaze. "What do you mean?"

"It's hard to explain, especially in French, but I'm feeling a bit lost and confused about the future right now. I miss my family and friends much more than I thought I would. The idea of being away from home for long periods of time makes me feel sad." I rolled my eyes toward the ceiling. "*Zut alors!* I felt certain that I wanted to become a flight attendant. That's why I came to France in the first place."

"You know what I think?"

I shook my head.

"It sounds like you've reached a point in your life where you're searching and trying to find your place in the world. It's not easy to leave the security of family and friends and move forward toward an uncertain future." Michel ground his cigarette in the ashtray and stretched his legs beneath the table. "You've had some rough times lately, with money, with Adam . . . and with me, so your insecurities are justified. You'll feel differently once things settle down."

"Hmm, you're probably right." I took a sip of my coffee and popped a piece of croissant into my mouth. "Well, one thing's for sure—I'm glad that we've worked things out."

"Me too, *ma belle.*"

A family of four entered the dining room, and we watched as the mother and father helped the young children into seats. Once they were settled, we refocused on each other.

"*Alors,* this brings up a question I've been meaning to ask." Michel picked up a croissant, buttered it and added jam. "How much longer do you think you'll stay at the institute?"

"I'll finish out the quarter, why?"

His expression turned serious as he reached across the table and grasped my fingers. "I'd like you to stay with me in Paris for a month or two. It's such an incredible city, and there are so many places I want to show you. Do you think your parents would agree to this?"

"I don't know." I paused and let his words settle in. *Paris with Michel. Ooh, wouldn't that be something?* "It's a good idea—a great idea, in fact—but my dad would probably freak out if I asked him for more money. They've been so generous already."

I closed my mouth and gnawed on my bottom lip. "I have to visit the Pan American Airline office in Paris to book my flight home, so maybe I could arrange to stay for a little while."

"*Parfait.*" Michel's face lit up and his words jumbled together. "I'll work on finding us a place to stay in the city. I can't wait to show you Paris, *ma belle*. I know you'll adore it as much as I do."

I smiled at his enthusiasm. "Okay, Michel, but don't do anything until I talk to my parents. They might say no."

"Well, then, you'll just have to convince them."

46

*W*e spent the rest of the weekend together, lounging and relaxing at Amir's apartment, and on Sunday afternoon, we made our way toward the train station. The overcast sky amplified our melancholy moods as we passed *la Place Plumereau* and continued toward *Saint-Pierre-des-Corps* across town.

"You're sure you put Jordan's phone number into your purse, right?" Michel's brow wrinkled as he glanced my way.

"Yeah, I have the number."

"*Bon.* You can call me anytime." When we paused at a light, he let go of my hand and moved his bag to his left shoulder. "If I'm not there, leave a message."

I met his gaze and offered him a gentle smile. *It's sweet that he's so concerned.* "Okay, I will."

He nodded, lit a cigarette, and we continued down the sidewalk.

Fifteen minutes later, on the train platform, Michel took me in his arms and held me close as we said our goodbyes. "I really enjoyed the weekend, Linda. Especially our stay at *Hôtel des Rois*."

My mouth went dry. "*Moi aussi.* I had a wonderful time."

He brushed his lips against mine and his whispered words

produced shivers. "I wish you were coming to Paris with me. I miss you already."

Both of us cringed when we heard the train attendant's announcement. "*On part pour Paris!*"

We clung to each other for a few seconds longer before Michel cupped my face in his hands. "I'll see you on Friday."

I stepped away and he boarded the car. "*A bientôt!*" He shouted over his shoulder as he slipped out of sight.

After the train pulled away from the station, I followed some passengers through the main doors and turned left toward home. While I walked along, my thoughts turned to Michel and our wonderful weekend together.

I still can't believe he took me to such a fancy hotel. It was such a romantic evening. The dinner was delicious and our room was so luxurious. I felt my insides ripple as my mind filled with sensual scenes—long drawn-out kisses and targeted caresses in all the right places.

When a group of tourists slowed my pace, I mumbled an apology, scooted around them and continued down the street.

Hmm . . . and what about Paris? I wish I could go, but my parents have been so generous already. I feel guilty just thinking about it.

I turned right onto my street and, off in the distance, I spied a black French bulldog tethered to a porch railing. He wandered over to sniff me as I walked past, so I stooped to pat him.

"Well, what do you think 'Frenchie'? If I can find the courage to ask, will my parents let me spend a couple more months in Paris?"

When he gazed up with his giant ears and round eyes, the corners of my mouth lifted. "I think you're right. There's only one way to find out."

After one last pat, I hurried across the street and dashed up the stairs to *chez* Martins.

47

*T*wo days later, after my Phonetics class, I headed north on *rue de la Grandière* toward the Tours Post Office to place a call to my parents. Shivering, I wrapped my scarf tighter around my neck and buried my hands in my pockets. *Brrr, the weather has turned cold again.*

When I reached my destination, I followed a couple into the building and turned left. There was only one vacant booth, so I squeezed inside and inserted my coins. When the operator came on, I effortlessly asked her to help me place a call to the United States. *My French is improving.* I used to dread this interaction, and now it is easy.

After four rings, someone picked up and my mom accepted the charges. There was a pause and I heard rustling noises.

"Hello, Lindy?"

"Hi, Mom."

"Lindy? *Yoy meni.*" I heard the usual scraping sounds and then mumbling. "Wait, my hearing aid is buzzing . . ." Seconds passed until she spoke again.

"Are you still dere?"

"I sure am. How are you and Dad?"

She grumbled. "Oh, not so good. We have to fix up the 'Big House' again."

One of my parents' rentals was a large home located on a major thoroughfare through town. This old house was a perfect rental for musicians because they could practice at all hours and no one could hear them above the roar of the highway. The bands usually left the place trashed, and it took great effort to get it fixed and ready to rent again. Over the years, I'd cleaned and painted the interior many times.

"Oh, that's a big job."

"Yeah, it's a lot of work, up and down, up and down, but good exkercise."

This was a common mispronunciation by my mom and it always put a smile on my face. "That's for sure."

"So, what's new with you? Are you eating enough?" Mom's voice was filled with concern.

"Yes. I even ate some scallops the other night."

She didn't respond, so I tried to explain it another way. "Kind of like clams. They were delicious."

"Good. Other way, things are okay?"

"Uh-huh. I'm feeling really confident with my French."

"Da, da, da." There was a long pause. "Would you like to say a couple words to your dad?"

"That would be great." My guts twisted as I pushed down the emotions—love, homesickness—threatening to close my throat. "I miss you, Mom."

"I miss you too, honey."

After a brief pause, I heard my dad's voice. "Hi, Linda. We were wondering when you would call again. We got a letter from you yesterday. It sounds like you had a good time at your class party."

Dad sounds better. I'm so relieved. "Yeah, it was a lot of fun."

"Before you ask, I'm going to the bank tomorrow and I'll send your money." I heard him sigh. "I meant to do it earlier, but we've been busy fixing the 'Big House' again."

Darn, my rent's due in three days. Now that I've paid Janice back, I only have 200 francs left. Oh well, I guess I should be used to this by now. "Yeah, Mom told me about the vacancy. Tomorrow should be okay."

"Thanks for understanding, honey."

I heard Mom's voice talking in Dad's ear. "Your mom wants to know how soon your classes at the institute end."

"The last day of the quarter is March twenty-first."

"Mmm, that's right. I think you mentioned that in your letter. Have you given your landlady your notice yet?"

My eye twitched. I reached up and rubbed it. "No. I'll do that in the next few days."

"Okay, good."

Moving on to other subjects, I asked about my brother, Bud, and we talked about other family members until the conversation lagged.

"Well, it's sure nice to talk to you," Dad finally said.

"It's nice to talk to you too." I ran my fingers down the metal phone cord. *Should I bring up Paris? No, I think I'll wait for a better time. Mom and Dad have a lot on their minds right now.* "Give my love to Bud."

"I will do that. Call us again in a week or two."

After class on Friday, I met Janice at *Café Moderne* for lunch. A waiter dropped off menus and we placed our orders—*soupe à l'oignon,* onion soup, for Janice and my usual, a *crôque monsieur.* While we ate, we brought each other up to date on current events.

"I'd love to hear more about your reunion with Michel." Janice pulled a Kleenex out of her purse and blew her nose. "Did you talk about the future?"

I felt my face heat with pleasure. Earlier in the week, during a phone call, I'd told Janice about my special night with Michel at *Hôtel des Rois*—the scrumptious dinner, his heartfelt apology, the lovely room—but I didn't get a chance to fill her in on his invitation the following morning. "Sort of—he asked me to spend a couple of months with him in Paris."

"That's so cool! Are you going to do it?"

"I'd like to, but I doubt my parents would agree to it."

Janice contemplated my words. "Hmm, you're probably right—it'll be tricky. You'll have to wait for the right moment."

I stretched my neck right and then left. "What about you? How long will you stay at the institute?"

"I don't know; it'll depend on my parents—another month for sure."

We moved on to other topics and, when the waiter returned to collect the dirty dishes, Janice glanced at her wrist. "What time does

Michel get in tonight?"

"He's coming over around eight." I lit a cigarette and placed the match in the ashtray. "Are you and Julie still meeting us at *Le Baron* for drinks?"

Janice reached in her purse and pulled out some money. "Yeah, but we won't get there until ten or so."

"Okay." I took a sip of water and met her gaze. "Can I ask you for a favor?"

"Of course."

I hesitated. "It's the last day of February, and I need to pay rent. My Telex hasn't arrived and I could use another loan."

"How much?"

I licked my lips. *I hate to put her on the spot.* "Ideally, two hundred."

"Sure, I can do that." Janice patted my arm and gestured to the waiter for the check. "We'll have to hurry, though, because I have a hair appointment at three."

We paid our bill, exited the restaurant and headed toward the bank at a brisk pace. Once we arrived at our destination, we dashed into the building and slid into a teller line three people deep. When the next available bank clerk yelled "*Suivant,*" we stepped forward and conducted our business.

I returned home a few hours later and discovered Madame Martin in the kitchen, her head in the oven.

"*Bonjour* Madame. Can I speak to you for a moment?"

She looked over her shoulder. "*Ah . . . bonjour,* Mademoiselle. Yes, of course." A deep V formed between her brows as she grabbed the edge of the stove and stood.

"I'm sorry, but I can only give you half the rent right now." I reached into my pocket and pulled out the 200 francs Janice loaned me. "I should have the rest for you in a few days."

Madame Martin removed her rubber gloves and shoved the bills in her apron. "Well, I guess this will have to do for now."

"I'd also like to give my notice. I'll be leaving at the end of March." Sudden, unexpected emotions roughed up my voice box and my words sounded grainy. *This is even more difficult than I imagined.* Madame Martin had been kind to me, and I felt guilty about giving notice and shortchanging her for rent on the same day.

"So soon? You've only been at the institute for a few months."

"Yes, I know, but my parents agreed to only one quarter, so I have no choice. I've learned basic French grammar and I'm feeling more and more confident with the language . . ." My voice trailed off.

"*C'est vrai.* I've noticed a big improvement." Sophie whined at her feet and she picked her up. "We'll be sorry to see you go. I've enjoyed having you."

"Thank you, Madame. I won't forget your kindness."

"*De rien.*" She brushed her arm across her forehead and glanced over her shoulder. "Well, I better get back to work—this stove won't clean itself."

"Hmm . . . yes . . . well, I've got a lot of homework tonight too. *Á demain*, Madame."

I wiped my sweaty hands on my thighs as I walked away. *Whew, I'm glad that's over.* I just wished I could have paid her all of my rent. Hopefully, my Telex transfer would arrive in the next few days and all of this business would be behind me.

Later that evening, Michel and I walked into *Le Baron*, and after a quick assessment, we settled at a table near the entrance.

The popular club catered to a younger crowd, mostly students. There was no DJ, but the bartenders mixed a strong drink for a great price, which kept the club packed on the weekends.

"What would you like to drink?" Michel asked me, anticipating our waiter's arrival.

"A Rose Cocktail, please. And can you ask them to go light on the strawberry syrup?"

"Of course."

A few moments later, the server delivered our drinks and I took a moment to admire the vivid pink cocktail before I brought it to my lips. "Mmm . . . this is delicious," I said, rolling my eyes. "Please don't let me have too many. I can only imagine the hangover."

Michel smiled and took a sip of his *Pastis* on ice. "Okay, I will keep my eye on you." He grabbed my fingers and brought them into the candlelight on the table. "I've wanted to ask you many times. Where did you get the ring?"

I relaxed into my seat and admired the gold band, fingering the etching with my left hand. "My mother gave it to me years ago. I think she brought it back from Croatia when she was a young woman."

"What a nice gift. It must mean a lot to you."

"Yeah, it sure does." It was one of my prized possessions. I never took it off my finger.

Absorbed in the moment, we didn't notice Janice and Julie's approach until they stood beside us.

Once I recognized them, I jumped in surprise. "Hi, guys!"

We greeted each other and then the girls removed their coats and draped them over nearby chairs.

"How's the service tonight?" Julie asked Michel, her blonde hair swaying.

"Not bad, but our waiter was just here." He glanced at the crowded bar. "What would you girls like to drink?"

"I'm not sure." Julie furrowed her brow. "A glass of white wine."

Grinning, Janice pointed to my Rose Cocktail. "I want whatever Linda's having."

"*Bien.*" Michel lit a cigarette and winked in my direction. "I'll be right back."

Julie ducked out to use the restroom and Janice and I took our seats. "You know what?"

I met her gaze. "What?"

"I'm so glad we met. Friends are so important, don't you think? I'm experiencing a whole new side of Tours, and it's all because of you." She folded her hands in her lap. "I just thought you should know that."

Her words struck a cord and unexpected emotions surfaced, blurring my vision. "What a nice thing to say. I'm really glad I met you too."

She was right. Without my friends—Lori, Julie, Adeela, Albert, Évelyne, Madame Bernard, and now Janice—my stay in the Loire Valley would have been much less enjoyable and, at times, unbearable. Soon, I'd have to say goodbye to all of them. *It won't be easy.*

Concern flitted across her face. "Linda, what's wrong?"

"Oh, nothing. I'm just getting sentimental about leaving Tours." I picked up my cocktail napkin and dabbed at my eyes. "Ah . . . here comes Michel with your drink." I narrowed my gaze and my voice rose with enthusiasm. "Hey, look who's with him! It'll be so good to spend some time with Albert tonight."

49

On Sunday, after a quiet Saturday—a home-cooked meal and a movie—I walked Michel to the train station. Sitting close together on a bench, he talked to me about his plans for the following weekend.

"I'll try to finish my translation job by Friday, but most likely you'll see me on Saturday."

I pursed my lips. "What a shame. That means we'll only have one night together."

"We'll have to use our time wisely," he teased, tickling my chin.

Both of us cringed when we heard the train attendant's announcement. "*On part pour Paris!*"

Michel pulled me to my feet, cupped my face in his hands and kissed me tenderly. "*Tu me manques déjà,*" he whispered. I miss you already.

"*Moi aussi,*" I replied.

He broke away, ran to the train car, climbed aboard and waved before disappearing through the coach door.

I returned home fifteen minutes later, my eyelids heavy as I put one foot in front of the other and climbed the stairs. When I rounded the corner to the second floor landing, I ran headlong into Thomas.

"Oh! *Je suis désolée.*"

"*De rien,*" he replied brushing aside his long bangs. "Um . . . I'm glad I ran into you. I thought you might like to know that there's a Paul McCartney special on TV tonight."

"Really? How cool." A few weeks ago, I mentioned that the Beatles were one of my favorite bands of all times. It delighted me that he remembered. "What time?"

"It starts at eight o'clock." Thomas shifted his gaze to his feet. "I'll have it on, if you want to come down and watch it with me."

Darn it. I'm exhausted, but I really want to see the concert. "Okay, that sounds like fun. Oh, and I wonder if you could help me with something? Some papers fell behind my desk a few days ago and I need to move it back from the wall so I can reach them."

"Sure. Right now?" Thomas asked.

"Yeah, that would be great."

He followed me up the next flight of stairs and into my room. "This should only take a minute."

We took our positions on either side of the desk, and after a "one-two-and-three," we inched it back from the wall. Thomas watched while I turned sideways, reached behind the desk, and gathered my papers.

"What the heck?" My mouth dropped as I scooped something off the floor. "Look what I found!" I spun toward him with a ten-franc note.

"Wow!" he said. "Today's your lucky day."

This unexpected event felt like a shot of espresso and, suddenly, I was wide-awake and determined to share my good fortune.

"Yours too," I replied impulsively. "Would you like to join me for pizza? There's this great restaurant down the street. I'll treat."

Thomas blinked, stunned. "Sure, that sounds great." He shoved his fists into his jeans' pockets and stood near the doorway while I grabbed my purse.

"We'll have to hurry, or we'll miss the concert."

"*Pas de problème,*" Thomas grinned. "I'm a real fast eater."

"I'm glad to hear it," I replied, my lips twitching with amusement as I followed him out the door.

50

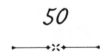

*T*he following Friday, after I checked to see if my money had arrived at the bank, I followed a familiar path home, my eyes watching the ground. *I can't believe I'm broke—again!* If I'd known how hard it would be for Dad to Telex funds to my account, I may not have stayed.

Argh . . . that's not true. I would have stayed no matter what, but maybe I would have learned more about the banking system in France, or found some way to earn money on the side. *Except working as an au pair!*

When I returned to my room, I shoved aside my worries and opened *Le Petit Prince.* Only a few pages remained, and I was anxious to see how the story ended. *Do we ever find out if the prince returned to his asteroid?*

Sometimes, I felt like the little prince searching for happiness. The fox taught him an important life lesson—one that resonated with me too—that important things in life reside inside the heart. Being far away from my family and friends made the memories of our times together even more special. I'd never take them for granted again.

Biting my lip, I translated several paragraphs and, just as I started the last chapter, I heard a knock.

"*Entrez!*" I called.

The door pushed open and I sprung off my chair into Michel's arms. "What are you doing here? I didn't expect you until tomorrow."

I heard his easy chuckle, and my insides melted as he pressed his lips against mine. "I finished my work early and decided to surprise you."

"Mmm . . . I'm so glad. I've missed you."

"*Moi aussi.*" His coffee-brown eyes searched my face while his finger outlined my jaw. "I hope you're hungry, because I ran into Bruno on the way here. He wants us to dine at *Le Café Vert* tonight."

"That sounds wonderful," I said, pressing my hand against his chest. "Much more appealing than four-day-old pizza on my windowsill."

"Huh?" His brow creased. "Who did you eat pizza with?"

"It's kind of a long story, so I'll tell you on the way to dinner."

"*D'accord.*"

Michel watched me gather my things before he led me out the door.

We didn't return to my room until well past midnight. Tipsy from the wine at dinner, we crept like thieves up the stairs. As we rounded the corner to the first floor landing, Michel grabbed hold of the banister and leaned in with a loud whisper. "I can't believe you're going to let me spend the night."

"Shhh," I placed my finger over his lips and then looked down the hall toward Monsieur and Madame Martin's bedroom. "You promised to keep your voice down, remember?"

"Oops, sorry."

I grabbed his hand, pulled him up the remaining stairs, and into my bedroom. After I closed the door, I watched, my chest heaving, as Michel removed his leather jacket and laid it on my desk chair.

"*Bien*, it looks like we avoided detection." Michel glanced toward the bed, and a slight dimple appeared as he walked over, sat on the edge and bounced a few times. "Your mattress feels good."

"Yeah, it's comfy, but it'll be a tight fit for two."

He patted the spot next to him. "Come here, *ma belle*."

My pulse leapt as I moved forward and lowered myself onto the bed. He slid off my coat, tilted my head back, and pressed his lips against mine. I melted against him and moaned as he maneuvered me onto my back.

"Mmm . . . I can't get enough of you. You're like an addiction."

"I feel the same way." I lost myself in his coffee-brown eyes as he slowly unbuttoned my blouse. *I love the way he takes charge. His confidence is so sexy.* "We'll have to be quiet, Michel."

He grinned seductively, his words filled with naughtiness as he unfastened my bra. "That will be more of a problem for you than for me."

51

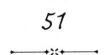

*A*t 6:00 a.m., I heard a rap on the door.

"Yes. Who is it?" I jumped out of bed at lightning speed and grabbed my robe off the chair.

The door creaked open and Madame Martin peeked her head

around the frame. "Linda, your father's on the pho..." Her eyes found Michel and she paused. "Er... Oh, I'm so sorry. I didn't realize you had company."

Damn, why didn't I lock my door last night? How embarrassing. I felt my face flush as I glanced at Michel's sleeping form. His back was turned to us, but half of his torso was exposed. Thank goodness his butt was covered.

"*Pas de probléme,* Madame." Concern diverted my attention. "Did you say that my dad was on the phone?"

"*Oui.*"

I slipped my feet into my slippers and followed her stiff form down the stairs to the second floor. Why was Dad calling me? *I hope it's not bad news.*

"*Bien,*" Madame Martin said, veering toward her bedroom. "I'll leave you to your phone call."

After a quick, "*Merci,*" I rushed down to the kitchen and picked up the receiver. "Hi, Dad. Is everything okay?"

"Yes... yes. Did I wake you?"

I relaxed my shoulders and glanced at the clock on the wall. "Yeah, it's pretty early here. Just past six o'clock."

"Oh, that is early. I'm sorry. I wasn't sure about the time difference." He paused, and I heard the TV in the background. "I've been concerned about you. Did your money arrive yet?"

Ahh... so that's why he called. "No, but my new friend, Janice, loaned me two hundred francs, so I was able to pay half of my rent."

"Goddammit! What's wrong with those banks in France? I sent a Telex transfer over a week ago."

I rolled my shoulders, waiting for him to finish his rant. We both knew he had every right to be frustrated. Hell, I felt the same way.

"Well, I guess there's nothing I can do about it over the weekend. I'll check with the bank on Monday morning," he finally said with a sigh. "Did you tell your landlady that you're leaving?"

"Uh-huh, last week."

"Good, so that means you'll be coming home in a few weeks. Your mother will be pleased."

My chest tightened. This was a bad time for me to bring up Paris, but I had no choice.

"Linda?"

Twisting the phone cord around my finger, I cleared my throat. "I wanted to talk to you about that. I . . . er . . . have this opportunity to visit Paris."

"Paris?" His voice sounded incredulous. "Now, you want to go to Paris?"

"Please just hear me out. My friend, Michel . . . I think I wrote you about him . . . is working in Paris and he wants to show me around the city. I'll probably never get this chance again. It would only be for a short time, and I'd only need a few hundred dollars."

"Linda, we've been patient with you, but don't you think it's time to come home?"

Disappointment clouded my eyes. "You're right, of course. You and Mom have been wonderful to me. I didn't really expect you to say 'yes.'"

There was a long silence. "I'll discuss it with your mom, but don't get your hopes up. Right now, I'm worried about this blasted transfer."

A tear rolled down my cheek. "Dad, have I told you lately that I love you?"

"Yes, you have," he said gently. "I love you too, honey. Take care of yourself. We'll talk again soon."

I replaced the receiver on the wall and slowly climbed the stairs to the third floor. That was the first time Dad had called me since I arrived in France. This transfer thing must really be bothering him. *And I had to ask about Paris! I wonder what Mom will say.*

Stifling a yawn, I entered my room, latched the lock, removed my robe and climbed into the small space beside Michel.

He flipped over and pulled me into his arms. "Is everything okay?"

"Uh-huh." I snuggled against his chest. "Go back to sleep and I'll tell you all about it later."

52

*W*e slept until one o'clock the following afternoon and then took turns freshening up at the sink while I filled Michel in on my phone call from home.

"*Alors,* at least your dad agreed to talk to your mom about Paris," Michel said, applying soap to his chin before grabbing his razor.

"Yeah, and it's nice to have it out in the open." I watched him from my viewpoint on the bed, admiring his slender build and the way his muscles moved as he shaved.

Michel caught me ogling and his reflection grinned. "How soon do you expect a decision?"

"I don't know. He wants me to call him back when my money arrives." I snorted as I pulled a sock over my foot. "Who knows when that will be?"

He joined me on the bed and passed me fifty francs. "Here. This should tide you over until your transfer arrives."

I looked at the bills. "What a nice thing do, Michel. I really appreciate it."

"I know you do." He caressed my cheek with the back of his hand. "I'm glad I can help."

Five minutes later, our bodies stiff with tension, we crept downstairs. Once I realized that we were alone in the house, relief swept over me.

"Whew. I'm glad I don't have to face Madame Martin right now. It would be a bit awkward, don't you think?"

"*Mais oui.*"

When we reached the sidewalk, Michel paused to light a cigarette. "*Bien.* Why don't we check out the street fair in *la Place Plumereau* today? The weather is spectacular and there are loads of things to see there. Maybe it'll take your mind off of your money troubles."

"I'd like that."

With a wink, he hooked his arm through mine and we crossed the street, smiling and bantering back and forth as we made our way toward *le Vieux Tours.*

53

*T*he sun came streaming through our bedroom window at Amir's apartment the following morning and, for once, Michel and I woke at a decent hour. After a leisurely breakfast of coffee and croissants, we decided to take a walk along the Loire River before I dropped him off at the train station.

We followed a familiar path south, passing restaurants, small businesses, apartment buildings and homes.

"When is your last day of class?"

"March twenty-first."

"*Eh bien,* that should work out well." Michel glanced over and squeezed my hand. "I'm sorry, *ma belle,* but I won't be able to come to Tours next weekend. I have some work to finish, and then I have to find a bed and maybe some sort of dresser for our room."

What? I stiffened. "The room doesn't come with a bed?"

There was a slight hesitation. "No, but don't worry, I'll find something."

"Good, because I don't want to sleep on the floor." I relaxed and lifted my eyebrows. "So, tell me about the people we'll be living with in Paris."

"Hmm . . . let's see. The apartment belongs to my friends Régis and Karine. They're traveling through Greece for three months and they've sublet their apartment to a girl named Marie-Christine. We'll be staying in the spare bedroom." He shrugged. "That's all I know at the moment."

"It sounds interesting. I can't wait to see the place." We walked along in silence for a while until an idea popped in my head. "If you're not coming to Tours next weekend, I'll have a chance to visit Songais and say goodbye to Évelyne. Maybe I'll invite Janice."

"*Bien*, that should work out well."

We maneuvered around a mother with a baby buggy and crossed the street to the tree-lined promenade along the Loire. The muddy gray river flowed past swiftly, but as we approached the edge, we noticed the faint smell of decay in the air. In the distance, water slapped against the shore of a heavily forested patch of land.

"I've never noticed that . . . island before. It's an island, right?"

"Yes, it's called *Parc de l'île Simon*. See the bridge over there?" He pointed to the left. "You take it across the river to the park."

"How nice. I can't believe that I've missed this sight until now."

"*Tant pis.*" Michel draped his arm around my shoulder. "If we had more time, I'd show it to you."

We passed a young couple, and when I heard one of them mention the Eiffel Tower, I glanced at Michel. "Tell me about Paris."

"Ahh . . ." His expression brightened. "The *Louvre* is in Paris. Have you heard of it?"

I nodded. "It's a museum, right?"

"Yes, one of the largest in the world. It houses Da Vinci's *Mona Lisa* and *Venus de Milo*, an ancient sculpture of the Greek goddess of love and beauty. Nearby is the *Arc de Triomphe,* a monument built to honor French soldiers who fought and died in the Revolution and Napoleonic Wars."

Michel checked to see if I was still listening. When I smiled, he continued. "Then there's *Notre-Dame*, the world-famous Catholic cathedral located on the *Île de la Cité*. I could go on and on."

I'd read about the *Louvre* and the Eiffel Tower, but the rest of the sights he mentioned sounded mysterious. "Can we visit some of these places when I come to Paris?" I asked, my voice full of yearning.

"Yes, of course." He spotted a bench up ahead and motioned for us to sit down. "Did you know that Paris is sometimes referred to as the 'City of Love'?"

"Why is that?"

"There are lots of reasons—the wonderful sights I just described, and the romantic language to name a few." Michel pulled out his pack of cigarettes, offered one to me and lit it. "It's also a popular honeymoon destination."

I coughed on smoke, and he patted my back until my lungs calmed down.

"Why does this subject make you so nervous?" Michel grabbed my hand and a deep V appeared between his brows. "I'm crazy about you, Linda. I want to spend the rest of my life with you, but I need to know how you feel. Do you see a future for us?"

"I don't know." My eyes studied the ground. "I care for you deeply, but we've known each other such a short time. Maybe I'll feel differently if we spend some time together in Paris."

Michel released my hand and the lines on his face softened. "Can I tell you how I feel about love?"

"Of course."

"I compare love to a trip on a train. True love—the forever kind—comes once in a lifetime. I believe that if you miss your 'Love Train,' you might be able to catch another one, but you'll regret that you missed the first one for the rest of your life."

My lungs pumped double-time as he waited for my response. "You may be right, but I've always believed that each of us has multiple soul mates in the world. They might not be easy to find, but they are out there, and you have to be willing to look for them."

"Yes, but what if you can't find that person when you're ready?"

"I don't know. That's the part that troubles me."

Michel helped me to my feet, and we walked along in silence for a few minutes. "I think I can make you happy, Linda. Will you just promise to keep an open mind?"

"Yes, I promise. I just think I need more time, that's all."

Later that afternoon, after I returned home from the train station, I settled at my desk, my shoulders slumped as I pondered my conversation with Michel. When my diary caught my eye, I turned to the last entry and picked up my pen.

What are my feelings for Michel? He asked me this question and I honestly could not answer him. If I return to the U.S. and never see this man again, will I have missed my love train? I feel so confused.

54

*T*wo days later, a rainstorm blew into Tours, but it didn't dampen my spirits. Humming a tune, I returned home from the institute and rushed up the stoop. Outside the entrance, I shook out my umbrella and pushed open the front door. Simultaneously, someone pulled from the other side.

"Oh! *Je suis désolée,*" Madame Martin." I said as soon as I recognized my landlady.

"*Bonjour,* Linda." She smoothed her coat and smiled tentatively. "How was school today?"

"Good. I took one of my first quarter exams today."

"What did that cover?" she asked politely.

"My least favorite—dictation. Thursday I'll take my Phonetics exam."

"I see . . ." She nodded. "Any news on your transfer?"

I broke into a triumphant smile as I reached into my purse. "Yes, my money arrived today." I handed her a pile of bills. "Thank you so much for trusting me."

She blushed. "*Je vous en prie.* I'm glad everything worked out."

We heard a dog bark and we glanced down the hall.

"Well, I should get to my shopping," she said. "Sophie doesn't like me to leave her for long."

"*Eh bien,* I'll see you later."

When I reached my room, I laid my bag on the desk and sat on the edge of the bed. *What a great day!* For the first time in weeks, I felt happy—really happy. I flopped back and closed my eyes, recounting the afternoon in my head.

Earlier, after discovering my money in my account, I placed a call home to tell Dad the news. It warmed my heart to hear the joy in his voice, but his next words sent me over the moon. I still couldn't believe my parents agreed to let me stay in Paris for six weeks. Six hundred dollars was more than generous. *Michel will be so pleased.*

I slid off the bed and fetched a glass of water and some cheese from my "fridge." As I wolfed down my snack, an idea formed. Maybe I should try to reach Michel. I promised to call him if I talked to my parents. *I can't wait to share my exciting news!*

An hour later, I made my way down to the kitchen where I found my landlady stirring a large pot of bubbly goodness on the stove.

"*Bonsoir*, Madame. Something sure smells good."

"Chicken soup," she mumbled over her shoulder.

"Ahh . . ." I shifted from one foot to the other. "Can I use the phone to call Michel in Paris?"

Her back stiffened. She laid down her spoon and pulled off her apron. "Okay, but not too long."

"*Oui. Merci.*"

I watched her leave the room, unraveled the piece of paper Michel gave me, and dialed the number. A man answered after three rings.

"*Salut.*"

"Hi. Can I talk to Michel?"

"Sure, I'll get him."

Seconds passed before I heard a familiar voice.

"Linda?"

"Yeah, it's me." I focused on a crack on the wall. "How did you know?"

"Jordan said that there was a girl on the phone. I was fairly certain that it was you."

"Oh, I see." I felt a surge of excitement and my words came out breathless. "I have some big news."

"Did you talk to your parents?"

"Yes! They've agreed to let me stay in Paris for six weeks."

I heard his sharp exhale. "*C'est merveilleux!* I can't believe it!"

"Me neither . . . I'm still in shock . . ." I filled him in on the details, the words pouring out of my mouth like a waterfall. "Oh, and guess what else happened?"

"I have no idea. Please tell me."

"My Telex arrived at the bank and Monsieur Toutain invited me to lunch at his home on Friday. Apparently, his wife is a fabulous cook. There will be three other professors from the school, but I'm the only student."

"*Bravo.* That's quite an honor."

"Thanks," I sighed. "It's been such an incredible day. I wish we could celebrate together."

"Me too."

There was a pause and I filled the space. "So...how's your translating going?"

"*Ça va très bien.* I'm trying to stay focused, but it's not easy." His teasing tone turned sexy. "I keep thinking about your soft lips pressed against mine."

I felt my face warm as I wrapped the cord around my finger. "If that's true, I'm surprised you're getting any work done at all."

When Madame Martin walked back into the room, I transferred the receiver to my other ear. "Listen, I have to say goodbye now. I'll try to phone you again next week."

"I'm so glad you called, *ma belle.* Sleep well."

I hung up, smiled at my landlady, and sprinted up the stairs two at a time.

55

*O*n Friday, at 12:15 p.m., Professor Toutain and I exited the *Institut d'Études Françaises* with three other professors in tow. Following his instructions, I climbed into the front seat of his light gray Citroën, while the other three squeezed into the back. Twenty minutes later, we arrived in the small town of Luynes, west of Tours.

"I know you lived in this area for a while. Did you get a chance to visit Luynes?" Professor Toutain asked, turning down the radio.

"No." I stretched my head around to catch a glimpse of a man on a bicycle with several baguettes tied on the rear rack.

"My wife and I have lived here for over thirty years." He coughed and then continued. "It's a quiet village, but that's one of the reasons we stay. Life stands still in a place like this."

I smiled at him. "I can see that." He was right. Luynes, with its narrow cobbled streets and historic castle from the thirteenth century, appeared frozen in time.

Professor Toutain turned left onto a private dirt road and we progressed slowly past fenced fields with cows and sheep. They raised their heads and watched us, chewing their cud, as we drove past. Eventually, we arrived at a modest two-story, gray stone house, half-covered with creeping vines. Deciduous trees and shrubs surrounded the building, while two rows of sculpted boxwoods framed the paved walkway leading to the entrance.

We climbed out of the car and Professor Toutain waved us forward. "Watch your step, please."

Single file, we progressed toward the house, our heels clicking on the pavers. When we neared the entrance, the blue-paneled door burst open. Madame Toutain, an ample, middle-aged woman with sandy blonde hair greeted us with a wide smile. "*Bonjour.* Welcome to our home."

She shook our hands and turned toward her husband with adoring brown eyes. He leaned forward for a quick kiss.

"May I take your coat?" Madame Toutain asked me.

"*Oui, merci.*" I deposited my wool coat into her arms and smoothed my periwinkle sweater over my black corduroy jeans. I was glad I dressed for the occasion because all the men sported suits.

Monsieur Toutain directed us into the salon, a cozy room filled with oversized furniture, family photos and heirlooms.

"Most of these treasures belong to my wife," Professor Toutain said, materializing by my side as I surveyed the room. "This vase, for example, belonged to her great-grandmother."

"It's magnificent." I peered closer, admiring the hand-painted detail.

Gently, he set down the vase and reached for a framed photo off the mantel.

"This picture was taken last year at Christmas." He pointed out the other people in the picture. "This is our oldest daughter, Gisèle, our youngest daughter Julia, their husbands and our two grandchildren, Louis and Emily."

"How nice. You all look so happy."

When Madame Toutain appeared with a tray of drinks, Professor

Toutain helped her pass them around the group.

"Mmm...this smells familiar." I took a sip and sudden recognition raised my eyebrows. "Is this a *Lillet*? I think I taste the orange liqueurs."

"Yes, you're absolutely right, Mademoiselle."

I took another sip and smacked my lips. "*C'est très bon.*"

Professor Toutain beamed. "Oh, I've been meaning to ask you, how is your translation of *Le Petit Prince* coming?"

"I can't believe I forgot to tell you. I finished the book a few days ago."

"Did you? I'm so happy to hear that." His eyes twinkled and he belly laughed. "Wasn't the prince a rascal?"

"Yes, he was."

We rejoined the group, and there was a brief question and answer session while everyone became acquainted. I learned that all three of the other professors—Girard, Facet, and Fontaine—had all taught at the institute for an impressive ten or more years.

When Madame Toutain announced lunch, Professor Toutain directed us into an intimate dining room with a round oak table and chairs. An intricate glass chandelier brightened the room, while blue-patterned china and a lace tablecloth added a bit of old country charm. A massive bouquet of yellow roses sat on the sideboard.

Professor Toutain ushered us into seats and circled the table, chitchatting and pushing his glasses up his nose, as he filled our wine goblets. "I hope you'll enjoy this *Pouilly-Fumé* from the town of Nevers."

A sublime aroma filled the air when Madame Toutain entered the room with the entrée, *tarte aux poireaux et tapenade*, leek tart with green olive tapenade. This was soon followed by the main course, *truite meunière aux amandes*—trout with brown butter and almonds, paired with roasted garlic potatoes. With each course, the room quieted as everyone sampled the exceptional cuisine.

After this, lightning-fast French commenced. I understood most of the conversations, but I knew it would be even more of a challenge to participate, so I drank the wine and enjoyed my food.

At one point, Professor Girard turned to me with a question. "So, Mademoiselle, as Professor Toutain's star pupil, what are your plans for the future? Will you move up to the next level at the institute?"

All eyes turned to me and I felt the heat rush to my cheeks. "No, I'm leaving after this quarter. I wish I could stay . . . but my parents agreed to only one quarter."

"What will you do with your French once you return to the United States?"

"I'm not sure." I fiddled with the napkin in my lap. "I came here to learn French so that I could get a job as a flight attendant with World Airways. I'm no longer certain that's what I want to do, but I may feel differently once I return home."

Sensing my distress, Professor Toutain came to my rescue. "*Eh bien,* I've changed my career path many times. I'm sure you'll come to the right conclusion, Mademoiselle."

"*Merci, Professeur.*"

While our host refilled our wine glasses, our hostess brought in the next course, a simple green salad, followed by a cheese board and baguette. Next, came a delectable dessert, *Île Flottante*—poached meringue floating on a vanilla custard sauce.

"This dessert is amazing." Professor Facet exclaimed, licking his lips before turning toward Madame Toutain. "I declare you the best cook in Luynes!"

"*Merci,* André," she said softly, her cheeks turning a pretty pink.

With lunch complete, we all filed back into the salon where Professor Toutain opened a bottle of champagne.

When he offered me a flute, I held up my hand. "*Non, merci,* I think I've had enough."

He paused, and a boyish grin appeared on his face. "Just one small glass for a toast, Mademoiselle?"

"Okay."

Once everyone had a flute in his or her hand, Professor Toutain raised his glass in the air. "*Á votre santé!*" To your health!

After another round of champagne, Professor Toutain glanced at his watch. "It's getting late. I think it's time I drove all of you back to Tours."

While we gathered near the front door, Madame Toutain retrieved my coat. "Here, I'll hold it for you."

Narrowing my gaze to focus, I pushed my hand in the general direction of the sleeve. When a loud hiccup escaped, I giggled. "Oops, I'm sorry," I said, covering my mouth. *I think I drank too much wine.*

Straightening and regaining some control, I managed a simple sentence with only minor slurring. "Thank you very much for the fabulous lunch, Madame Toutain."

Her lips twitched, and she exchanged a look with her husband. "*Je vous en prie*, Mademoiselle."

Professor Toutain offered me his arm. "Yes . . . well, why don't you let me escort you to the car?"

"Would you?" I looped my arm through his. "You really are the kindest professor I've ever had."

The corners of Professor Toutain's mouth lifted slightly as he puffed his chest and led me though the door. Professors Girard, Facet, and Fontaine followed, their faces reddening as they swallowed back laughter.

56

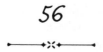

*T*he late morning skies were overcast as Janice and I caught the 11:10 train to Songais. As we disembarked, I searched the platform and, when my eyes found Évelyne in the crowd, my center shifted with joy.

"*Bonjour, mon amie!*" She engulfed me in a warm embrace. "*C'est bon de te revoir!*"

"It's good to see you too," I whispered into her brown hair.

There were introductions and a brief conversation, and then Évelyne turned to me with a suggestion. "Let's have lunch and then we'll visit the *Château de Songais*. You mentioned once that you'd like to take the tour."

"Yes, I've always wanted to see the interior, but somehow I never got the chance while I lived with the Dubois family." *This will be such a treat.*

"*Bien*, then it's settled." She nodded. "We'll get a bite to eat at *Chez Henri* and then we'll catch the two o'clock tour."

I glanced at Janice and she smiled. "That sounds great."

As we ambled along narrow streets, Évelyne filled Janice in on some of the town's history, including the Saint-Jean-Baptiste Church and the Songais suspension bridge. Even though I'd heard most of it before from Madame Dubois, I enjoyed the lesson anyway.

The sidewalk narrowed and we progressed around a bend, single file. When I heard Janice's sudden, sharp intake of air, a feeling of *déjà vu* washed over me.

"Is that the *Château de Songais?*" she asked, her eyes wide with wonder. "It looks like it belongs in a fairytale."

Ah . . . yes, now I remember. I felt the same way when I first saw the château. That seemed like three lifetimes ago.

Évelyne laughed. "Many people feel that way when they see it for the first time. Maybe it's the multiple towers and the drawbridge."

"How old is it?" Janice asked, unable to tear her eyes away.

"I believe it was built during the fifteenth century. You'll learn all about it in a few hours." Évelyne pointed to a restaurant a short distance away. "There, that's where we're going to eat."

Cranberry-colored awnings with *Chez Henri* spelled out in large white letters sheltered the restaurant's paned windows. Purple and blue winter pansies, in built-in wooden flower boxes below the windows, added old-world charm.

We strolled over, passed the empty outdoor seating area, and entered the idyllic restaurant. Moments later, a waiter ushered us to our seats, handed us menus, and then rattled off the specials before walking away.

Évelyne unfolded her napkin and laid it in her lap. "I don't even need to look. The *bouillabaise* special with *salade d'endives aux noix et Roquefort* sounds delicious, don't you think?"

"Uh-huh," I lied. Fish soup? I wasn't so sure. My mom always left the heads on. *I think I'll pass.*

The server returned, and Janice and I both ordered *poulet Provençal aux citrons confits*—roasted chicken with a sauce of shallots, tomatoes, white wine and preserved lemons. When we passed him our menus, he addressed Évelyne once again. "*Et comme boisson?*" And to drink?

She glanced at Janice and me. "Shall we have some wine with the meal?"

We nodded in unison. "*Oui.*"

Évelyne ordered a bottle of sauvignon blanc and, a few minutes later, the waiter poured three glasses of the fragrant wine.

"*Á votre santé!*" We all cheered, raising our glasses in the air.

During the meal, we chatted nonstop—about the institute, Michel, my birthday, and the Songais *Collège*. I learned that all was well with Madame Bernard, Director Moreau and the students. When the waiter brought dessert, *croquembouche*, caramel-glazed cream puffs, Évelyne moved the topic in a surprising direction.

"So . . . I've been thinking I might take a trip to the United States next year, maybe during summer."

I blinked twice and sat up straight. "Really? Do you think you'll make it to the West Coast?"

She glanced at Janice and shrugged. "I'm not sure. I'd love to see California . . . but Washington would be a marvelous place to visit too."

Unexpected emotions caused my voice to crack. "Well, if you do come to Seattle, you'll have a place to stay for as long as you like."

Her eyes glistened and she placed her hand on my arm. "Thank you, Linda. That's a very kind thing to say."

"*Excusez-moi, s'il vous plaît.* Can I get you anything else?"

We all shook our heads and then Évelyne asked the waiter for *l'addition*. He returned immediately and we split the check three ways.

We exited *Chez Henri* onto the cobbled lane and strolled toward the *Château de Songais* for the tour. The sun broke free from the clouds, and a discussion ensued between Janice and Évelyne about the best cities to visit in California.

Since I had nothing to add, I focused on the familiar sights around me—the butcher, the baker, the town square. Without warning, melancholy thoughts entered my mind and my throat swelled. Would I ever see this town or the Loire Valley again? And what about my French friends? Would we keep in touch once I returned home? *It'll be so hard to say goodbye.*

57

*F*ive days later, on the second to the last day of class, I arrived at the institute early, eager to speak with Professor Toutain. Peering inside the room, I discovered him alone, writing at his desk.

As soon as he recognized me, his face lit up and he stood to greet me. "*Bonjour*, Mademoiselle Kovic. How are you?"

"I'm good. Can I talk to you for a moment?"

"*Bien sûr*," he said, whipping off his glasses and peering at me closely. "What's on your mind?"

"I was wondering about my certificate from the institute. I'm heading to Paris in a few days, and I'd really like to have it with me when I leave town."

"Ah, I see." His brow creased in concentration. "It usually takes a few days for the office to put those together, but I'll see what I can do."

"Thank you." I smiled and adjusted my purse on my shoulder. "Are you going to the show tonight?"

Earlier in the week, an advertisement for a Dinner Show at *Club 81* appeared on the Student Notice Board. Intrigued by the description titled "Female Impersonators," Janice and I purchased tickets immediately.

"*Non!*" he waved his hands in front of his face. "That's not my thing, but I've heard that it's very entertaining."

"Yeah, well . . . we'll see."

When classmates entered, I slipped into my seat.

"Good morning, students," Professor Toutain said, clasping his hands together while he scanned the room. "I know you're all looking forward to the end of the quarter party tomorrow . . ."

There were "whoops" and "shouts" from around the room, but when Professor Toutain raised his hand, everyone quieted. "Do any of you need more time to practice your performances?"

Several hands flew into the air.

"Aha! That's what I thought." He scratched his forehead. "I tell you what. I'll take care of some paperwork in my office while you all work on your skits for a couple hours. Then, if you'd like, we'll all head down to *Café Moderne* for coffee and cake."

Fresh cheers erupted. Professor Toutain smiled and raised his hand once again. "*Bien*. Please find your group and get started."

Later that evening, with excitement cursing through my veins, I walked into *Club 81*. Rising onto my tiptoes, I surveyed the crowded lobby, but I didn't see Janice until she materialized by my side.

"Hi. I'm glad you're here," she said, giving me a quick, tight hug. "I've already checked us in."

I followed her to the reservation desk, where a willowy, white-haired woman escorted us through double doors into a large room with a curtained stage.

"Here you are," she motioned.

We slid into seats next to each other and greeted the students around the table. There were a few familiar faces from my classroom, including Tomoko and her sister Akiko. When I spotted Professor Girard at a table nearby, he waved.

Janice leaned toward me. "Is that Professor Toutain?"

"No, he couldn't make it. Is your professor here?"

"I don't see her either."

Conversations buzzed, and two waiters dressed in black slacks and white shirts arrived with red wine. Slow and meticulous, they strolled around the room, serving guests with a slight bend at the waist. Task complete, they left the room and returned with the main course, *fricassée de volaille au Vouvray,* chicken with a Vouvray-wine sauce. "Mmms" commenced around the room as the appetizing aromas filled our nostrils.

The room quieted as everyone ate and, twenty minutes later, Janice laid her fork on her plate and declared, "That was delicious, but I can't eat another bite."

"I'm done too." I pulled a cigarette from my purse and lit it.

Janice watched me for a moment and then her expression turned serious. "I have something for you." She pulled her purse onto her lap, extracted a small package, and placed it in front of me.

I slowly blew the smoke from my mouth. "Janice, I—"

She held up her hand, palm out, forestalling my protests. "I know I know . . . you didn't get me anything. It's really not a big deal, just open it."

My fingers trembled as I unwrapped the present, reached in and pulled out a black oval pin embellished with a drawing of a roaring-twenties French woman.

"It's so cool," I said, peering at it closely before pinning it on the cowl of my navy sweater.

She smiled tentatively and her voice faltered. "I know we've known each other a short time, but I wanted to give you something to remember me by."

I gave her a hug. "Thank you, so much. I'll treasure it always."

The waiter refilled our glasses, and at ten o'clock, the lights dimmed and all eyes focused on the stage.

When the curtains opened, a lone dark-haired man with a slight build, dressed in red robe, sat highlighted at a vanity table. He broke into a humorous song in English. We watched, mesmerized, as he applied makeup—eye shadow, blush, mascara—slipped a wig on his head, and clipped on earrings. Taking his time, he rose, placed his foot on the chair, and slowly, very slowly, pulled on fishnet stockings over his briefs. A short tuxedo jacket, white shorts, a white top hat with sequins, and a large flamboyant pink feather fan completed the outfit.

I heard Janice's exhalation. "Wow! I've never seen anything like this before."

I couldn't tear my eyes away from the man. "Me neither."

Another female impersonator, with an identical outfit, joined the first performer on stage and, over the next hour and a half, they sang and danced to familiar show tunes. Pockets of laughter erupted around the room and, when the two men finished their routine, everyone rose for a standing ovation. Fanning their faces, the cheeky impersonators returned to perform one last cabaret song before the curtains closed for good.

When the lights came on, Janice turned toward me with eyes like saucers. "That was really off the wall, but I'm glad we came."

"Me too." *I can't wait to write Carline and Cindy about it.*

We pulled on our coats and then exited to the lobby.

"What now?" Janice asked, her voice hopeful. "Do you want to check out the club downstairs?"

I hesitated. I'd probably regret it in the morning, but this would be one of the last nights to party with Janice and my other friends from school. I couldn't resist.

"Okay, let's go for it." I looped my arm through hers, and grinning like a couple of impish schoolgirls, we descended into *Club 81 Underground.*

58

*M*idafternoon, the following day, a few hours after I returned home from the party at the institute, a knock on the door woke me from my nap.

"*Entrez,*" I shouted, throwing my legs over the side of the bed.

The door opened and Thomas peeked in around the frame. "Michel is on the phone."

My stomach fluttered. "*Merci.*" *I can't wait to talk to him.*

I hurried down the stairs into the kitchen and picked up the receiver. "Michel?"

"*Bonjour.* How was your last day of school?"

"Good . . . really good. Professor Toutain hosted another celebration and the students sang and performed skits. It was so much fun." The corners of my mouth twitched. "You'll laugh when I tell you the part I played in *Cinderella.*"

"Were you the princess?"

"No. I was the prince."

There was silence, and then Michel let out a loud guffaw. "That is hilarious. I wish I could have been there."

"Yeah, I thought you'd get a kick out that."

He chuckled a few more times before his tone turned serious. "So, now that school is over, when are you coming to Paris?"

"I'm not sure. How soon do you want me?"

"Yesterday."

Mmm . . . perfect response. "Well, I've said goodbye to Évelyne, Janice and Professor Toutain." I bit my lip and then continued my musings aloud. "I can pack tomorrow. I suppose I could be ready by Sunday morning."

"Really? That would be fantastic!" There was a pause. "What about your luggage? How will you get to the train station?"

"Évelyne's sister, Valérie, offered to give me a lift. I'll call her tomorrow and make the arrangements."

I heard him exhale. "Then it's settled. I'll meet you at *Montparnasse* on Sunday morning."

An image of Michel waiting impatiently for me at the train station came to mind and my insides quivered. "I can't wait to spend time with you in Paris."

"I'm looking forward to it too, *ma belle*. Once you get to know the city, you'll never want to leave." When his voice suddenly pitched lower, I strained to hear his next words. "As a matter of fact, I'm counting on it."

Part Three

Paris

59

———•✕•———

*W*hen my alarm sounded on Sunday morning at 7 a.m., I pushed the covers aside and rolled out of bed, anxious to start the day. As I walked to the sink, I spotted my suitcase sitting near the door, and my pulse quickened. *In a few hours, I'll meet Michel in Paris. Six weeks together. I can't wait.*

It had been almost two weeks since I'd seen him and I wanted to make a good impression. I brushed my hair until it shone, and then I shimmied into my burgundy sweater and faded blue jeans, two of Michel's favorites. It was a day for blush, mascara and lip gloss—the works. After a backward glance in the mirror, I picked up my luggage and walked through the door.

When I reached the bottom of the stairs, Madame Martin appeared in the kitchen doorway. "*Eh bien*, it looks like you're ready to go. Did you check the room carefully for all of your things?"

"*Oui*, Madame."

"*Bon*." Her eyes glistened as she hugged me. "I've enjoyed having you, Mademoiselle. I hope you have a pleasant stay in Paris and a safe trip home."

Emotions clogged my voice box. "Thank you for everything. You've treated me like part of the family. I won't forget your kindness."

Madame Martin patted my shoulder and stood aside while Monsieur Martin and their youngest son, Frédéric, shook my hand. Thomas was the last to say goodbye.

"*Bonne chance, mon ami.*" Good luck, my friend.

"Thanks." Thomas's face reddened and he pushed his hands into his pockets. "Good luck to you, too."

I studied their faces, just as I had when I said goodbye to my other friends from Songais and Tours. Somehow, I wanted to sear all of these images in my memory so they would stay with me forever. I'd endured both heartache and happiness while I lived in the Loire Valley, and without the benevolent support from people like the Martins, I may have given up long ago and returned home.

Blinking hard, I picked up my suitcase and rushed out the door to Valérie's waiting car.

"Put your things in the back seat," she said out the window.

I stowed my bags and climbed into the passenger seat. As she pulled away from the curb, I wiped a tear from my cheek.

Hours later, when the brain-rattling train arrived at the *Gare Montparnasse* in Paris, I leapt up, grabbed my suitcase, and slid into the queue to exit. As I disembarked, I searched the platform. My breathing halted until my eyes found their mark. *Ahh . . . there's Michel. It's so good to see his smiling face.*

I set my luggage down and watched him maneuver around a group of people. Once he reached me, he pulled me into a tight embrace and his ardent kiss produced shivers. "I've missed you, *ma belle.*"

"I've missed you too," I sighed.

His brows lifted as he studied my face and pushed strands of hair out of my eyelashes. "Are you hungry? There's a café around the corner."

"No, not really. I had a bite to eat at the train station in Tours."

"*Bon,* then why don't we go directly to the apartment?" He picked up my suitcase, curled his arm through mine, and with an easy stride led me out of the station.

"Is your apartment close by?"

"No. It's located at *place de la Bastille,* which is about four kilometers from here. An hour's walk."

My forehead wrinkled. "Maybe we should get a cab, Michel? My bag is heavy."

"I think I can manage. You'll enjoy the walk." He winked his reassurance. "Oh, and I should warn you to watch where you step.

There's dog shit everywhere."

What? I quickly checked the pavement in front of us and my jaw dropped. There were reeking piles of dog poop every few feet. "Ugh! Why don't people clean up after their dogs?"

"Because they don't have to. The city sweeps the sidewalks daily."

That's crazy. I had no idea.

We progressed down the sidewalk onto the tree-lined *boulevard du Montparnasse*, sharing stories and discussing recent events, while I marveled that I was actually in Paris.

Four-, five- and six-story stone structures, both old and new, towered above us. Many of these aged buildings boasted tall multi-paned windows, intricately railed Juliet balconies, and rooflines decorated with medallion or leaf designs. Retail establishments of all kinds—quaint cafés with open-air seating, grocers with colorful fruits and vegetables on outdoor displays, jewelers with sparkling baubles in the window—beckoned people to enjoy a meal or to come in and purchase their goods. Musicians and street performers, solo or in small groups, claimed a street corner, and offered passersby a song for a few coins.

"*Alors*, it sounds like you've had a busy two weeks," Michel pulled me into a doorway, laid down my bag, and rested his arm.

"I sure have. Saying goodbye to my friends was much harder than I thought it would be."

Michel assessed me with a slight frown. "*Mais oui, c'est très difficile.*"

Duh. Of course it's difficult, Linda. It'll be ten times worse when you have to leave Michel behind. I stepped into the intersection without looking for cars and, when a horn honked, Michel grabbed my arm and jerked me back onto the curb.

"Careful, *ma belle*. I need to warn you about the drivers in Paris too. They rarely stop for pedestrians."

I brushed my arm across my forehead. "Thanks for the warning."

Continuing along, an old woman with a small, hyperactive, black poodle exited a chocolatier and blocked our progress. We smiled and maneuvered around her with Michel mumbling "*Pardon*, Madame," while her dog yapped.

"See that café up ahead? That's *Le Dôme Café*, a famous gathering spot for many Parisian 'intellectuals.'"

"Such as?" I asked.

"Picasso and Hemingway both frequented the place."

"Wow, that's amazing." I craned my neck to get a look inside the restaurant and noted the tourists snapping photographs nearby. "Have you eaten there?"

"*Ouais*, many times," Michel replied. "Maybe we can go one evening."

"That would be wonderful."

We crossed the street onto a wide boulevard lined with universities, and Michel pointed out the famous *Sorbonne*. Immediately, I noticed younger, livelier pockets of people—girls dressed in lacy white tights, short skirts and red high heels, and guys wearing pastel sweaters or blazers, and scarves.

"What part of Paris is this?" I asked, my voice rising with excitement.

"It's called the Latin Quarter. You'll like it here. There are lots of great bistros and bookstores that cater to students."

"Hmm . . . sounds like fun."

Two heavily armed French soldiers walked past and my eyes widened. "What's going on? Why are they carrying machine guns?"

He shrugged. "The Iranian Revolution and the hostage crisis has the French government on edge. You'll get used to seeing them after a while."

"Oh . . ." I doubted that, but he was indifferent so I swallowed my concerns.

Fifteen minutes later, we spotted the *Pont de Sully* bridge over the *Seine*. "Wait until you see the view." Michel urged me forward with a hand on the small of my back. Once we reached the middle of the bridge, he lowered my suitcase to the ground and pointed west. "There's *Notre-Dame* Cathedral on *Île de la Cité*."

I lifted my right eyebrow. "That's an island?"

"Yes, and we'll cross over *Île Saint-Louis* to reach the Right Bank on the other side."

We stood there for a few moments and I drank in the scene. Peaceful rustic gray barges—one trimmed in bright orange and blue—rested alongside the river's seawall. Random terra-cotta flowerpots filled with purple winter pansies or miniature pine trees rested on a few decks. Off in the distance, a second arched bridge, *Pont de la Tournelle*, offered people another route on and off the island, and the multi-towered *Notre-Dame* Cathedral, proudly displayed its French Gothic architecture.

Wow, what a view. I can't believe I'm actually here in Paris, seeing all of this in person. "It's incredible, Michel."

"*Ouais, c'est vrai.*" He gave me a quick kiss and picked up my bag. "We should go—we have about a kilometer left."

I reluctantly followed his lead.

Throughout the rest of our journey, Michel pointed out interesting sights—a medieval church or a historic structure—until we finally arrived at a five-story stone building in a modest neighborhood.

"Well, here we are."

I glanced up at the structure. "*Génial.* I can't wait to see the apartment."

Michel didn't move. Instead, he rubbed the back of his neck and his brown hair fell forward as he studied the ground. "I have something to tell you first."

Uh-oh. I moved my purse from one shoulder to the other. "Go ahead."

"I'm really sorry, but we don't have a bed yet." Michel finally looked me in the eye. "But I've made a pallet for us."

I felt the sting of yet another disappointing confession. "So we're sleeping on the floor?"

"*Ouais,* but not for long. I'm getting a large payment from Amir in a few days."

His expression, resembling a scolded puppy, tugged at my heartstrings. *This is a drag, but I don't want to ruin our first night together in Paris. Now that I'm here, I'm sure he'll buy a bed.* "Okay, we can pretend that we're camping."

Michel's face relaxed and he brought my hand to his lips. "I knew you'd understand." He led me into the building and hefted my suitcase up three flights of stairs.

Fiddling with the lock, he opened the door and stood aside for me to enter. "As you can see, it's quite roomy. Here is the salon, the kitchen is through there, and this is the bathroom. The bedrooms are down that hall."

He was right. The high ceilings and sparse furniture in the salon gave the room a lofty feeling. A well-used burgundy couch, matching stuffed chair, and oak coffee table were the only items "floating" in front of a beautiful stone fireplace ornately carved with vines. In the kitchen, a timeworn oak table and four chairs rested under a tall leaded-paned window and, on the opposite wall, a matching buffet offered additional kitchen storage.

I gave Michel an approving nod. "It's nice."

We proceeded down the hallway, past a large framed poster of the world, and he pointed to a closed door on the right. "This is the bathroom, and this room belongs to Régis and Karine."

He opened the door and I peered inside. A mirrored mahogany dresser and matching queen-size bed dominated the pale blue room. Sheer lavender drapes, a dark burgundy bedspread and throw pillows in similar hues gave the room an exotic, bohemian vibe.

Michel grabbed my hand. "I know what you're thinking. I wish it belonged to us too."

I lifted my chin. He was right, but I'd already decided to accept the situation. "So, where is your room?"

Michel ushered me through the door across the hall and laid my bag on the floor.

My eyes skimmed the empty room to land on the mattress in the corner. *Thank goodness he bought blankets and pillows. It actually looks kind of cozy.*

"Do we have a view?" I strolled to the window and pulled back the curtain.

"*Ouais,* into the apartment across the courtyard."

I felt his fingers move my hair aside and when his lips caressed my neck, goose bumps erupted on every inch of my skin. With a firm grip, he turned me around and kissed me, exploring my mouth with his tongue. I moaned and pressed my body against his. *Mmm . . . I've missed his touch.*

"I want you," Michel said roughly, continuing his ravishment as he maneuvered me toward the pallet.

"Shouldn't you close the door?" I whispered.

"That won't be necessary." He released me and explained while we shed our clothes. "Régis and Karine are gone, and Marie-Christine doesn't move in until the fourteenth of April."

"How convenient."

Michel's gaze locked mine and I lost a breath as he wrapped muscled arms around me, tipped my head back, and kissed me passionately. Slowly, we sank to our knees and, when his hands slid like silk down the length of my lower back, I felt dizzy with longing. "I have to say, you really know how to welcome a girl to Paris."

"*Mais oui, ma belle,* I'm half French, after all."

60

$\mathcal{T}$ he next morning, I woke up in bed alone. Bewildered, I slipped into my clothes, found the kitchen and discovered Michel working on his translations at the table.

"*Bonjour.*" He waved me over and pulled me onto his lap.

Yawning, I lay my head on his shoulder. "How long have you been up?"

"A couple of hours."

I twisted around to meet his gaze. "Promise you'll wake me next time."

"Okay."

I gave him a quick kiss, rose and then poured myself a cup of the aromatic coffee on the stove. After I stirred in milk, I settled in the seat across from him. "How are your translations coming along?"

"Good." He leaned back in his chair and laced his fingers behind his neck. "I'm almost done with this job. In a few days, I'll have to return to Tours so I can get paid."

I blinked. "How long will you be gone?"

"Just for the day. I'm sure you can find something to do while I'm gone." He tore a few pieces from a baguette on the table and handed them to me. "Here, have some breakfast. After I finish my work, we'll go out and visit some of the sights."

"Okay." I nodded, spreading some jam on my bread. "Can we stop at the American Express office too?"

Michel's brow furrowed. "*Pourquoi?*"

"That's where my dad said he'd wire my money. I want to check to see if it's arrived yet."

"*Eh bien.*" His elusive dimple appeared as he stared at me. "Have I told you how pleased I am to have you in Paris with me?"

I felt my face warm. "Uh-huh, about a hundred times last night." Leaning forward, I laid my hand on his arm. "I'm happy to be here with you too." I meant it. Michel was charming, intelligent, and he knew how to please me in bed. I wasn't sure what the future would bring, but six weeks with him in the "City of Love" sounded marvelous.

Two hours later, after a visit to the American Express office, we caught the metro to the *Charles de Gaulle-Étoile* station to see the *Arc de Triomphe*.

"It's much larger than I thought it would be," I said, straining to look beyond the sea of tourists in front of us.

"Hmm . . . sometimes it's hard to imagine the scale of something until you see it in person." Michel shoved his hands in his pockets as he gazed at the monument. "A man named Charles Godefroy flew his biplane through the arch in 1919."

My eyes rounded. "Really? That would have been cool to see."

"I think so too. It was an illegal act, but eventually he was deemed a hero for it."

He grabbed my hand and we strolled down *avenue des Champs-Élysées*, conversing easily and greeting passersby with an occasional "*bonjour.*" From time to time, we stopped to peer in fancy storefront windows or read sidewalk signs in front of delicious-smelling restaurants.

After we left the main shopping areas, we passed two massive historic sites, the *Grand Palais* and the *Petit Palais,* and five minutes later, we entered *la Place de la Concorde.* As if drawn by invisible strings, we approached the ancient obelisk. When my eyes swept skyward, up the shaft to the gold-leafed pyramid cap, a shudder ran through my body.

"Where did this come from?" I asked, breaking the silence.

"It was a gift from Egypt to France in the early 1800s, and the fountains over there, and there," Michel pointed left and right, "were erected at the same time."

We moved closer for a better look and Michel's voice turned wistful. "This fountain is one of my favorite sights in Paris. The symbolism of the "rivers and the seas" of France speaks to me."

Six bronze, half-nude figures, seated in the prow of a ship, supported the lower basin of the fountain, while four statues held an inverted upper basin with a mushroom-shaped cap. Surrounding the fountain were six additional bronze and iron tritons, perhaps eight feet tall, holding gold-colored fish. Water spurted from the fishes' mouths and the fountain's cap, splashing and mingling with the water bubbling and running down the basins.

"It's impressive. I can see why you feel that way."

I looped my arm in his and we advanced toward the *Tuileries* Gardens, with Michel pointing out a few more sights. "There's the top of the *Tour Eiffel*, and over there is the *Musée d'Orsay*, currently under construction." He scratched his head for a moment before gesturing left. "I believe that's the Madeleine church."

Glancing at my blank expression, he added, "If you'd like, we can try to find you a book that describes some of these places in English."

What a sweet suggestion. "Thank you. I would like that very much."

As we approached a large shallow basin with a central fountain, I noted a small arch off in the distance, similar to the one we admired hours ago. Puzzled, I glanced at Michel and he offered a simple explanation. "That's the *Arc de Triomphe du Carrousel*. It's a smaller, older version of the arch we saw earlier."

"And what about that building straight ahead?"

"That's the *Louvre* Museum, but we'll save that for another time. There are so many things to see inside, we could spend a whole day in there." His coffee-brown eyes searched mine. "I know it's a lot to take in. What do you say we get a bite to eat and I'll tell you more?"

"Okay." I touched his arm. "Thank you so much for the tour today. You were the perfect guide."

He brushed his fingers against my cheek. "*Tout le plaisir était pour moi.*" My pleasure.

Lifting my brows, I scanned the people around us and pulled out my Kodak pocket Instamatic camera. "Do you think someone would take our picture?"

"Oh, sure."

Michel walked over to a nearby couple, handed them the camera, and we posed in front of the fountain. When they passed it back to me, I offered them a quick "*Merci.*"

As we moved forward, I glanced over my shoulder and my breathing paused. Between the budding trees, in an impressive, tidy row, I saw the obelisk, the large basin, the fountains, and finally, the extraordinary *Arc de Triomphe*. It was a spectacular view and I had a hard time turning my back.

When I stumbled, Michel laughed and righted me. "You don't have to memorize the view, *ma belle*. We'll return to the *Place de la Concorde* again and again over the years to come."

61

*T*he temperature dropped dramatically in Paris over the next three days, and I was glad I picked up my burgundy scarf and gloves before we exited the apartment into the frigid air.

"Brrr, it's chilly." A strong gust of wind blew open my coat, and I stopped to secure it as we proceeded toward the *métro* that would take us to *Montparnasse* train station.

Michel draped his arm around my shoulders. "People have been talking about a cold front coming into Paris."

"I think it's arrived, *n'est-ce pas?*" I said snuggling close to him.

"*Oui*, I think you're right." We separated and maneuvered around a sidewalk bench and then reconnected again. "So, *ma belle*. What are you going to do while I'm in Tours today?"

"Well . . . now that my money's arrived from home, I think I'll do some shopping." I tossed him an impish grin and my tone turned playful. "Someone has a birthday coming up on Tuesday."

Michel's eyes twinkled as he met my gaze. "*Eh bien*, something from one of those fancy shops on the *Champs-Élysées* would be nice."

"Ha! I wouldn't count on it." I laughed as we descended the stairs into the *métro* station. "More than likely, I'll shop in the Latin Quarter."

When we arrived at *Montparnasse*, Michel secured his ticket and we walked onto the platform. He wrapped his arms around me and held me close as we said our goodbyes.

"What time do you think you'll get home tonight?" I asked.

"I'm not sure—late evening. It'll depend on Amir." Then with a labored sigh against my ear he said, "*Ma belle*, what have you done to me? Do you realize that it's hard to leave you for even one day?"

His words sounded so sincere, a lump formed in my throat. "I feel the same way, Michel."

We stood there for several seconds, Michel stroking my hair and, when our eyes locked, he tipped my head back for a tender kiss. "I'll see you later tonight."

He climbed the stairs and disappeared after a final wave.

Two hours later, I returned to the apartment and laid my packages on our mattress. I'd found some great shops on *boulevard Saint-Michel* where I'd purchased a new pastel blue shirt and V-neck sweater for Michel. I couldn't wait to give him his presents.

What now? I wandered into the kitchen and looked inside the refrigerator. *Hmm . . . maybe I'll have some of the duck pâté Michel brought home yesterday.* Thank goodness I grabbed a baguette on the way home.

Once I finished my meal, I got up, poured myself a glass of water and lit a cigarette. When I sat back down at the table, I wrote a few entries in my diary and penned two short letters to Janice and Évelyne. I knew they'd be anxious to hear my news—the apartment, the sights, the scenes—and I was excited to share it with them.

Janice's letter in English was easy, but Évelyne's took a bit more thought. When I finished, I double-checked my work and smiled as I sat back in my seat. *I can't believe I wrote that in French all by myself.* With each passing day, I felt my confidence growing with the language. Michel was right; a second interview with World Airways just might land me a job.

After this, time seemed to pass slower and slower and slower. I straightened the apartment, cleaned the kitchen and swept the floors. When I checked the clock again, it was only seven o'clock. *Darn it. I sure wish the apartment had a TV.* It was strange how many young French people didn't have phones or televisions. *Oh well, I guess I'll study some French to pass the time.*

I fetched *Le Petit Prince* out of my suitcase, sat on the couch and curled my legs under my side. An hour and a half later, I heard the apartment door slam.

"*Salut!* Linda?"

My adrenaline surged and I jumped to my feet. "I'm in here, Michel."

When he entered the room, I wrapped my arms around his neck. "I'm so glad you're home," I told him, squeezing him tight.

He held me close and I heard his easy chuckle. "What a nice reception."

I pulled away and searched his coffee-brown eyes. "Did you get your money from Amir?"

His body tensed. "Yes . . . yes, I did."

"*Bien.* And did you eat dinner?"

Michel removed his black leather jacket and laid it on the back of the couch. "I ate a late lunch, but I could use a snack."

"There's a bit of *pâté* left in the refrigerator," I said, waving my hand toward the kitchen.

"*D'accord.*"

His stiff demeanor raised my eyebrows, along with my suspicions. "Is everything okay?"

Michel ran his right hand through his hair, walked over and leaned against the fireplace mantel. "I didn't get paid as much as I thought I would for this last job. In a week or so, we'll have to make a trip to Grigny so I can finish another project."

"Is that far away?"

He shook his head. "No, it's just outside of Paris, but we'll have to take the train, and the job could take a few days."

I frowned and shifted from one foot to the other. "They won't mind if you bring me?"

"No, of course not."

I walked over and grabbed his hand. "Well then, it sounds like everything will turn out okay."

Michel's smile came and went. "*Mais oui.* Between your money and mine, we should be fine."

I drew a breath to remind him how much I had left, but he cut me off.

"Linda, we'll manage. You don't need to worry."

When he pulled me into his arms, his kiss was more convincing than his promise.

62

*O*n April 1, 1980, Michel turned thirty years old. Given the special occasion, we decided to splurge and go to dinner at his friend's Greek restaurant in the Latin Quarter. At first, I felt guilty, my stomach churning as I pondered our limited funds. In the end, I convinced myself that a special birthday like this one warranted a memorable celebration.

When we entered the bedroom to dress for the evening, I rummaged through my suitcase and pulled out his package. Unable to squelch a nervous giggle, I shoved the present in his direction. "*Bon anniversaire,* Michel."

A wide grin appeared on his face. "*Merci, ma belle.* I was wondering when you were going to give me my gift." I watched as he ripped off the paper, pulled out the blue shirt and sweater, and then met my gaze. "These are fantastic." He gave me a quick peck. "Would you like me to wear them tonight?"

"*Oui.*" My cheeks heated with pleasure. "I sure hope they fit."

His muscles flexed as he inserted his arms into the sleeves and buttoned the shirt. Next, came the V-neck sweater and then he turned to me with his eyebrows lifted in expectation. "Well, what do you think?"

"You look very handsome."

Michel reached out and cupped my face. "I'm glad you think so." His lips skimmed lightly over mine and his spicy cologne filled my nose. "I'd like to thank you properly for these . . ."

I grinned and placed my hand on his chest. "Later, birthday boy—I don't want to be late for our reservation."

"*D'accord.*"

He helped me with my coat, slipped into his trench, and we exited the apartment. After a short *métro* ride, Michel directed me down a narrow, pedestrian-only lane and then pointed to a restaurant.

"There it is."

The peach-colored restaurant trimmed in bright orange, was easy to spot. Above the doorway, in large blue "Heorot" font letters, *Gia Sas* proclaimed Greek cuisine, and the colorful photographs near the entrance depicting specialty dishes left no doubt. As we approached, delicious aromas—coriander and allspice—filled the air.

"Mmm ... something smells good." I glanced at Michel and inhaled deeply.

"*Ouais,* I'm sure you'll enjoy the food here."

He waved me through the door and we immediately noticed the increase in volume inside the busy restaurant. Along with chatter and laughter, a trio played Greek folk music in the far corner of the room.

"Michel! *Salut!*"

A powerfully built, mustached man grabbed Michel's hand, and clasped the other one over it while they conversed in rapid French. Seconds later, a middle-aged woman with curly dark hair and dancing eyes, joined them.

"It's good to see you," she said, folding him in her ample arms. "It's been quite a while since you've paid us a visit."

"Yes, well it feels good to be back in Paris."

"But of course." She narrowed her eyes, focusing on me. "And who is this?"

Michel stepped aside. "Delia, Angelo, this is Linda. Linda, this is Delia and Angelo."

Taking turns pumping my hand, they greeted me and then Delia showed us to a booth in the far corner of the room, opposite the band. Mahogany woodwork, checkerboard tablecloths, and glass vases filled with yellow wildflowers created a cozy, homey atmosphere.

"I think you'll like this table," she said with a wink. "You'll have a bit more privacy."

"*C'est parfait. Merci.*"

Delia took our coats, we slid into our seats and she laid two menus on the table. "What can I get you two to drink? A couple of ouzos?"

I glanced at Michel and raised my eyebrows.

"Bring us a bottle of Kourtaki retsina and some black bean

hummus, please."

"Okay . . ." Delia's lips thinned and she mumbled something unintelligible as she walked away.

"What did you order? Delia seems skeptical."

"Retsina is a traditional Greek white wine. It's not for everybody, but I thought you might enjoy trying something different."

"Sure, why not." I shifted in my chair and fiddled with the menu. "How do you know these people?"

"Years ago, when I traveled from Lebanon to France, I lived in Paris for a few years, and I acquired a taste for Greek food. Angelo, who is the cook in the family, and Delia became friends after several visits."

"I see."

Delia returned with our wine and the hummus, and poured two glasses. "I'll return in a little while to take your order."

"Very well, thank you."

After she left, Michel picked up his glass. "*Santé,*" he said softly, watching me carefully. "Do you like it?"

"Well . . . it's definitely different." I set down my glass. "A bit strong for me." *Ack . . . and it smells like turpentine.*

"It's an acquired taste." Michel scanned the restaurant and waved Delia over to the table. "Can you please bring a glass of your house white for Linda?"

"*Bien sûr.*" An amused "I could have told you that" expression settled on her face as she removed my retsina from the table.

Michel and I perused the menu and he made a few suggestions. When Delia returned with my wine, he ordered grilled fish with a lemon-mint sauce, a platter of rice and vegetable-stuffed dolmades, and an order of Angelo's famous baklava for dessert.

I took a sip of my wine. "Mmm . . . this is better."

"*Bon.*" Michel relaxed in his seat and studied my face. "Have I told you how radiant you look this evening?"

"*Merci,* Michel," I mumbled, tucking a strand of unruly hair back into place. *He's so romantic.* None of the guys back home would ever use that word.

We chatted while we ate and our wine disappeared quickly, so Michel asked Delia to bring me another glass. When the main course arrived, we savored the meal, commenting on the exceptional flavors, and taking our time as we cut and chewed each mouthwatering bite.

Halfway through dinner, Angelo paid us a visit. "You two seem to be enjoying your meal."

"It's delicious, as usual," Michel said, wiping his mouth with his napkin.

"Good, I'm glad to hear it." The two men exchanged a few more pleasantries, and before he left, Angelo patted Michel on the back and refilled his glass of retsina.

Once we finished our dinner, Delia cleared the table and then brought our baklava. Laughing aloud, Michel and I fed each other bites of the delicious, syrupy-sweet cake until the plate was clean.

"Mmm . . . that was fantastic." I placed my fork on my dessert plate.

"Yes, it sure was."

When Delia returned to refill Michel's glass, he placed his hand over the top of it. "No thank you. I think I've had enough."

"*Bien.*" A victorious smile appeared on her face. "Can I get you anything else?"

"No, but will you cork this retsina so we can take it with us?" Michel handed her the bottle. "And bring the check, please."

Delia nodded and, a few minutes later, she delivered a heavily discounted bill.

"*Mais non*, this is too generous." Michel stood and pulled out his wallet just as Angelo materialized from the kitchen, having anticipated a confrontation.

"Consider it a 'welcome back' present." He crossed his arms and shook his head.

Seconds elapsed, and then Michel shrugged and laid a few bills on the table. "Thank you, my friend. I promise to return as often as I can."

"*Naturellement*," Angelo chortled, before turning to me.

I stood and extended my hand to Angelo, and then, Delia. "It was a pleasure to meet you both. Thank you for a lovely meal."

Delia's lips twitched as she placed her hands on her hips. "You are welcome, Linda. Please come again."

After helping me with my coat, Michel took my hand and we walked out into the cool night air.

"What a beautiful evening," Michel said, gazing up at the moon and stars as we strolled along.

"Yes . . . it is." Our eyes locked and earnest emotions surfaced. "I'm so glad I was able to celebrate this special birthday with you."

He paused our progress and pulled me into his arms. "It's only special because you're here with me. *Je t'aime*, Linda."

His declaration of love produced shivers and I almost repeated the phrase, but the words got stuck. "Michel, I'm—"

He silenced me with a finger to my lips. "It's okay, *ma belle*. I'm not trying to pressure you into saying something before you're ready. Let's blame it on the retsina." Then with a goofy grin he said, "Now, what do you say we take a walk along the river Seine?"

"I'd like that very much." Pleased that he dropped the topic, I rewarded him with a gentle kiss and then we continued down the cobbled lane holding hands, our arms swinging between us.

63

*F*our days later, Michel and I caught the late afternoon train to *Grigny-Centre,* a commune twenty-two kilometers south of the city, so he could finish his translation job. As we disembarked at the tiny station, I heard someone call his name.

"Michel!" A dark-haired, stocky man and an attractive woman with two children stepped forward to greet him warmly. They all spoke to each other in Arabic, and then Michel introduced me in French.

"Nice to meet you." I shook hands with Mahir, his wife Nadira, and their twin boys, Omar and Ali.

"*Eh bien*, I hope you two are hungry." Mahir cleared his throat and waved Michel forward. "Nadira has prepared a special meal for us."

The men led the way out of the station, and when we turned right onto *avenue des Sablons,* Nadira gripped her children's hands firmly. As we walked along, I snuck a glance her way. *She's pretty.* Her tawny brown hair, cut in a short shag with bangs, perfectly matched the color of her eyes. Full figured and a bit thick around the middle, I wondered if she was still carrying a bit of baby weight.

Steadying my voice, I attempted communication. "How long have you lived in Grigny?"

Nadira tilted her head in my direction, and her zesty citrus perfume drifted my way. "A little over three years. Omar and Ali were only babies at that time."

I looked at the boys. Chubby-cheeked and well dressed, they looked healthy and happy. "Were they born in France?"

She nodded shyly. "Yes. We lived in Paris at the time."

On our train trip from Paris, Michel told me a bit about Mahir and Nadira. Originally from Baghdad, they moved to France four years earlier, searching for a better life. Mahir had trouble finding a job, so he started a business translating books from French to Arabic.

"What about you?" Nadira asked. "Michel told us that you're American. What brings you to Paris?"

I hesitated. *Where should I begin?* "It's a long story, but I came to France seven months ago to learn French."

"Why?" Her voice was filled with curiosity.

"So that I could get a job as a flight attendant with World Airways."

Omar yanked on her hand and she murmured a few words to him in Arabic before refocusing on me. "So you already have a job?"

"No. I have to reapply once I return home."

"Ahh, I see." The group paused at the light, and after we crossed the street, Nadira glanced my way. "I have to tell you that you speak French very well now. As a matter of fact, I thought that you were French."

"Really?" Warmth spread through my body and I felt my lips lift at the corners. "I can't tell you how pleased I am to hear that. I've just finished a quarter at the *Institut d'Études Françaises* in Tours.

"Well, it appears that you took your studies seriously."

"*Vous êtes très gentille.*" You are very kind.

Mahir paused in front of a four-story building, waved us inside, and the six of us crowded into the elevator. We got out at the third floor and entered a spacious, modern-looking apartment.

A television, along with a large rust-patterned couch and easy chair, filled the living room. An oak table and six chairs added a homey feeling to the dining room. There was no artwork on the white walls and no embellishments on the coffee tables and end tables. Toys of all shapes and sizes—balls, trucks, and building blocks—littered the rug.

Whooping it up, the boys immediately hurled their jackets onto the floor and raced to a large basket of toys.

Nadira blushed, and then scolded them in Arabic. "Sorry for the mess," she said, bending down to pick up the jackets, along with a stuffed bear.

Michel walked up behind me, wrapped his hands around my waist and rested his chin on my shoulder. "*Pas de problème*. Children need to play."

"Especially boys," Mahir added with a grin. "Michel, why don't you and Linda put your things in the guest room? Then you and I can talk business while the girls prepare dinner."

Michel glanced at me and raised an eyebrow.

"Sure, that's fine." He was concerned. He didn't need to be.

While Nadira settled a toy dispute with the boys, I watched the men walk away; their Arabic words faded as they progressed down the hall and entered a room on the left. *It must be nice for Michel to speak to someone in his own language.* I certainly enjoyed speaking English with my friends back in Tours. Memories of Lori, Julie, and Janice swamped my mind and my guts twisted. I missed them.

Nadira's voice brought me back to the present. "The kitchen is this way."

"Yes, of course," I said, pushing my hair back as I followed her lead.

Two hours later, after a delicious Iraqi meal—lamb with rice, followed by a salad and flatbread with apricot jelly—Nadira and I cleared the table and then washed and dried the dishes. Task complete, she glanced my way. "Thank you for your help, Linda. Why don't you join Michel and Mahir while I make some coffee?"

"*Bien*." I laid my dishtowel on the counter, walked into the living room and squeezed in beside Michel on the couch. Deep in an Arabic discussion with Mahir, he didn't acknowledge my presence.

"What are you talking about?" I bumped his shoulder.

Michel looked my way and I noted his stiff jawline. "The Middle

East."

"Hmm . . . I see." I knew very little about the topic.

They changed to French, but given the complex subject matter, I didn't understand much of the conversation, only that they disagreed. When Nadira arrived with a tray of coffees, Michel ground his cigarette in the ashtray.

"We've discussed the revolution in Iran many times, Mahir. I don't want to get in an argument with you tonight."

Mahir shrugged his shoulders. "Okay, my friend. We'll drop it for now."

We moved onto other topics—our hometowns, our families—and the minutes slipped by unnoticed until Mahir checked his wrist. "Nadira, it's ten o'clock. The boys should be in bed."

"You're right. I hadn't noticed the late hour."

Mahir reached out and grabbed her hand as she rose. Mischief sparkled in his brown eyes. "When you return, maybe you'll dance for us?"

The corners of her mouth lifted as she shared a private moment with her husband. "*D'accord.*" She shifted her gaze to me. "And maybe Linda will join me."

Huh? I licked my lips. *What kind of dancing? I hope this doesn't get weird.* "I'll probably just watch."

After Nadira left, Mahir put an Arabic record on and the three of us listened, tapping our feet or moving our bodies as the repetitive rhythmic melody got under our skin.

Ten awkward minutes later, when Mahir went to check on Nadira, Michel draped his arm over my shoulder and pulled me close. "What do you think of this music?"

"I like it—it's different." *Kind of exotic . . . sexy. I wish we were alone.*

His lips brushed against mine. "I'm glad."

Nadira and Mahir returned and he switched to another album while his wife moved to the middle of the room.

Hmm . . . she's barefoot and wearing a different outfit.

As soon as the music started, Nadira swung her hips back and forth while a *kanun*, a middle-eastern stringed instrument, a goblet drum, and flute played in the background. Repeatedly, she twisted and turned in her light peach shift, her shoulders lifting and dropping, her ribcage and belly undulating under the thin fabric, as her citrusy perfume drifted our way.

When the song ended, we clapped while Nadira grinned and bowed her head. A new song came on and she grasped my hand, pulling me to my feet. Laughing, I joined her. *Why not give it try.*

Mahir and Michel watched with interest, their eyes bright and focused, as Nadira taught me how to rock my hips, turning forwards and then backwards, while throwing an occasional grin over my shoulder. Eventually, the men joined in the dance and the temperature rose in the room.

"I can't stand another minute of this," Michel whispered, his voice urgent as he wrapped his hands around my waist. "We need to say goodnight."

"All right." My words were barely audible.

He glanced at Mahir and pointed toward the bedroom, and the two men smiled at each other in a way that suggested mutual understanding. With a firm grip on my elbow, Michel led me down the hall while my heart thumped loudly to the beat of the Arabic music.

64

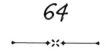

*O*ver the next three days, while Michel and Mahir worked on translations late into the evening, I stayed busy helping Nadira with household chores and meals. Occasionally, I turned on the TV, and although I was thankful for the distraction, the programming was severely limited during the day. *Argh . . . I wish there was more to do inside the apartment.*

Late afternoon on the second day, while I sat on the sofa and thumbed through an old French magazine, Nadira approached and cleared her throat. "*Excuse-moi.*" She fidgeted with the dishtowel in her hands. "Can I ask you for a favor? Could you watch Omar and Ali while I run some errands?"

"Yes, of course." I laid the magazine aside and swung my feet to the floor. "I'm glad you asked." I meant it—this would be a welcome distraction.

Once Nadira left, the boys and I played with their trucks for a while—building roadways and towns—until they grew tired of the game and knocked them down. Looking for a second option, I grabbed a book about animals from the toy box and plopped down on the couch. Even though Omar and Ali's first language was Arabic, I knew they would enjoy my next activity once they got the hang of it.

"Come sit," I said, patting the seats beside me.

The two boys scampered onto the sofa and settled against my thighs. I turned to the first page and pointed to the animal. Using my singsong voice, I asked, "What does the cow say? The cow says, 'moo'!"

Delighted, the boys laughed as they turned the pages, pointing to each picture with saucer eyes. "What does the duck say? The duck says, 'quack'!"

This went on until we finished the story. Then the boys flipped back to page one and we started the process all over again. When Nadira returned home an hour later, we were still "reading" on the couch.

Midmorning on day three, trying to stay busy at the apartment, I lay on the bed and penned a letter to my dad. Then I wrote an entry in my diary.

> *The reason I have mingled these days is simply because there is not much to say about them. Although I find Nadira gentle and kind, my surroundings are sometimes more than depressing.*

When I reread my words, my vision blurred and I pushed my diary aside. I missed my family. I missed my friends. Most of all, I missed my stable life back home.

Given my unhappy state of mind, gloomy thoughts materialized. Would life in France always be like this with Michel—moving around, wondering where we'd get our next dime? I cared for him deeply, but it was difficult to consider a future with him under these circumstances.

What if he came to America? Would I have to support us? *I'm not sure that I want to become a flight attendant anymore, so where would that leave us?* Things would be so different if he had a reliable profession. And what about his psychology degree? *Every time I bring it up, he tells me, "It's on hold for the time being." What does that mean?*

I paced the short distance between the bed and dresser. *I wish there was more to do here. I feel like I'll go crazy. I need to talk to him.*

I walked down the hall and knocked on the office door. After a few seconds, Michel answered.

"I'm sorry to interrupt you," I said. "Can we talk for a moment?"

"Of course."

He murmured some words in Arabic over his shoulder and I heard Mahir's muffled response. He followed me into the bedroom and closed the door.

Swallowing hard, I tried to control my emotions. "It would be nice to get out of the house for a while. Maybe we could get a cup of coffee somewhere?"

A muscle twitched in his jaw. "I'd like to, *ma belle*, really I would . . ." He combed a slender hand through his unruly hair. "But we're nearing the end of the project and I can't stop now."

My lip quivered and, when I looked away, Michel grasped my chin and turned my face toward his. "I know you're unhappy here. If things go as planned, maybe we can return to Paris tomorrow. Would you like that?"

"*Oui, je veux bien.*" I rested my head against his chest and he held me close as I cried into his sweater. Eventually, he passed me a Kleenex, and I dabbed at my eyes and blew my nose. "I'm sorry, Michel. I don't mean to be such a baby. I think I'm just feeling a bit homesick."

"That's okay. I know it's been boring for you here." Then with a bit more enthusiasm, he said, "Hey, why don't you take a walk? It's a nice day, and there's a café a short distance away. Maybe Nadira and the boys will go with you?"

My spirits lifted and I managed a weak smile. "Yes, I think I'll do that."

"*Bien.*" He gave me a quick peck and left.

Leaning against the closed door, I thought about Michel's reaction. He was trying hard to please me. Maybe I just needed to be more patient.

65

————◆:◆————

*W*hen our train arrived back in Paris the following afternoon, moderate temperatures and blue skies heightened my good mood. *I'm so glad Michel finished his project with Mahir. It feels great to be back in the city.*

"Hey, I've got an idea." Michel squeezed my hand as we neared the apartment. "Why don't we cook at home tonight?"

"Okay. Do you have something in mind?"

Michel pursed his lips and I could almost see his thoughts churning. "How about *Kofta*? It's a Middle Eastern meatloaf."

"I have no idea how that differs from regular meatloaf, but I'm willing to give it a try."

"*Bien*. There's a grocer up ahead."

We entered the store, I grabbed a basket and we gathered ingredients, both of us giggling as Michel tried to maneuver our bulky suitcase down narrow aisles. Once we found our meatloaf essentials—onions, garlic, parsley, cumin, coriander, and chili flakes—we moved on to the side dish.

"How about eggplant?" he asked.

I shrugged. "I've never had that either."

"Ha! Then you're in for a double treat." Michel grabbed an oblong purple fruit. We added a can of crushed red tomatoes and parmesan cheese to the basket and made our way to the cash register.

Back out on the sidewalk, we popped into three more places—a bakery for a couple of baguettes, the butcher for half a kilogram of ground lamb and the local wine shop for two bottles of *vin rouge*, red wine.

"Thank goodness we're close to home," I said, my triceps quivering with the heavy load.

Amusement flickered across Michel's face as he adjusted his packages. "Yeah, but we still have three flights of stairs."

Once inside the apartment, we unpacked the groceries in the kitchen. I stood close by and watched while Michel mixed the lamb and spices together, formed four large oblong balls and set them aside. The sauce for the eggplant came next—crushed tomato puree, garlic, basil and sugar. When it came to a boil, a delightful aroma filled the air.

"How long before dinner's ready?" I asked glancing at the clock on the wall.

"About an hour."

"That's perfect. I think I'll take a bath."

Michel pulled me into his arms and his voice turned husky. "*Bonne idée.* Maybe I'll join you."

I smiled. "That's not exactly what I had in mind. I was looking forward to a relaxing bubble bath."

"*Tant mieux,*" Michel said brushing his lips against mine. "I'll scrub your back . . ."

Laughing, I shook my head, wiggled out of his embrace, and scurried down the hall to the bathroom.

Two hours later, after we consumed his fabulous meal, we both sat back with sated grins.

"That was delicious, Michel—moist and flavorful." I downed my last gulp of wine.

Michel nodded. "I'm so glad you liked it."

When the doorbell rang, both of us startled.

"I wonder who that could be?"

My pulse jumped as I followed him down the hall. When he opened the door, two strange, dark-haired men stood there, one of them holding a bottle of ouzo in the air. It took Michel a few seconds to react, but then he laughed and pulled them into an embrace while excited Arabic punctuated the air.

"Linda, this is Jordan, and this guy . . ." He slapped the back of taller man. "Is my old friend Rahim."

"*Enchantée,*" I said, shaking hands.

After a short, polite conversation in French, both men turned to Michel and resumed speaking Arabic. He led them into the kitchen, leaving me to trail behind.

Feeling out of place, unable to understand the discussion, I stood to the side and watched as Michel pulled three glasses from the cupboard, added ice and poured big measures of ouzo. There was joviality and backslapping as the three men drank and bantered back and forth.

He didn't even ask if I wanted one. It was like I didn't exist. *I get that these guys are old friends, but come on!*

"Linda, can you find something for my friends to eat?"

I plunked Camembert, Brie, and baguette on a wooden tray and laid it on the counter.

Michel didn't thank me as he gestured at the food. "*Bien*, dig in guys."

Okay, now I'm getting mad. I drew slow, steady breaths, walked to the wine bottle and refilled my glass. When the trio moved toward the salon, I grabbed Michel's upper arm and he waved Jordan and Rahim forward.

"You're all ignoring me. Are you guys going to speak Arabic all night?"

"I'm sorry if you feel left out, but I haven't seen Rahim in years. Maybe you can find something else to do?"

"Like what?" My words came out harsher than I intended.

Michel stiffened and his right eyebrow lifted. "I don't know . . . maybe you can wash the dishes."

"Fine. Go ahead and join your friends."

He shrugged and left the room.

What a drag. The evening was going so well, and now this. I frowned and downed my glass of wine.

After I cleaned the kitchen and wrote a few letters, monotony drove me down the hall toward the salon. As I approached the arched entrance, a familiar, unmistakable smell wafted my way. *Somebody's smoking pot.*

Three glassy-eyed men turned and stared at me. "*Salut*," Michel finally said with a grin, patting the seat next to him.

An uneasy feeling settled in my stomach as I sat down. "What are you guys smoking?" I raised my eyebrows at the strange-looking cigarette in the ashtray.

It took Michel a few seconds to respond. "Rahim brought over some hashish. It's been a long time since I've smoked Black Lebanese and this is good stuff."

During my teenage years on Whidbey Island, and beyond, I'd smoked my share of pot. On a few occasions, I even tried hash. At parties and clubs, someone would pass around a joint, and "*voilà*," the atmosphere changed—music sounded clearer, jokes and stories appeared funnier, and food tasted better. Unfortunately, on occasion, it made me intensely paranoid.

"Do you want to try a hit?" Michel asked, sluggishly reaching for the hash.

I hesitated. *It's probably not a good idea.* I was still irritated with him and I didn't want to risk magnifying those feelings. "No, thank you. I think I'll go to bed."

I waited for him to ask me to stay, but instead he wiped his hands on his pants, and said, "*D'accord.* I'll see you in a little while."

When he leaned in for a kiss, I resisted the urge to pull away. Forcing a smile, I turned to Jordan and Rahim. "*Bonne nuit.*"

They paused their conversation and mumbled a few polite phrases. I rose from the couch and left the room.

Wouldn't you know it? Our first night back in Paris, and we spend it like this. Michel was so weird around his friends. Tomorrow, we definitely had some things to discuss.

66

*T*he following morning, I felt a nudge on my arm. When I opened my eyes, I discovered Michel crouching near my shoulder. "*Bonjour.*"

I sat up and a rush of nausea brought my hand to my lips. *Damn. Why did I down that fourth glass of red wine before bed?* "What time is it?"

He stood and shoved his hands into the front pockets of his gray pants. "Almost ten o'clock."

Memories from last evening swamped my mind, and I felt my stomach lurch. "What time did your friends leave?"

"Around midnight."

"Oh . . ."

Michel's coffee-brown eyes followed me as I tugged on blue jeans and a purple V-neck sweater. The moment I stood, pain spiked my head and I massaged my temples. "We need to talk," I said, keeping my voice low. "But first I need some pain medicine and I'm out of Tylenol. Do you have any?"

He nodded. "There's a packet of *Doliprane* in the bathroom."

I followed him out of the bedroom and, five minutes later, I tracked him down in the kitchen, seated at the table. Pausing at the stove, I poured myself a cup of coffee, stirred in milk and rested my back against the counter. "You and your friends were very rude to me last night."

Michel took out a cigarette and rolled it between his fingers, taking his sweet time before responding. "So, you're not angry about the hashish?"

I blinked. "What . . . no." I shook my head, gently. "I was surprised to find you guys high in the salon, but that's not why I'm upset. I've smoked pot lots of times."

He relaxed and lit his cigarette. "I'm relieved to hear that. So, what exactly are you mad about?"

I felt my face heat as I walked over and took the seat opposite him. "After your friends arrived last night, why didn't you insist that everyone speak French? You all ignored me . . . it was like I wasn't even in the room. I never did that to you when I was around my American friends."

Michel blanched. "I'm sorry." The words sounded contrite. "It was such a surprise when they showed up. I must have got caught up in the moment."

"What about Jordan and Rahim?" I asked, wrapping my fingers around my coffee cup. "Why would your friends treat me that way? Is it because I'm a woman?"

He stiffened and looked away. "I suppose that's possible. I'm not sure."

"I didn't like it, Michel."

"Okay, I get that. I promise to pay more attention next time," he said, tapping his cigarette against the ashtray.

We both sipped our coffee in silence and, when I stood to refill my cup, Michel came up behind me and wrapped his arms around my waist. "Are we okay now?"

"I suppose so." I turned to face him.

He lightly kissed my lips. "And what about your headache? Do you feel better?"

"Yeah, it's almost gone."

"*C'est bon.*" He scattered random kisses on my lids, my nose and forehead. "Why don't you let me make up for last night? It was our first evening back in Paris and I didn't get a chance to welcome you properly."

Our eyes linked and I couldn't stop my smile. "Michel, I can't believe you've managed to charm me out of my bad mood. I think you must have been a poet in a past life." My snort surprised both of us. "Or maybe a gigolo."

He threw his head back and guffawed. "*Mais non*—not a chance. I've always been fussy about my women." As his finger outlined my jaw, his eyes darkened. "And right now, all I want is you, *ma belle.* Only you."

67

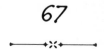

*T*hree days later, early in the afternoon, Michel and I huddled under his umbrella and walked outside into a downpour. As we rushed toward the *métro*, avoiding puddles, people scurried for the nearest shelter.

When we passed a bakery, scrumptious aromas wafted our way and Michel turned to me with a welcome suggestion. "Why don't we stop in here for a moment?"

"Okay."

We parked our umbrella at the door and entered the fragrant shop, inhaling deeply as we maneuvered around display cases filled with breads. There was a short line at the cashier's and we slid behind a woman at the end.

"What would you like?" Michel asked.

I peeked around the customers in front of us and searched the shelves, drooling, until a favorite pastry caught my attention. "Can I have a chocolate brioche, please?"

"*Bien sûr.*"

When it was our turn, Michel placed our order and we ate our pastries near the entrance, waiting for the downpour to subside.

"I can't wait to see *Notre-Dame*," I said taking a bite of my brioche. "Too bad it's raining. I've been looking forward to this for days."

Michel smiled. "*Je t'en prie.* The weather is supposed to improve. I just hope there's not a long line."

The downpour subsided, but a drizzle remained as we descended the stairs into the Bastille station. Five minutes later, we arrived at the west façade of the cathedral and slipped into the end of the short queue.

"Wow!" My voice filled with wonder as my eyes followed the massive, grandiose structure heavenward, pausing to admire the vertical and horizontal lines and the huge, round rose carved in the center of the church. "How old is the cathedral?"

"Twelfth century, I believe."

"*Vraiment?* I think the *Cathédrale Saint-Gatien* in Tours was built around that same timeframe."

"Yeah, I think you're right." Michel pointed up. "See those statues perched on the ledges?"

"Uh-huh."

"They're called *gargouilles* and they aren't just ornamental. They actually help drain water off of the roof."

I raised my eyebrows. "Really? How clever."

The line moved quickly and, moments later, we entered the building through a wooden door, nestled inside one of the three large, heavily decorated portals. It took a few seconds for my eyes to adjust to the dim lighting and, when I saw the holy water stoup near the door, I immersed my fingers and made the sign of the cross. Out of the corner of my eye, I saw Michel grimace.

"You take your religion seriously, don't you?" He whispered over my shoulder.

I felt a surge of adrenaline. "Yes, I do." *What a strange question. He already knows that. I'd really like to hear his view on religion someday, but not while we're inside the cathedral.*

We moved forward, past the pews, and my mouth went dry as I took in the nave's towering heights filled with graceful carved arches. A massive altar, embellished with a flamboyant organ that looked like a wall of pipes, and intricate, rainbow-colored stained glass windows, filled the apse.

"It's beyond beautiful," I finally said, unable to find the right words for something so incredible and spiritual.

Michel nodded. "*Ouais.*"

I moved away from him and over to the candle-lighting area, placed some coins in the slot, lit three candles and bowed my head in prayer. *Please keep my mother, father and brother safe from harm.*

When I rejoined Michel, I noted his compressed lips, but he kept his thoughts to himself as we exited.

Once we were outside, I glanced his way. "Are you hungry? Shall we get something to eat on the way home?"

"Sure. Why don't we stop in the Latin Quarter for lunch?"

I worried my lip for a moment and then looped my arm through his. "Michel, we haven't talked about religion since Christmas day. I'd like to hear your point of view."

"It's really quite simple," he said, steering me around a puddle. "I dislike all organized religions. I believe that God exists not in churches, mosques or synagogues, but everywhere, and in everything."

"Can you please repeat that?"

He repeated his viewpoint and then watched me, his eyebrows lifting expectantly as I mulled it over in my mind.

"If God exists everywhere, then he's also in the churches, mosques and synagogues, right?"

Michel stopped and turned to face me. "I suppose, but with organized religions, it's all or nothing."

My throat tightened. "Well, I enjoy going to church, especially at certain times of the year, like Christmas."

"Ha! Christmas is the biggest sham of all." He released my arm and his tone turned challenging. "Certainly you can see that?"

Hmm, he's getting irritated. I got that he felt strongly about this subject, but he needed to accept my point of view too. I raised my chin and my words came out firm. "Your argument isn't unreasonable, Michel, but you can't expect me to change my mind so easily, or so quickly."

He threw his cigarette on the ground and I noted the pinched, angry expression on his face. "Why don't we drop this for now?"

I was glad he wasn't pushing me, but this was a real bummer. I'd hoped to attend a Catholic Mass while I was in Paris, but now I was certain Michel would disapprove. *I don't like this side of him.*

We didn't speak for a few minutes, and then Michel rolled his shoulders and grabbed my hand. "*Bien,* why don't we go and see a movie after lunch? There's a new Jerry Lewis film in town called *Hardly Working.* I think we both could use a bit of levity right now."

Michel was right. A good laugh might lighten the mood and put us back on track.

"Good idea," I replied, hurrying to keep up with his robust stride.

68

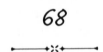

*O*n the evening of April fourteenth, Michel and I heard a knock on the door. "That must be our new roommate," he said, laying his book aside and rising off the couch.

Curious, I followed him to the door and looked over his shoulder as he pulled it open.

"*Salut!* I'm Marie-Christine."

A pretty, young woman in her mid-twenties, with shoulder-length, wavy auburn hair and sky blue eyes, offered her gloved hand to Michel, and then me. Her stylish red coat opened slightly and I noted her voluptuous figure—large breasts and tiny waist.

"*Enchantée,*" I said with a smile. "Please come in."

She reached for her suitcase and Michel's brow furrowed. "Here, let me help you with that."

"Thank you," Marie-Christine said, moving to the side. "Lugging my bag up those stairs almost killed me."

"*Mais oui.*" Michel picked up her suitcase and followed her inside.

"Wow!" She paused at the arched entrance to the salon and her hand flew to her chest. "It's been a few months since I've been here. I forgot how big this room is."

"Yeah," I said with a nod. "The high ceilings make it look even bigger than it is."

We continued single file down the hall while Michel talked to Marie-Christine over his shoulder. "Just to refresh your memory, the kitchen's straight ahead. That's the bathroom, next to our room. This one belongs to you."

Marie-Christine walked through the entrance and a subtle grin crossed her lips as she removed her leather gloves. "Yes. I remember the lovely decor."

Michel placed her bag on the floor. "*Alors,* I suppose you'd like to settle in."

"Thanks for the help." Her forehead wrinkled and a note of concern colored her words. "I should warn you that some friends are dropping by later this evening with the rest of my things. I hope you don't mind."

He shrugged. "It's nice of you to ask, but the apartment belongs to all of us now."

"*Bien.*" Marie-Christine reached down and slipped off one black, high-heeled shoe. "I have a feeling that this arrangement will work out perfectly."

Just after eight o'clock, a crowd filed through the door—two girls, each holding boxes and bottles of wine, a man with a guitar, and two men, carrying a large television.

"Wait a minute." Marie-Christine stopped the guys with the TV and turned to Michel. "Where do you want them to put this? In the salon?"

I shifted my gaze to Michel. *Right on!* I couldn't believe it—we'd be able to watch television. My wish had come true.

"*Je veux bien.*" He quickly cleared an end table. The two guys stumbled forward, set the TV on the table, and straightened, gasping for air.

After this, Marie-Christine introduced her friends and greetings ping-ponged between us. None of them spoke more than a few words of English and I tensed as I tried to answer their rapid-fire questions in French. I couldn't wait to break up into smaller groups.

When Michel wrapped his arm around my waist and made an announcement, I sagged against him. "Hey everyone, follow me and we'll get some drinks."

I moved toward the kitchen, but Marie-Christine and her friend, Brigitte, caught my eye, beckoning me with little waves.

"Michel, I'll meet you in the kitchen."

"Okay." He released me and I joined the two girls. "What's up?"

Marie-Christine leaned in with a secretive tone. "Is it okay with you and Michel if we smoke some hashish tonight?"

"Yes, of course." *Hmm . . . hash again. It must be easier to find than pot.*

I heard the relief in her voice. "Good. I thought so, but it's always better to ask first."

Everyone returned to the salon with his or her drink and the impromptu party got under way. The couch and chair filled up quickly. The rest of us settled for the floor with our backs against the wall.

"What do you think of Marie-Christine and her friends?" I whispered, squeezing in next to Michel.

"They seem nice. What do you think?"

"I agree."

Conversations commenced and soon the smell of pot permeated the air. When the hash reached me, I took a big toke before passing it on to Michel.

"Are you sure you're okay with this?" he asked, inhaling deep.

I nodded and coughed slightly. "*Oui* . . . I just hope I don't forget how to speak French."

He patted my thigh and passed the hash to Marie-Christine. By the time it came around for the third time, I started to catch a buzz.

"This is good stuff," I told Michel, unable to hold back a giggle.

His slow smile stretched clear across his face. "It sure is."

The volume and laughter in the room increased. Eventually, Serge brought out his guitar, and the group sang familiar folk songs, like "Mr. Tamborine Man" by the Byrds and "Bridge Over Troubled Water" by Simon & Garfunkel. I was so absorbed in the music, I didn't notice Michel was missing until someone asked about Marie-Christine. *I wonder where they are.*

I found them in the kitchen, facing each other, drinking ouzo, deep in a discussion. They barely glanced my way when I entered the room. A surge of jealousy clenched my jaw.

"What are you guys talking about?" I asked, cuddling against Michel and grabbing his bicep.

The corner of his mouth twitched and he raised a brow. "Marie-Christine took two psychology classes in college. We've been discussing some of her textbook cases."

"Oh . . ." There was an awkward silence while I tried to think of something else to say. *Damn, now I wish I wasn't high.* Of course he found this subject interesting. I would have found it interesting, too, if he would have brought me into the conversation. "Well, I didn't mean to interrupt. I'll just grab some more wine and you two can continue your chat."

Back in the salon, I took a seat next to Brigitte and, for the next hour, we sat mesmerized in front of a television series called *Médecins de Nuit,* Night Doctors. When the next program came on, I checked my wrist. *What? No wonder I'm tired. It's almost one o'clock.*

I walked back into the kitchen and laid my head on Michel's shoulder. "It's getting late. Don't you think it's time for bed?"

"You go ahead. I'll be in shortly."

My body tensed. "I'd really like it if you joined me."

Marie-Christine's eyes darted back and forth between Michel and me. "Actually, it's getting late." She walked over and placed her glass in the sink. "Tomorrow's my day off, but I have a ton of errands to run."

Michel downed the rest of his ouzo. "*Bien,* then I guess we'll see you in the morning. *Salut.*"

"*Salut.*" Marie-Christine nodded.

I followed Michel into our bedroom and, as soon as I closed the door, he crossed his arms and glared in my direction. "Did you have a problem with me and Marie-Christine?"

"No . . . er . . . maybe."

"Why? We were only talking."

I felt my face flush. "I know that, but when I found you in the kitchen with her, you certainly didn't make me feel welcome. How would you like it if I did the same thing to you with a man we just met?"

"Oh, come on. It's been a while since I've talked with an intelligent woman, and I was fascinated with her perspective."

I felt my chest tighten. "Oh great—now I get to hear how clever she is compared to me?"

"Ack . . ." He threw his eyes to the ceiling and approached me. I stepped back and he stopped. "*Merde!* I didn't mean it that way. I've told you many times how smart I think you are, but you don't have the French vocabulary that she has. Honestly, I think you're overreacting."

My vision blurred and my voice cracked. "It doesn't feel like it to me."

"*Eh bien*, I can see that." Michel rubbed the back of his neck, pulled out his pack of Marlboro Lights and lit a cigarette. I watched him walk over to the window and draw back the curtains as he took a deep drag.

Maybe he's right. My emotions felt out of control these days and I was sure the pot made me super sensitive. I grabbed a Kleenex and blew my nose.

"Michel?"

His coffee-brown eyes met mine.

"Can we just go to bed now? I'm so sleepy—I can't think straight."

"That's probably a good idea."

He ground his cigarette in the ashtray and after we took turns in the bathroom, Michel clicked off the light and crawled into bed. He didn't kiss me goodnight, but I was too tired to care.

69

I woke up alone the next morning and my eyes immediately flew to the clock. *Hmm . . . just past ten. I wonder where Michel is.* I pulled on my jeans and a long-sleeved T-shirt, and pushed a brush through my hair before slipping into the kitchen.

"*Bonjour,* Michel."

His head jerked up from a newspaper and he attempted a smile. "*Salut.*"

"Have you been up long?" I poured myself a cup of coffee from the pot on the stove and added milk.

"No, about a half an hour."

I took a sip and then slid into the seat across from him.

"How do you feel this morning?" His eyebrows formed a knot above his nose. "Would you like to continue our discussion from last night?"

Memories swept through me and I froze with indecision. "No, Michel. I probably overreacted because I was stoned. I think we should let it go."

"*Comme tu veux,*" as you wish, he said with a shrug. His eyes followed me as I sipped my coffee. He appeared to be assessing my mood. "Did you remember that I'm going to Grigny today?"

"Oh, no . . . I'd lost track of that." I felt my shoulders slump. "How long will you be gone?"

"Three nights."

"Mmm . . ." I bit my lip as competing thoughts raced through my mind: *I hate to be away from him for that long, but I'd rather stay in Paris. I hope Marie-Christine and I get along while he's gone.* "Well, I'm glad that Mahir has another translation job for you."

"*Ouais.*" He ran his hands through his hair and pulled it into a ponytail. "It's a small job, so I'm hoping he'll give me an advance on the next one."

I sat up straight. "Why? Are you running low on money?"

He hesitated, and I noticed a muscle twitch in his jaw. "No . . . not really. I'm just thinking about the future."

"Good, because my two hundred francs has to last for three weeks."

He averted his eyes. "Like I said, I don't think that'll be a problem."

After Michel left for Grigny, I took a walk to explore Paris on my own. I caught the *métro* line 5 up to *République* and tip-tapped up the stairs to *Canal Saint-Martin*.

As I strolled along the canal, my thoughts turned to Michel. *I'm pretty sure he's broke again. I sure hope things go well for him in Grigny. What a shame—our life would be so different if this weren't a constant concern.*

London plane and horse chestnut trees awash with spring buds swayed in the breeze as I passed tourists toting cameras and young lovers entwined on benches. Ornate iron bridges spanning the gray-green waters came into view, and I stopped, fascinated by the interplay of a series of locks allowing boats to navigate through the narrow canal.

Curious about the melodious sounds coming from a group up ahead, I veered off course and peeked around a couple of bystanders. The enthusiastic musicians—a jaunty male accordionist and a tall, gangly female violinist—almost danced as they played one polka song after another while the crowd kept time. When they paused to rest, I deposited a few coins in their instrument case.

Continuing along the canal, I admired a woman sitting in front of an easel painting. She paused, smiled at me and then refocused on her palette, her paintbrush dipping into blues and greens before returning to her landscape. Mesmerized, I watched as a nearby tree came to life on the canvas.

"*Bien fait*," I said, my voice filled with awe.

The artist's chubby round cheeks turned pink as she shifted in her seat. "*Merci*, Mademoiselle. You are very kind."

After this, I ventured over and took one last look at the canal before returning to the apartment. According to Michel, Napoleon ordered the canal's construction in the early 1800s to ease barge congestion on the Seine and bring fresh water into Paris. During the 1960s, when boat traffic declined, officials considered filling it in and making it into a highway, but reason prevailed. I was so thankful they left it alone. It was such a wonderful place to lose yourself. *I'm glad I came.*

70

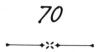

*T*hree days later, Michel returned home from Grigny and I met him at the train station. He was the last person to exit the coach and when I saw his familiar face, I felt my cheeks flush with pleasure. *He looks good . . . perhaps a little tired.*

We hugged and, after a quick kiss, he engulfed me in a warm embrace. "It's so good to see you. Mmm . . . and you smell nice too."

I relaxed in his arms. "I'm glad you're back, Michel."

He pushed me away gently and his voice was filled with concern as he searched my face. "Is everything okay? How did you and Marie-Christine get along?"

"Better than I expected. The TV is a great distraction."

"*J'imagine bien.*" I'll bet. He entwined his arm in mine and we headed toward the exit. When a runaway toddler crossed in front of us, pausing our progress, his mother swooped him into her arms. We shared a mutual smile with her and continued on our way.

"Did you get out of the apartment while I was gone? Michel asked, glancing my way. "I think you mentioned a visit to *Bois de Vincennes* Zoo."

"Uh-huh, yesterday. It was such a pretty day. I saw lots of animals. The elephants were fantastic and I spent an hour watching a panda bear eat bamboo."

I heard Michel's soft chuckle. "Yeah, animals can be very entertaining. I wish I could have joined you."

A second errand came to mind. *Should I bring this up now? I might as well get it over with—there'll never be a good time.* "I also stopped at the Pan Am office and arranged my flight home on May sixth."

"I see." His smile vanished and his mouth settled into a thin line.

"I won't pretend that makes me happy. I'm just glad we still have a few weeks before you leave."

"*Bien sûr.*" I squeezed his arm and quickly changed the subject. "*Alors,* how are things with Mahir and Nadira? Did he advance you the money?"

He stiffened. "No, he refused. I'm afraid we'll need to use your money after all. Oh, and I think you should ask your dad to send more."

My jaw dropped and I stopped in my tracks. "I can't do that, Michel. He's been so generous to me already, and . . ."

Michel didn't let me finish my sentence. "I realize that, but things have changed."

Our reunion was turning into a disaster. I was looking forward to seeing him today and now, we were arguing again. "It doesn't matter, Michel. I've already told you that my parents aren't rich. They had to scrape together this last six hundred dollars." I felt my emotions surge and I swallowed hard to keep my voice from quivering. "I promised them that was the last transfer I'd need."

We walked in silence for a while and when we neared the post office, Michel released my arm and faced me. "I'm sorry about this, really I am, but we're in a jam right now. Can't you just go inside and call your dad? A few hundred dollars is all we need to tide us over."

I saw the distress in his eyes and my heart lurched as an internal battle raged inside of me. *I know he's trying to find more work. I'd like to help, but it's too much to ask.*

"No, Michel." I let my hands drop to my side. "We'll just have to come up with another solution."

He gave me a troubled nod. "Okay, *ma belle,* you win. Things will be tight, but we'll get through it."

Frowning, we continued toward his apartment, both of us watching the sidewalk as it passed beneath our feet.

71

*T*he next six days blurred into one another. Since Michel and I were on a strict budget, we barely left the house except to get a cup of coffee at a nearby café or to take a walk. With limited options for entertainment, we fell into bad habits—staying up late, sleeping in until noon, getting high during the day, and watching TV for hours on end.

Early afternoon on the seventh day, I'd finally had enough. *I need to talk to Michel. We only have eleven days left together. I don't want to waste it like this.*

Following a familiar smell, I tracked down Michel in the salon smoking hash with Marie-Christine. When I entered the room, they both looked at me with blank expressions, and my stomach dropped. *Darn it, I wanted to catch him before he got stoned. Oh well, I don't have a choice now.*

I plopped beside him on the couch and leaned forward for a kiss. "*Salut. Ça va?*"

"*Ouais, ça va bien,*" he replied.

I smiled at Marie-Christine and then patted his thigh. "Can I talk to you for a moment please?"

Michel nodded and offered me the hash. "Sure, but do you want a toke first?"

I shook my head. "No thanks, not right now."

He followed me into the kitchen and we faced each other. "What's up?" he asked, shoving his hands into his pockets.

"I'm worried about our money situation. I only have fifty francs left, and I'll need some of that for my trip home."

Michel stiffened and studied his shoes. "*Alors,* I guess I'll have to ask Jordan for a loan. Do you want to come along?"

I shook my head. "No, I think you should go alone. That way you and Jordan can talk to each other in Arabic."

"You're right. I'll take a shower and head out."

"*Bien.*" I pushed my hair behind my ears. "Have you talked to Amir about that translation job in Tours? Didn't he ask you to call him at the end of April?"

"Yeah, you're right. I'll do that too."

When he started to leave, I placed my hand on his chest and forced a smile. "When you get back, maybe we can go grocery shopping? You've prepared a few meals for me, but I've never cooked for you."

A slow grin appeared on his face. "And what will you prepare?"

"How about stuffed peppers? It's one of my specialties."

"*Bonne idée.*" His coffee-brown eyes studied me for a moment, and then he cupped my face and brushed his lips against mine. "And afterwards . . . I'll show you my appreciation and we'll head over to the Latin Quarter for dessert."

Good, we need to reconnect. "I'd like that, Michel. It'll be so nice to have an evening out for a change."

72

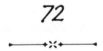

*A*s we approached *Montparnasse* station four days later, sunlight glinted off storefront windows and busy sparrows fluttered in and out of the honey locust trees lining the boulevard.

"It feels like spring, don't you think?" I smiled and unfastened the first few buttons on my coat.

"*Oui, c'est agréable.* April is one of my favorite months in Paris."

Once we arrived at the station, Michel purchased his ticket and we sat on a bench to discuss his timeline.

"*Bien*, I'll try to return from Tours tomorrow on the five o'clock train, but I can't promise." He paused and lit a cigarette. "If Amir has a translation job for me, it could be a bit later."

I smiled and snuggled against him. "That's fine. I'll be waiting for you at the apartment."

Michel lifted his chin and blew his smoke to the side. "So, tell me, what are you going to do today?"

"Well . . . on my way home, I'm going to stop at a travel agency and find out the best way to get from Paris to London on the sixth."

"Oh . . ." Michel stiffened and grabbed my hand. "You know, one of these days, we need to talk about our future plans. I've tried not to push you, but we don't have much time left together before you leave."

My stomach flip-flopped and I reluctantly met his gaze. "*Mais oui*, you're right, of course. Like I've said before, our money issues . . . especially lately . . . are a big concern."

"Yes, but what about love?" I could hear the impatience in his voice. "I want to spend the rest of my life with you. Everything else is secondary. First, you have to decide if you love me."

"*Départ pour Tours quai dix-huit!*" we heard over the loudspeaker, startling us. Departure for Tours platform eighteen!

"I have to go." Michel's hands cupped my face and he kissed me as we rose from the bench. "I'm sorry, *ma belle*, this was not the right time to bring this up. We'll talk more when I return from Tours."

"Okay," I replied, holding back a sigh.

When he reached the top of the stairs, Michel turned and waved before he slipped through the door.

Later that afternoon, I settled at the kitchen table and penned my last letter from France to my mom and dad, giving them my arrival date and time back in the US. When my diary caught my eye, I picked it up and held it, caressing the edges as I contemplated Michel's impassioned question a few hours earlier. He deserved some answers. Was I ready to give them to him?

I picked up my pen and wrote from the heart.

> *Do I love this man enough to marry him? Are his good qualities enough to make me forget his bad ones? Have I been as honest with him as I should have, and furthermore, have I been honest with myself?*

73

The following evening, I watched the kitchen clock strike six and then seven, but there was still no sign of Michel. Where was he? I hoped everything was okay.

I lit a cigarette and poured myself a glass of sauvignon. When the doorbell rang, I almost jumped out of my skin. *Who could this be? Michel has a key. I sure hope Marie-Christine remembered to tell her friends that she'd be out of town until Friday.*

When I opened the door, I forgot to breathe.

"Janice!"

I hugged her with gusto. "What are you doing here? Why aren't you at the institute?" Before she could answer, I turned to Michel, my eyes wide with wonder. "I can't believe it. Ringing the doorbell was sneaky."

Janice and I laughed and hugged each other again.

"*Entrez, entrez.*" I stepped aside and leaned over to give Michel a kiss. "This is such a wonderful surprise. Thank you so much."

His smile was triumphant. "I knew you'd be pleased."

After we toured the apartment, Michel poured two glasses of wine, a white for Janice and red for himself, and we settled in the salon.

"*Alors*, how did you two meet up?"

"We ran into each other yesterday at *Café Moderne*," Janice replied, setting her glass on the table. "It's the strangest thing. I was thinking about you, and when I looked up from my coffee, Michel was standing in front of me."

I slapped my thigh. "I still can't believe you're here. How long will you stay in Paris?"

"Actually, I'm done at the institute. I'll be heading home to California at the end of the week."

"Oh, I see. Do you have somewhere to stay tonight? You're welcome to use our couch—right, Michel?"

"*Oui, bien sûr.*"

A grin spread across her face. "I was hoping you'd say that. Tomorrow, I'll catch the train to Orly so I can spend a few days with my grandmother."

When I opened my mouth to speak, Michel interrupted me. "Listen, I can see that you two have a lot to catch up on. Why don't I take a shower and when I'm finished, maybe we can walk over to *boulevard Saint-Michel* to get a drink and a bite to eat."

My eyes flew to my friend. "Is that okay with you?"

"It sounds like fun."

After Michel left, we quickly resumed our conversation—in English this time. "I had no idea you had relatives in France."

"Yeah, well, I guess it never came up. She's my dad's mom. Years ago, she married a Frenchman and has lived here ever since."

"That's so cool. So, when is your flight home?"

"I'm not sure." She removed her shoes and curled her feet under her side. "I have to stop at the Pan Am office tomorrow to confirm my seat. What about you?"

"My plane leaves at 4:05 p.m. on May sixth. Hey, I just thought of something. I've already booked the channel hovercraft for that morning. Maybe we can go to London together?"

Janice shrugged. "Why not? It's worth a try."

Our conversation continued nonstop as we discussed one subject after another—the institute, Julie, Albert, the sights I'd seen in Paris, and my trip to Grigny.

"I can't believe you tried belly dancing," Janice said, shaking her head as she took a sip of wine.

"Yeah, well, unfortunately, it was the highlight of that trip."

"What do you mean?"

I glanced at the salon entrance and lowered my volume. "I don't want to get into right now, but Michel and I have had some rough times in Paris, especially with money."

Janice paled and averted her eyes. "I . . . I'm sorry to hear that."

Huh? Why would that upset her? Before I had a chance to ask, Michel rejoined us in the salon.

"*Eh bien,* are you girls ready to go?"

We stood and Janice glanced my way. "Um . . . where's the bathroom again?"

"Down the hall, third door on the right."

After she left, I cuddled up to Michel. "Thank you so much for bringing Janice home with you," I purred.

"You're welcome." His lips caressed my forehead. "I knew it would make you happy. I'm so glad it worked out."

The tender kiss that followed warmed my insides. "I almost hate to ask, Michel, but did Amir find more work for you?"

"Yes, and it's a large job so it should last a while."

I released my breath. "Good. That must be big relief for you."

"*Mais oui.*"

When Janice returned, we slipped on our coats and exited the apartment, rattling down the three flights of stairs. Arm in arm, jesting back and forth, we ambled down the street toward the *métro*. For the first time in days, I felt content. Content to be with Michel and Janice. Content to be in Paris on such a lovely night.

74

*T*he following afternoon, after Michel and I dropped Janice at the train station, we stopped for coffee at *L'Oiseau Bleu*. The quaint, royal blue restaurant, nestled under one of the grand old buildings in the Latin Quarter, was a popular destination on *boulevard Saint-Michel*. Red awnings sheltered three large, paned windows and an open-air section offered guests a prime seat to people watch while they ate a meal.

Given the mild temperatures, Michel asked for a seat outside.

"Will this be okay, Monsieur?" the waiter asked, escorting us to a table nearby.

"Yes, this will be fine."

Once we took our seats, Michel ordered two coffees. The waiter nodded and walked away.

"*Alors*, when does Janice return to Paris?" Michel lit a cigarette and laid his pack on the table.

"The morning of the fourth."

"*Bien.*" He leaned back and the smell of smoke drifted my way. "Why don't we visit the *Tour Eiffel* and *Louvre* that day?"

"That would be fantastic! She mentioned that she wanted to see those sights." The entrance fees came to mind and my stomach lurched. "Do we have the money?"

Our waiter arrived with our coffees. Michel offered him a quick "*merci*" before plopping in two sugars and stirring. "Yes . . . well . . . I didn't mention this yesterday, but Janice loaned me one hundred and fifty francs."

My cup hit the saucer. "What? I can't believe you did that!" A jolt of anger surged through my body. *That explains her odd reaction when I mentioned our money problems yesterday.* "How will you pay her back? You still owe money to Jordan."

"Like I said, I have a big job coming up. I'll send her a bank check in a couple of weeks." We stared at each other for a few seconds, and then Michel looked away and took a sip of coffee. "You don't have much faith in me, do you?"

"It has nothing to do with faith, Michel." Weeks of pent-up frustration surfaced and heated words spilled from my mouth. "As far as I'm concerned, you need to find a real job and learn how to follow a budget. Last night, I suggested we split a meal, but you wouldn't listen." I grabbed a cigarette from his pack, lit it and hurled my match in the ashtray. "*Zut alors*, I'm not great with money, but you're impossible."

He winced and his body sagged. "You're right. My translation jobs are becoming less and less stable. I should have finished my psychology degree a long time ago . . ." His words trailed off. "Maybe I needed someone like you to come along." He sat up straight. "With your help, I still might be able to do it."

"What do you mean?"

"Once you become a flight attendant, I could enroll in college—either here or in the United States—and you could support us until I finish my studies."

My mouth went dry. "Whoa, Michel. I'm still stuck on the fact that you asked Janice for money. And if you recall, I'm no longer sure that I want to become a flight attendant."

"I know, I know, but this is only one option." Michel exhaled and rubbed the back of his neck.

"*Voulez-vous autre chose,* Monsieur?" Would you like something else? Our waiter's sudden appearance turned our heads.

"*Non, merci.*"

Once our server moved on, Michel reached in his pocket and threw some money on the table. "Let's get out of here."

We walked along the sidewalk, neither one of us talking. Finally, Michel pulled me into a doorway and broke the silence. "I'm sorry, *ma belle.* I knew that you'd be angry with me about the loan. That's why I didn't tell you yesterday. You know I'll pay her back, right?"

"Yes . . . yes, I know you will. It's just a shock, that's all."

"And what about the things you said? I know that you're frustrated with me. I'm afraid that you'll leave Paris in a few days and I'll never see you again."

His words sounded so earnest, a lump formed in my throat.

"Michel, I don't want that to happen any more than you do." I swallowed hard to keep my voice from cracking. "It's just that we've had so many arguments lately, especially about money. The pressure is really getting to me . . ."

I laid my head on his shoulder and he held me close, stroking my hair. "Listen, *ma belle.* Why don't we avoid these heavy conversations and just enjoy these next three days together alone."

"Can we?" I met his gaze. "I'd like that very much."

We stood there for several seconds, and then he draped his arm around my shoulders and we continued down the street. Now that I had spoken my mind, I felt a renewed closeness with Michel and, for the first time in weeks, I looked forward to spending some quality time with him. Our future together was still uncertain, but at least now, I could collect my thoughts without the added pressure of his persistent questions.

75

*L*ate in the morning on May fourth, Janice returned to Paris. After a quick *petit déjeuner* at the apartment—baguette, jam and coffee—we caught the *métro* to the *Tour Eiffel*.

"I can't wait to see it up close," Janice said, her smile jubilant as we walked along the Seine.

"Yeah, me too."

All three of us turned our heads toward the river when we heard people shouting on a *Bateaux-Mouche,* tour boat, passing by the bulkhead. Given the moderate spring weather, crowds had formed on the upper open deck, many of them pointing and waving toward the iconic monument that loomed above us.

Following their lead, my eyes tracked the tower's lines all the way to the top and my breath caught. The elegant, sleek structure, composed of thousands of triangulated iron sections, looked as though it might rocket into the sky.

"*C'est magnifique!* Does anyone know when it was built?"

Michel tilted his head and scratched his day-old beard. "*Alors*, I believe that it was an engineer named Gustave Eiffel who designed and built it for the 1889 World Fair."

"Hmm . . ."

As we approached the base of the tower, two heavily armed French soldiers dressed in khaki, gripping submachine guns, came into view. They appraised us from top to bottom and gave us an authoritative nod.

"I don't think I'll ever get used to that," Janice said softly.

"Yeah, I've had a hard time with it too."

Once we were directly below the monument, I noted the flaking paint and rusting bolts. "It looks like it could use some paint."

"*Oui*," Michel said. "Apparently, there's been some mismanagement of funds. I think they're back on track and talking about a complete renovation in a few years." He walked over and stood directly under the monument. "Check this out."

Janice and I joined him. We all looked up through the iron latticework, marveling at the layers of crossed metal bars arranged in a distinct repeating-diagonal pattern.

"Can we go up to the observation level?" Janice asked.

Michel wandered over and joined the small crowd reading a sign near the elevator. "Normally we could, but it appears to be out of order today."

"*Tant pis.*" When an alternative route came to mind, I spun toward Michel. "Have you ever climbed the stairs?"

He shook his head. "*Mais non*, there must be hundreds."

"Oh, come on. I know we can do it."

Michel rolled his eyes and reluctantly followed us toward the staircase. It took us about fifteen minutes and our legs burned, especially near the top, but we were all smiles once we saw the incredible view.

Across the Seine to the northeast, we spotted *Trocadéro* gardens and the *Palais de Chaillot*, and from the southeast, down the *Champ de Mars*, we could see the *Tour Montparnasse* in the distance.

"Wow!" Janice exclaimed, pulling out her Pentax camera. "I'll be right back."

When she disappeared around the corner, I looped my arm through Michel's and laid my head on his shoulder. "The views are incredible. I'm so glad I saw this before I left Paris."

I felt him flinch. *Damn, why did I have to bring this up right now?*

I'd felt so close to Michel over the last three days. Every morning, he worked on his translations while I read or watched TV, and then in the afternoon, we'd make love or take a long walk. Most days, we'd shop for groceries and cook dinner at the apartment, and twice we invited Marie-Christine to join us. It had been a magical time, but now that Janice had returned, we both knew the end was near.

"*Je suis désolée*, Michel. I didn't mean to spoil the moment."

"It's okay, *ma belle*." His fingers brushed against my cheek. "We'll have to face reality sooner or later."

After we descended the stairs, we explored the *Champ de Mars* greenspace and then caught the *métro* to *place de la Concorde*. Once again, we toured the sights, walking past the *Obélisque de Luxor* and the fountains before entering the *Tuileries* Gardens. Soon the *Arc de Triomphe du Carrousel* came into view and, beyond that, the *Louvre Palace*.

As we advanced toward the imposing structure, Michel voiced his concerns. "Where are the crowds of people? I hope it's open today."

"I was thinking the same thing. It's Sunday, but that shouldn't matter."

We walked past the large, mostly empty courtyard and when Michel announced that the *Louvre* was closed, I felt my body slump with disappointment.

"What a shame. I was looking so forward to this." I gnawed on my bottom lip. "What should we do now?"

Michel shrugged and buried his hands in his coat pockets. "How about the cinema? *The Electric Horseman* starring Robert Redford is playing nearby."

I looked at Janice.

"Sure, why not?' she replied. "I haven't been to a movie while I've been in France."

"*On y va.*" Michel grabbed my hand and we retraced our steps back through the *Tuileries* Gardens where we caught the *métro* to the Latin Quarter.

After the movie, we ended up at a club and didn't return home until 2:00 a.m. Tipsy from the large quantity of wine we consumed, noisier than we should have been, we entered the apartment.

"Shhh." Michel placed his forefinger in front of his lips and then looked down the hall toward Marie-Christine's bedroom. "We need to be quiet."

"Okey dokey." Janice's giggle, followed by a hiccup and another giggle, threw everyone into a fit of laughter. When we finally recovered, Michel shushed everyone again, walked over to the hall closet, pulled down a pillow and blanket, and placed them on the couch.

Janice swayed and placed her hand on my shoulder. When she finally spoke, her words came out wobbly. "Thanks so much for today. I had such a good time."

Ooh . . . she is going to feel bad tomorrow. "Yeah, it was fun."

After a few quick hugs, Michel and I tiptoed down the hall and entered our bedroom.

As soon as he closed the door, I wrapped my arms around him and kissed him. "You taste good," I whispered against his lips.

Michel glanced at the clock. "It's kind of late, *ma belle.* Tomorrow's a big day."

Huh? Not really. "Come on. It won't take me long to pack." I pressed my body hard against his and kissed the hollow areas around his collarbones. "We only have two nights left."

He groaned. "*D'accord,* but I think you'll be sorry in the morning."

I smiled and pulled him toward the bed. "Oh, I doubt that very much."

76

"*L*inda?" Someone said, then again, a little louder. "Linda?"

I opened my eyes and discovered Michel on his side, watching me, with a slight smile on his face. "*Bonjour.*"

"*Bonjour.*" I glanced at the clock. *Nine o'clock?* "Why so early?" I asked, rubbing my eyes.

"Well . . . I'd like you to do something for me today. It might take a while."

I scooted closer to Michel and wrapped my arm across his chest. "Okay, what?"

I felt his body tense. "Visit the American Consulate with me?"

I pushed myself up to a sitting position. "Why?"

"So I can find out what kind of visa I'll need to get into the United States. I think we should do this while you're still here, don't you?"

My lungs compressed and I tried to think of a response. *What's wrong with me? This should make me happy.* "Yes . . . yes, you're right, of course."

Michel flipped the covers to the side, his demeanor suddenly turning jubilant as he pulled me to my feet. "Good. Then let's hurry and get dressed. We can grab some breakfast along the way."

"What about Janice?"

His lips twitched with amusement. "I have a feeling she's going to want to sleep in today. We'll leave her a note and sneak out quietly."

Four hours later, Michel and I wound our way back toward the apartment. His good mood had vanished and he barely spoke as he steered me around passersby, his long purposeful strides a challenge. *Damn, this is not how I imagined we'd spend our last day together.*

"*Alors,* that wasn't very helpful, was it?" I tried to keep my voice light and cheerful. "I can't believe they made us wait three hours for a ten-minute meeting with the consulate. Tell me again what you need to do to get a student visa in the US."

Michel frowned and combed his hand through his hair. "Like I said already, to start the process, they want me to return in July with a letter from the *Université François-Rabelais,* stating that I am a current student there."

"What exactly does this mean? Will you have to sign up for classes again?"

"No. I'm afraid that's impossible." His words were barely audible.

"Why?"

I felt his grip tighten around my arm. "Let's finish this discussion back at the apartment."

My stomach pitched and I stumbled. "Michel. Are you in some kind of trouble?"

"*Mais non* . . . well . . . sort of." He paused and his brow furrowed. "Once we get home, I'll explain everything, okay?"

Twenty minutes later, when we returned to an empty apartment, our note was gone, and we found a new one from Janice.

"*Bien,*" I said with sigh. "I'm glad we'll have the place to ourselves so we can finish our conversation."

Michel led me into the salon and we took a seat on the couch. "Would you like a smoke?"

"*Non, merci.*"

I watched him pull a cigarette from his pack. His hand trembled as he brought it to his lips and lit it.

"So, why can't you sign up for classes?"

"Because my residency—" His words came out scratchy, so he

cleared his throat and tried again. "Because my residency card is expired. It has been for years. That's why I work under the table doing translation jobs. No one else would hire me."

"Oh . . ." I suddenly felt light-headed. Had I understood him correctly? "Are you saying that you don't have a current visa?"

"Yes." Michel stood, walked over to the fireplace and flicked his cigarette ash. "I should have renewed it long ago. Now, I'm worried that they'll send me back to Lebanon if I bring it to their attention."

"But your mother is French?"

"Yes, but there are other complications."

This was unbelievable. "Why didn't you tell me about this sooner, Michel?" I almost choked on my words.

"I wanted to—really I did—but I was worried that if you learned the truth too soon, it would keep you from falling in love with me." His troubled gaze met mine. "In the end, it didn't matter."

My vision blurred instantly, and through the haze, I watched as Michel threw his cigarette in the fireplace and rejoined me on the couch.

"It's time for honesty, *ma belle*." He held my hands in his. "It's time to speak our minds."

Tears rolled down my face and an ache gripped my heart. "You're right, Michel. I care for you deeply, but I don't love you. Not the forever kind. You have so many qualities I admire—"

He stopped my words with a tender kiss, and then he pulled me into his arms and held me close while I quietly sobbed against his chest. "I'm sorry, really I am."

"You have nothing to be sorry for. As much as I hoped otherwise, part of me knew all along that it would end this way. I want you to know, I'm thankful we had this time together. I wouldn't have missed it for anything."

Fresh tears emerged and I choked out a response. "*Moi aussi.*"

We sat there on the couch, holding each other for a long time, and then I drew away and looked into his coffee-brown eyes. "What are you going to do about your visa?"

"For now, I'll leave things as they are."

My shoulders slumped. "There has to be more you can do."

"Don't worry about me." He brushed strands of wet hair from my cheeks. "I'll get by and, maybe one day, I'll find an answer."

Michel helped me to my feet and I excused myself to use the bathroom. I blew my nose and splashed cold water on my cheeks repeatedly, attempting to soothe my red, swollen eyes. After a while, I dried my face and exited the room.

When I heard a familiar voice in the kitchen, I lifted my chin, squared my shoulders and walked toward the sound.

"*Salut,* Janice. Where have you been?"

Our eyes met and concern flashed across her face, but she didn't ask any questions. "I bought some souvenirs and cashed in my francs."

"Good for you." I snuggled up next to Michel and he draped his arm around my shoulder. "I purchased a few things the other day too, but I have no idea where I'll put them. Are you all packed?"

"Yep."

"Listen, I have an idea," Michel said, turning to face me. "Why don't you finish packing while Janice and I go grocery shopping? I'd love to cook for you girls tonight."

"What a sweet suggestion. Thank you."

Janice frowned and shook her head. "Sounds good to me, but after last night, I'm laying off the wine."

As promised, Michel prepared a fabulous *boeuf bourguignon,* a beef stew to "soothe my soul." Succulent aromas filled the apartment as the beef simmered in a savory wine sauce with carrots, mushrooms, pearl onions, and diced bacon. Marie-Christine joined us for dinner and the *vin rouge* flowed freely. True to her word, Janice didn't touch a drop. I probably should have followed her lead because the alcohol only added to my melancholy.

"That was one of the best meals I've ever had," Marie-Christine said, dabbing at her lips with a napkin.

"Yes, it was." I raised my glass for a toast. "To Michel."

When our eyes linked, I saw his anguish and my lips trembled as I took a sip of wine. In an attempt to distract myself, I stood, collected the plates from the table, and filled the sink with soapy water.

Janice joined me and her whispered words only added to my misery. "You're definitely not yourself. You must be upset about leaving Michel."

I nodded and continued washing dishes while she patted me on the shoulder.

The rest of the evening progressed in slow motion, with Michel and me staring off into space and barely participating in conversations. At ten o'clock, we finally decided it was time to say goodnight.

"So, what time are you guys leaving in the morning?" Marie-Christine asked.

"We have to be at the *Gard du Nord* train station at 7:00 a.m., so we should probably leave around five-thirty, right, Michel?"

"Yeah, that will leave us plenty of time."

Janice's brow furrowed. "I don't have an alarm clock, so you'll have to wake me."

"Of course."

I turned to Marie-Christine. "Since I doubt I'll see you in the morning, I'll say goodbye now. Thanks so much for sharing your apartment with me."

She smiled. "You need to thank Michel, not me, but it was fun getting to know you. Have a safe trip home."

77

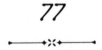

*W*hen the alarm sounded the following morning at 5:00 a.m., Michel clicked it off, reached over and pulled me into his arms.

"Well, I guess this is it."

I winced and tightened my grip. "I've been dreading this day for weeks."

"At least we made some memories last night, huh, *ma belle*?" His words were whisper soft against my hair.

"We sure did." Entangled in each other's arms, we stayed awake until 2:00 a.m. reminiscing about our time together, and then we made passionate love, both of us crying softly afterwards. It was a tender, poignant moment that would stay with me forever.

Michel kissed my forehead, shoved the covers aside and pulled on his clothes. I reluctantly followed his lead, my body shivering with anxiety as I stretched a turtleneck over my head and tugged on my blue jeans. Once we were dressed, I woke Janice and we took turns in the bathroom. A half an hour later, we all walked out the door with our suitcases in tow.

Given the early hour, the *métro* was empty and we arrived at the *Gard du Nord* forty-five minutes early.

"Let's get a cup of coffee," Michel said, surveying the area.

We jaywalked across the street and entered a tiny café nestled under a four-story building. In a private booth near the back, Michel ordered an espresso for himself and two *café au laits* for Janice and me.

"I don't know about you guys," Janice said, stifling a yawn, "but this is a crazy time to be up and about."

I rolled my shoulders and stretched my neck. "Yeah, it's too early for me too."

Our orders arrived, and we listened to Janice's chitchat while we smoked cigarettes and drank our coffees. She was a great distraction, but as our departure time approached, my stomach tightened with nervous energy.

"Listen, I'm sure you two would like some time alone together. Why don't I go and buy our train tickets?"

I exhaled and gave her a weak smile. "Thank you. That would be awesome."

After she walked away, I scooted closer to Michel. He wrapped his arm around me and pulled me close.

"What will you do after I leave? Will you go back to the apartment?" I fingered my ring as I spoke.

Seconds passed and I wondered if he heard me. When he finally answered, his voice sounded odd, almost dreamlike, prompting me to look at him.

"Once your train pulls away from the station, I'm going to go to the nearest bar and order a beer. While I'm waiting for it to arrive, I'll write the words 'I am sad' on a piece of paper. After I finish my drink, I'll put that piece of paper in my pocket and walk out of the bar feeling very much alone."

My vision blurred at his words. The image of Michel standing at a bar feeling dejected and forgotten, left my emotions raw and torn. *There must be something I can give him. I don't have much.*

With a trembling hand, I pulled my mother's ring from my finger and passed it to him. "Here. I want you to have this."

He looked at the ring and his brow furrowed. "Are you sure?"

A tear slid down my cheek and I swiped it away. "Yes."

Michel's coffee-brown eyes glistened as he slipped it onto his little finger. "I'll keep it forever and, whenever I look at it, I'll remember our time together."

Janice returned, he paid the bill and we walked toward the train station at a pace much slower than the hammering in my chest. Once we reached the platform, Janice said goodbye to Michel and then she stood to the side.

"I want you to believe me when I say I have no regrets. You were one of the best things that ever happened to me." His voice quivered as he pressed a note into my hand. "I wrote this poem for you the other day. You can read it later."

"Thank you." I tucked it carefully into my purse.

Michel kissed me, the kind of bittersweet kiss you want to last a lifetime. When we broke apart, I stifled a sob. "I'm going to miss you so much," I said, clinging to him.

"I'm going to miss you too, *ma belle*. More than you'll ever know."

Janice put her hand on my shoulder. "We need to go, Linda."

I picked up my bag and followed her to our coach. Before I slipped through the door, I turned and waved at Michel for the last time.

Janice led the way, and I followed, numb and blinded by tears. Once we stowed our luggage, I took the seat across from her, pulled out my Kleenex and blew my nose.

"That was rough, huh?"

I nodded and bit my lip to keep from crying. "Yeah."

She frowned and looked at me the way a psychologist looks at a patient when they're worried about them. "Do you want to talk about it?"

"Not right now." My mind felt cloudy with sorrow and fatigue. "I have some things to tell you, but I need to pull myself together first."

She patted my knee. "Okay."

I watched as she pulled a book from her suitcase and retreated into her own thoughts. Then I retrieved the paper Michel gave me. One line at a time, I translated his note.

le 4 Mai, 1980
  Place du Tertre
   Butte de Montmartre

Beaucoup de gens passent . . .
Many people pass by
the world is immobile,
the earth doesn't turn
I am outside time
I think of your eyes

Michel

I reread the words again and then dabbed at my eyes with the sodden tissue. *Oh dear, this man has definitely left his mark on my life.*

As the train slowly pulled out of the station, I turned to stare at the world beyond my window. Vivid, happy memories with Michel—our dinners at *Le Café Vert*, my birthday party, our stay at *Hôtel des Rois,* our visits to *place de la Concorde,* his birthday celebration—swirled inside my mind.

In spite of Michel's recent announcement, he'd been good to me. From the very beginning, he'd shown me great patience with my awful French, generosity when I was broke, and affection when Adam bruised my heart. I admired him for his intelligence, kindness and remarkable way with words.

I let my head drop back against the seat and closed my eyes. Eight and a half months had passed since I arrived in the Loire Valley. I'd experienced enough drama to last a lifetime—with the Dubois family, Adam, Michel, and my friends. In the end, I'd accomplished my goal to learn French and I'd grown as a person. From here on, I would be more thoughtful and honest, especially with life-changing decisions that affected other people.

Images of Madame Dubois and my father came to mind, and I shifted in my seat and re-crossed my legs.

After living abroad for months, the idea of becoming a flight attendant no longer appealed to me. I wasn't sure what career I'd pursue next, but I knew that it would have to be close to home, near my family and friends. If I traveled in the future, it would be on my own time and with plenty of money. Above all else, the serial dating scene no longer appealed to me. My close relationships, first with Adam, and then Michel, had reminded me how rewarding it could feel to be committed to one person. I wanted to find a stable partner and share my life with him. I wanted to fall madly in love. I wanted to live happily ever after.

The train attendant's voice brought me out of my reverie. Moving down the aisle, he checked our tickets and then exited to the next car.

After he left, I refocused on the view out the window. As I watched the sky turn tangerine and then segue into a magnificent burnt orange above Paris, I whispered "*au revoir*" to the city of light.

Author's Note

What happened after I returned home?

Michel and I exchanged a few letters and I pined for him for weeks. We spoke on the phone once, but the conversation felt forced and awkward. I never heard from him again.

I kept in touch with Évelyne for several months, but we never saw each other again. Two weeks after I left France, she sent me a beautiful framed print of the *Château d'Azay le Rideau*. She had inscribed it with "*En Souvenir d'un après-midi, d'hiver, 1979,* A Souvenir of an afternoon, winter 1979. I only exchanged a few letters with Janice and I never heard from Lori again.

Monsieur Toutain and I corresponded for almost two years. Always the professor, he returned all of my letters corrected. I never heard from Madame Dubois, but my parents received a communiqué from her shortly after I left the château in December. The note informed them—in French—that they'd spawned a horrible daughter.

I never became a flight attendant, but I attended travel agent school and worked for a tour company. A year later, I left my job, went back to college and acquired my business degree. That's when I met my dreamy husband; we married and had two daughters.

To this day, I tell people that I've lived a storybook life.

CPSIA information can be obtained
at www.ICGtesting.com
Printed in the USA
BVHW081517121218
535437BV00010B/988/P